Folens

Applied A2

Health and Social Care

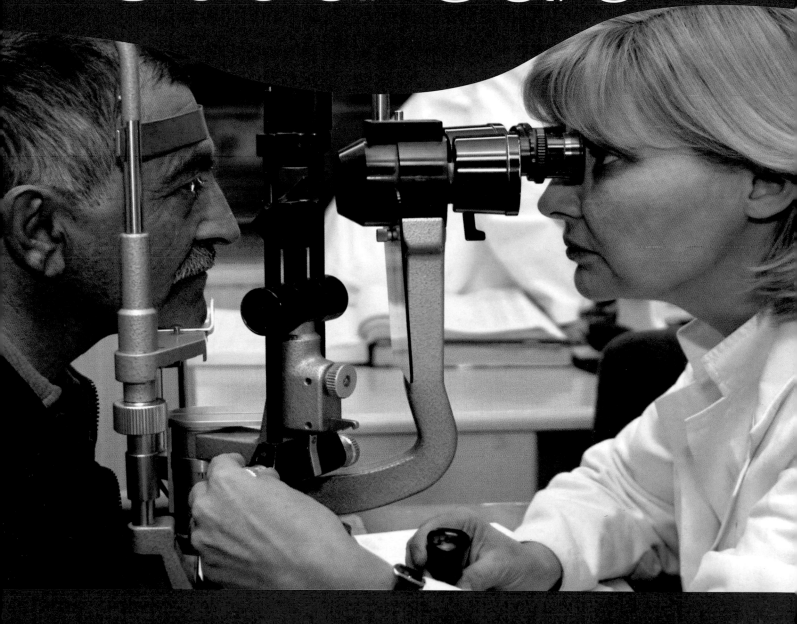

Contents

About the A2 Course

When combined with **three** units from the AS level and **three** units from the A2 level the award is known as Advanced GCE; while for the whole twelve unit award, **six** units from AS level and **six** units from A2, the qualification is known as Advanced GCE (Double Award). The A2 course will provide the opportunity to achieve a full advanced level qualification in Health and Social Care. The A2 units are equally weighted and aggregation across units means that if a candidate fails a unit, they may still pass overall. Therefore the GCE is a two-tiered qualification containing AS and A2 level units.

The units within the A2 level are:

Unit No.	Unit Title	Mode of Assessment	Mandatory/Optional
(F919) Unit 10	Care Practice and Provision	Portfolio	Mandatory
(F920) Unit 11	Understanding Human Behaviour	**External Examination**	Optional
(F921) Unit 12	Anatomy and Physiology in Practice	**External Examination**	Optional
(F922) Unit 13	Child Development	Portfolio	Optional
(F923) Unit 14	Mental-Health Issues	Portfolio	Optional
(F924) Unit 15	Social Trends	**External Examination**	Optional
(F925) Unit 16	Research Methods in Health and Social Care	Portfolio	Optional

A2 candidates must complete Unit 10; the mandatory unit. The optional units chosen will depend on individual interest and desired career routes. However, a minimum of two units that are externally assessed must be included if the Double Award is being followed, one if the Single Award is being taken. The content of A2 will address knowledge and skills that will enable candidates to move to higher education or to careers in the workplace.

A2 units can be studied in the following ways:

Advanced GCE (Double Award = 12 Units)					
AS	AS	AS	AS	AS	AS
A2	A2	A2	A2	A2	A2
Advanced GCE Single Award					

For the Advanced GCE (Single Award) **four** units will be assessed internally through teacher-assessed portfolio and **two** units will be assessed externally by examinations. These **six** units will be equally sized and equally weighted.

For the Advanced GCE (Double Award) at most **eight** units will be assessed internally through teacher-assessed portfolio and at least **four** units will be assessed externally by examinations. These **twelve** units will be equally sized and equally weighted.

How to use this book

Throughout the book there are a number of features that are common to all units. For example:

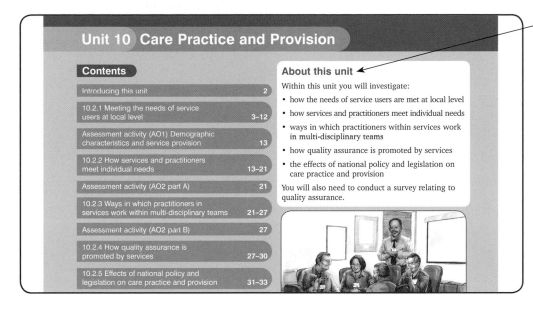

About this unit

This will list the knowledge and skills that will be covered within the unit.

Introducing this unit

This is a broad outline which gives some focus to the content of the unit. This is intended to help focus on the scope of the unit and what the study may involve.

Key words

Throughout each unit 'key words' are evident. These key words are in bold within the text. The meanings of such words are given in the glossary at the end of the book. You should check that you understand the meaning of these words.

Discussion point

While working through each section of the book there are questions to help check understanding of the knowledge that has been given.

Discussion point

Identify some of the barriers that might face people in society today. What types of services would the social model promote?

The traditional model is the 'medical' model. Using the medical model a person tends to be seen as having a medical problem because part of the body is not working properly. The response is to try and cure or manage the problem, using medical means. This then becomes the responsibility of the medical and associated experts, e.g. doctors, physiotherapists, support workers, social workers and care staff.

Discussion point

What might be the advantages and disadvantages of this approach?

Holistic health means considering the whole person:

Antonnia — CASE STUDY

Antonnia has a well paid job as a section manager of a large hospital department. She finds the job very demanding and when she is off duty she drinks quite a lot as she finds this helps to reduce her stress. Antonnia realises that if she continues to drink five units each evening she is eventually going to have liver problems. Already she is depressed, is often sick and finds it difficult to get up in the morning. She is also having rows with her partner and is beginning to worry that he will leave her.

Antonnia's drinking is affecting her physical, emotional, social, spiritual and intellectual health and is having an effect on societal health because she is not doing her job properly and her relationship with others is being affected. Solutions when found will similarly reflect the holistic approach.

Case studies

These are used periodically throughout units. Sometimes they have questions attached and at other times they will be used to try and explain a point that is being made.

A lifestyle that includes becoming more active and improving diet can greatly benefit the heart. Taking more exercise helps reduce blood pressure, improves cholesterol levels and boosts metabolism, thus reducing the risk of CAD.

Stress has long been linked to ill health. A study of 10,000 civil servants found a link between stress and metabolic syndrome, which involves obesity and high blood pressure. Factors such as social class, smoking, high alcohol consumption and lack of exercise were all recorded as part of the study.

Heart dysfunction — Activity 2

Dysfunctions of the heart can occur in many forms.

1. Choose **one** heart dysfunction and carry out research to show the causes, the effects and diagnostic treatment.

2. Give a presentation to the rest of the group using your findings. Include speaker notes.

Theory into practice

Carry out primary or secondary research to find out how radio-diagnostic imaging actually works.

Blood pressure monitoring

Monitoring blood pressure is an essential way of checking for hypertension. It is now common place for people to have their own monitor at home as they are now inexpensive, non-invasive and simple to use.

ECG

ECG (electrocardiogram) is a test that measures the electrical activity of the heart. The signals that make the heart's muscle fibres contract come from the sino-atrial node, which is the natural pacemaker of the heart. In an ECG, the electrical impulses made while the heart is beating are recorded on a piece of paper. This is known as an electrocardiogram and records any problems with the heart's rhythm and electrical impulses. The

Theory into practice

These are activities that can be conducted individually or in groups to help obtain information or to enable the application of theory to practice.

Activities

These have been included in each unit to help to check understanding of the text and could also help to build up evidence for the portfolio. Sometimes these are preceded by a short scenario.

Assessment activity

This will occur at the end of each piece of underpinning knowledge for the unit. The purpose of the assessment activity is to help focus on what is required as portfolio evidence from a particular strand in the Assessment Evidence Grid. This will form part of the evidence collected by you for the portfolio and should be completed individually. Sometimes the Assessment activity will begin with a short scenario and will be followed by tasks that must be completed, preferably individually.

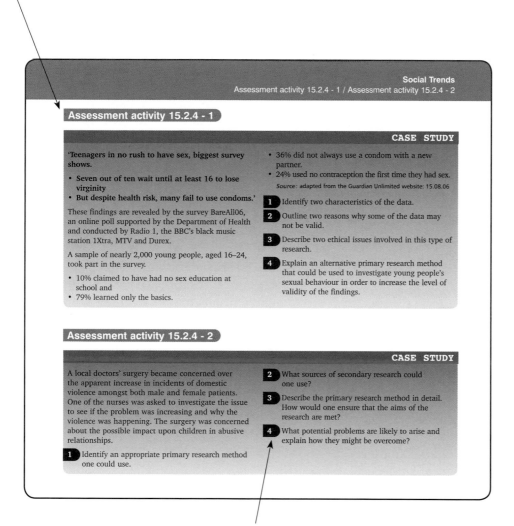

Social Trends
Assessment activity 15.2.4 - 1 / Assessment activity 15.2.4 - 2

Assessment activity 15.2.4 - 1

CASE STUDY

'Teenagers in no rush to have sex, biggest survey shows.

- Seven out of ten wait until at least 16 to lose virginity
- But despite health risk, many fail to use condoms.'

These findings are revealed by the survey BareAll06, an online poll supported by the Department of Health and conducted by Radio 1, the BBC's black music station 1Xtra, MTV and Durex.

A sample of nearly 2,000 young people, aged 16–24, took part in the survey.

- 10% claimed to have had no sex education at school and
- 79% learned only the basics.

- 36% did not always use a condom with a new partner.
- 24% used no contraception the first time they had sex.

Source: adapted from the Guardian Unlimited website: 15.08.06

1 Identify two characteristics of the data.

2 Outline two reasons why some of the data may not be valid.

3 Describe two ethical issues involved in this type of research.

4 Explain an alternative primary research method that could be used to investigate young people's sexual behaviour in order to increase the level of validity of the findings.

Assessment activity 15.2.4 - 2

CASE STUDY

A local doctors' surgery became concerned over the apparent increase in incidents of domestic violence amongst both male and female patients. One of the nurses was asked to investigate the issue to see if the problem was increasing and why the violence was happening. The surgery was concerned about the possible impact upon children in abusive relationships.

1 Identify an appropriate primary research method one could use.

2 What sources of secondary research could one use?

3 Describe the primary research method in detail. How would one ensure that the aims of the research are met?

4 What potential problems are likely to arise and explain how they might be overcome?

Assessment questions

These are provided for Units 11, 12 and 15, where portfolio evidence is not required. Questions have been prepared to help focus on the knowledge acquired and on the style of writing needed for the external assessment. Sometimes questions will be set in the classroom and on other occasions students may be asked to complete a number of questions for homework. Whichever is the case, it is important to attempt these questions as in doing so, it is likely that confidence will be gained.

Bibliography

A bibliography is provided at the end of each unit. This gives a full list of references so that further reading and research can be undertaken.

We hope that you will be successful in the GCE Health and Social Care course and that this book may help you to achieve your goals.

Author details

Angela Fisher is a former Senior Manager of a comprehensive school. She has worked for an awarding body for a number of years as a very Senior Examiner and has helped to develop a variety of qualifications. She has also been a consultant for QCA. Angela has been a major contributor to a wide range of textbooks and learning resources which includes Folens at GCSE and AS level. She has also written for Heinemann for GNVQ and OCR Nationals at Level 2 and Level 3.

Mary Riley introduced First and National Health and Social Care into her current comprehensive school in 1989. She still teaches across the spectrum of Health and Social Care courses as Head of Department. She has worked as a Senior Moderator and Examiner for many years. She has trained as an Ofsted Inspector. Mary is also a major contributor to the Folens AS book, OCR National L2 and L3 with Heinemann.

Stephen Seamons is a retired Superintendent Radiographer with over 25 years of clinical and managerial, health service experience. He currently teaches Health and Social Care in the south west of England and is a Senior Examiner for examination boards in a variety of subjects. Stephen has contributed to Folens textbooks for GCSE and AS level as well as the L2 OCR Nationals for Heinemann.

Marjorie Snaith is a manager in a large college of further education. She is the co-author of several health and social care books and is an External Verifier and Moderator for a number of awarding bodies where she has helped to write national standards for qualifications.

Stuart McKie is an External Verifier and Moderator for a major awarding body. As well as being a qualified Probation Officer and FE lecturer in Health and Social Care he has worked extensively in the voluntary sector, including for a London-based homeless charity, a homeless and ex-offenders residential care charity and Age Concern.

Michael Ancil is a Senior Examiner at Advanced Level in Health and Social Care with a major awarding body. He also has considerable experience as an Examiner and Moderator in Sociology. Michael has worked in a number of comprehensive schools teaching Sociology and Health and Social Care at both GCSE and A Level, and for a number of years was Head of Sixth Form in a large community college.

Marion Tyler is an award-winning health professional. Her innovative training in stress management has meant working with individuals and organisations nationwide for over 20 years. Marion's training guides people to improve their knowledge and understanding of common problems and to find their own solutions.

Unit 10 Care Practice and Provision

Contents

About this unit

Within this unit you will investigate:

- how the needs of service users are met at local level
- how services and practitioners meet individual needs
- ways in which practitioners within services work in multi-disciplinary teams
- how quality assurance is promoted by services
- the effects of national policy and legislation on care practice and provision

You will also need to conduct a survey relating to quality assurance.

Working together to meet the needs of service users

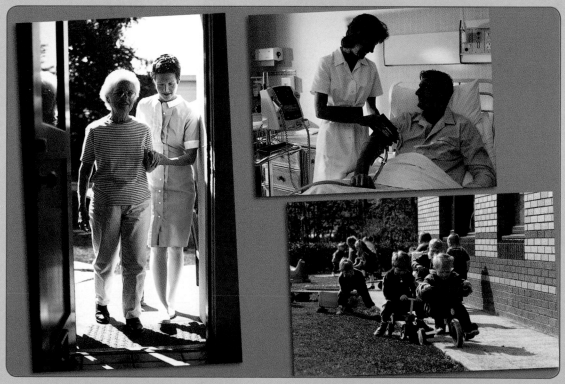

We all need health, social care and early years services from time to time

Introducing this unit

Think about the number of times that you have used different services that provide health and social care or childcare. You may have used dentists, a GP, a hospital, nursery school or social services. Most of us have used at least one of these providers and found we have a better quality of life as a result of the care given. The practitioner working in the service may have stopped pain by filling a tooth, by repairing a broken limb, or helped with a personal problem. Whatever the situation, our lives will have been improved by the service received.

Providing care for the local community takes a great deal of planning. This must take into consideration complex and ever-changing needs. Planners will be influenced by **demographic** factors, by national targets and standards as well as by the needs of individual service users. Planning has to consider all who live in the local community, not just one section of the population.

Once services have been established, those who work in them, the practitioners, have to respond to the individual needs of service users. These are not just the service users' physical needs, but the intellectual, emotional and social needs of individuals. Practitioners have to set targets, maintain standards and use different approaches in order to meet the individual needs of those who require care.

Budgetary requirements have to be considered by purchasers and providers of care. In order to make the most of financial provision and to provide a **seamless** service, providers will work together in multi-disciplinary teams to assess, plan and implement care and to monitor and evaluate the care given. They also have to understand and accept the consequences if the care provided goes wrong!

How does all of this affect us? It is the quality of service that we receive when we are in need of health and care that will influence how we 'rate' the service. How good is it? What was good practice? What needed improving? We, the service users, should have every confidence in the quality of service that is being provided. Have the goals or standards set by the organisation or service been met? If the answer is negative then a good complaints system should be in place for both service users and staff enabling them to make suggestions for improvement.

In this unit consideration will be given to exploring how national attitudes, policy and legislation affect the care that is provided. We will also need to recognise that personal accountability for our own health will contribute to the approaches used by qualified practitioners.

10.2.1 Meeting the needs of service users at local level

Working in the health, social care or childcare sector means understanding the concepts of 'need', in order to be able to respond and provide effective care. Needs include:

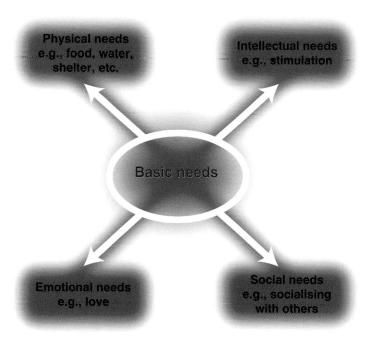

Abraham Maslow considered that 'the goal of living is **self actualisation**'. That means that one needs to fulfil one's full potential. Self actualisation is at the top of Maslow's hierarchy of needs. A person cannot reach this point unless all their other needs are met. The diagram below shows the sequence of fulfilled need that Maslow considered essential to achieve self actualisation.

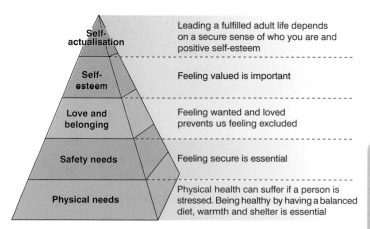

Maslow's hierarchy of needs

Services work together to identify the different types of needs within their local community. Their planning is influenced by a number of considerations, for example demographics and government standards.

Local demographic characteristics

What is demographics? Demographics is being concerned about the facts relating to the population. Those who are planning health, social care and childcare provision for their local communities must research and find out about the **elements** and size of those living in their area, taking their health needs into consideration. For example:

- the number of births that occur in any one year or part of a year and whether there is an increase or decrease in these rates
- the number of single parents
- the number of children below compulsory school age
- the number of children who are of school age
- the number of people living in their area who are registered disabled
- the migration figures, e.g. those moving out of their area and those moving into an area (emigration and immigration of movement within society)
- the number of people who are unemployed
- the death rate and ages of those who die.

These are demographic characteristics that will influence the planning of services. For example, if a local population has a high number of children living in its area who are under the age of 5 years, services such as playgroups, nursery schools and health care for children are likely to be a focus that will need careful planning. On the other hand, if a large number of the population are older adults, i.e. over the age of 65 years, then residential homes, nursing homes, health care and community care and support will need to be high on the planners' agenda.

Very often the demography of a local area will have more than one high priority, particularly if there are, for example, both large numbers of children under the age of five years and large numbers of older adults living in the community.

Theory into practice

Find out for your own area which demographic factors will take priority with planners. Which services will need to be incorporated in the plan to meet this need?

National standards, targets and objectives

The standards, targets and objectives of today's health and social care systems are continually undergoing change. For example, life-saving medicines, neo-imaging technology and non-invasive treatments have combined to produce effective, albeit costly, health care. People are living longer and the traditional patterns of family life have changed, all of which must be taken into consideration by those involved in planning health, social care and childcare services.

As a result of such changes government standards, targets and objectives have also changed, which has meant a radical alteration in the way that care is organised and operated.

A change in standard is given in the table below with an example of the target:

Standard	Target
To encourage individuals to accept some responsibility for their own health and well being.	To encourage the use of the **preventative approach** designed to address problems before they become a crisis.

From the example given it is possible to see that **standards** are concepts which when implemented will produce quality care outcomes. **Targets**, on the other hand, are the goals to help achieve the standards set.

What then are the **objectives?** The objectives are the steps taken, when the target has been set, to help the concepts to be implemented and the targets to be achieved. Below is a simple example of a standard, the target and some of the possible objectives:

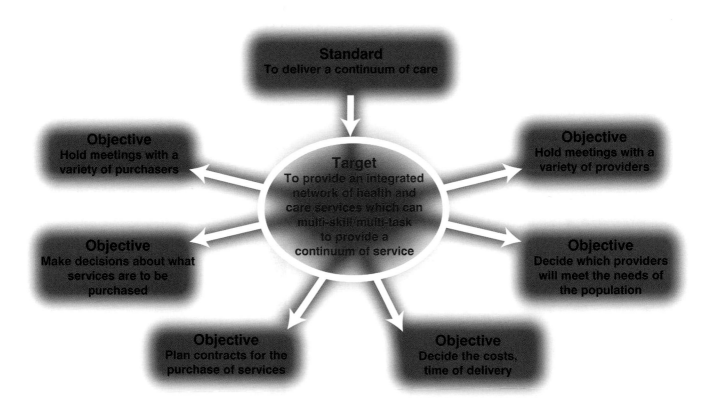

Within the diagram the standard has been set, the target is given and the various objectives that will help achieve the target have been put into place.

The challenge for those who are in planning is how to constantly manage a changing system.

To do this planners have to work with teams of administrators and providers to deliver quality health, social care and childcare services in a cost-effective manner in order to meet the needs of service users.

Petroc — Activity 1

Petroc lives in a county town in Dorset. He is 35 years of age and has a disability which prevents him from working full time. He is confined to a wheelchair when moving around.

Petroc lives with his parents, who are older adults and who are in need of health care on a regular basis. Petroc is just one example of many living in the area who have a disability. Similarly, there are a lot of older adults living in the area.

1. Identify **two** different demographic factors that would influence planners when planning health and social care services for service users like Petroc and his family. Explain how each demographic factor could influence the planning of services.

2. Identify a national standard that is likely to influence planners when planning services for service users like Petroc and his family. Explain the standard, the target, and the possible objectives that would be set.

It is important to consider a more complex standard that has been set by the government which has targets and objectives. Such a standard is contained in *'Every Child Matters: Changes for children in schools'* (DfES2004e).

Childcare is such an important matter

The standard

A standard is a written statement that defines the level of performance or a set condition determined to be accepted by an authority, e.g. the Department of Health.

'Every Child Matters' identifies that children and young people cannot learn unless they feel safe nor can they learn if they have ill health. Five outcomes are the focus of ensuring that effective, joined-up, children's services, from education and health and social care; provide 'wraparound' care on the site of a school or early education centre. The aim is to ensure that children:

- stay healthy
- stay safe
- enjoy and achieve
- make positive contributions
- achieve economic and social well being.

This approach makes the commitment that the 'education of the whole child' is the main focus of attention. Education settings will not be the sole site for learning but will become the 'gateway' to a number of learning opportunities and activities that offer a range of extended services. Closer working relationships between educational settings, health and social care services and parents will occur earlier and will be effectively supported. The government standard is to 'remove barriers to achievement'.

In the White Paper: *'Higher Standards, Better Schools for All'*, the government has stated: 'It will no longer be acceptable for young people to be denied the opportunity to achieve their full potential, whatever their abilities or talents…'

The government's *'Change for Children'* programme gives many new opportunities for this to be fulfilled.

Targets

The government wants to ensure that *'Sure Start Children's Centres'* are available in every area by 2010. This is one target for the standard set.

Such Centres open from 8 am to 6 pm all the year round and provide **seamless, holistic, personalised** and **integrated** services for children aged under five years and their families. All *Sure Start Children's Centres* are part of the government's *'Ten Year Strategy for Childcare'*. This enables all families with children to have access to affordable, flexible, high quality childcare places for their children.

A second target for the standard is to put in place *'Full-Service Extended Schools'* and *'Extended Schools'*. The former will have key professionals such as health workers, psychologists and youth workers based on education sites who will work closely alongside teachers so that children's problems can be addressed without too much disruption. Extended Schools too will offer a wide range of activities beyond the school day to help meet the needs of children and other individuals who live in the local community. Examples would be after-school clubs, holiday clubs, leisure activities.

The diagram below gives an overview of the different types of services that are likely to be in and around education centres, e.g. schools:

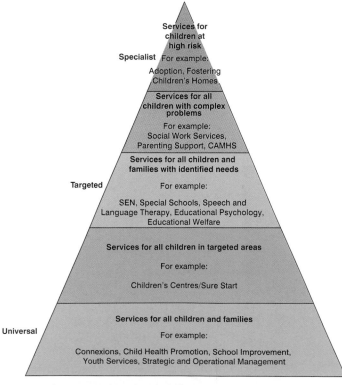

Universal, targeted and specialist services in and around schools

Objectives

The table below shows examples of the objectives for specific targets for *Every Child Matters*:

Target	Objective
Promote being healthy	Stress management programme for learners and staff Healthier eating options in school canteen Education about leading healthier lifestyles
Staying safe	Peer mentoring programme to reduce bullying Linking with police liaison/crime prevention panels
Promoting good health	Informing young people of how to access health and social care services promoting healthy lifestyles and how to reduce risks Improving information sharing between agencies
Making a positive contribution	Setting personalised learning plans Improving access to diagnostic testing Improving the opportunity for assessment Addressing disengagement Befriending scheme
Achieving economic and social well being	Engagement in mini enterprise projects Developing literacy and team working skills Developing problem solving skills

These examples show how teachers, health and social care professionals, **paraprofessionals** and parents can all work together to improve the quality of life and learning for the child.

Theory into practice

Take one aspect of the five targets or outcomes included in *Every Child Matters* and investigate how it is being applied in either an early years learning centre, e.g. a children's centre or a primary school.

Give a presentation to others highlighting the standard, the target and the objectives. Explain how these will be applied in the setting.

Who are the planners?

These are the people who are known as the 'stakeholders'. They are individuals who have the responsibility and interest in seeing that the service that they represent has the resources to provide an effective service. Examples of the main planners could include:

Local authorities
Representatives of local authorities who provide finances for community services

Social service purchasers
Representatives who are responsible for buying services

Private fund holders
Insurance companies who pay for care

Patients and the public
Includes those who are using the service as well as those who may use it

Stakeholders

Voluntary and community sectors
Charities, Support Groups, Forums

GP services
Representatives who purchase services on behalf of local GPs

NHS
Executive members of Primary Care Trusts/ Groups/Organisations who have money for the purchasing of services

Local education departments
Providers of services within Sure Start Centres and Full Extended Schools

Service users
Those who use the services

An integrated meeting of stakeholders

Planners are involved with *'Building Local Strategic Partnerships'* through closer joint working with the key stakeholders. Planning takes place for a three-year cycle in advance. Primary Care Trusts/Organisations/Groups (PCTs/PCOs/PCGs) and local authorities are required to lead the community partnership. The group are to follow the *'Local Strategic Partnership' (LSPs)* to prepare *'Local Delivery plans'*, for example for 2007 to 2008.

The *'NHS Improvement Plan'* (2004), set out the stages in the government's plan for the next three years. These are:

- putting patients and service users first through more personalised care
- putting a focus on the whole health and well being – not just considering illness
- developing strategies to provide further **devolution** of decision making to local organisations.

This change means that planners now have to move away from a system that is driven by national targets to one where:

- there is greater scope for addressing local provision
- standards become the main driver for continuous improvement in quality
- all organisations play their part in modernisation of the services
- incentives are in place to support the system.

This planning system brings together an integrated approach which involves:

- the planning framework
- national standards
- Payment by Results system.

The *'National Service Framework'* emphasises the need to set local targets alongside a smaller number of national targets. The quality of service provision is supported by the *'National Service Framework'* (NSF) and *'The National Institute for Clinical Excellence'* (NICE). The local planners have to demonstrate that they are achieving the levels of quality described by both these standards.

Theory into practice

Carry out research in groups to find out about either the National Service Framework or The National Institute for Clinical Excellence.

Give a short presentation to others about your findings.

The principles for local planners, for local target setting are:

- targets are in line with population needs
- the targets address local service gaps
- the targets deliver equity
- the targets are evidence based
- the targets are developed in partnership with others
- the targets offer value for money.

In order to achieve these targets the planning group must have access to data showing the needs of the local population, they must consider recent trends in needs, they need to examine what is already available and project what might be necessary for the future. Cost will also be an important factor to be considered.

Theory into practice

Invite a member of the local planning group to your Centre to talk about one plan that they have developed. Try to find out who was involved with planning and how the plan was implemented.

If you are unable to invite a member of the group to the Centre, you may be able to access the information through the Internet by accessing your local PCT/PCG.

The way in which services are commissioned

What can you offer? Have you considered the contract?

What is commissioning? Commissioning is purchasing a range of services for the local population. For the NHS this means Primary Care Trusts/Groups (PCTs/PCGs) purchase resources for community health services and for GP practices from a **unified budget**. Funding is based on a population of around 100,000 which is for approximately 50 GPs. The organisation of commissioning is very complex, but the table below will give some idea of how this works:

Level 1	PCG is an advisory sub-committee of the local health authority
Level 2	PCG is a sub-committee that manages a budget devolved to it by the local health authority
Level 3	PCG is a free-standing body accountable to the health authority for commissioning services for primary community health, and hospital services for its patients
Level 4	A free-standing body accountable to the health authority for commissioning primary community health and hospital services and for providing primary and community health services

The commissioning (purchasing) of services is still part of the **purchaser-provider** system that was worked prior to the 'New Labour' era (prior to Labour's election victory in 1997), but is designed to focus on the positive aspect of fund holding. The purchaser-provider system meant that organisations such as the health authority or local authority social services would purchase services from those who agreed to provide the service, e.g. community home care.

In April 2004 the *Commission for Health Improvement* (CHI) came into being, whose main purpose was to monitor the quality of services purchased and to publish reports. The name of this group has since changed to *Commission for Healthcare Audit and Inspection* (CHAI), their work being fairly similar in that they are checking the concept of *'clinical governance'*.

'**Clinical governance** is a system through which NHS organisations are accountable for continuously improving the quality of their services and safeguarding high standards of care by creating an environment in which excellence in clinical care can flourish.'

Commissioning now means paying attention to the new financial incentives introduced by the government, known as 'Payment by Results'. These are attached to '**commissioning levers**' which include:

- appropriate contracting, monitoring and performance management arrangements to ensure that sustainable out of hours services are commissioned which meet quality standards
- using the new *'General Medical Services'* (GMS) and *'Personal Medical Services'* (PMS), to deliver preventative services and high standards of care to people with chronic diseases
- using core flexible contracts for people requiring planned hospital care. Such contracts to support the flow of funds to alternative providers where patient choice demands them
- agreeing explicit criteria for referral and treatment.

The commissioning process involves all stakeholders. Some commissioning will be through joint arrangements whereas others will involve the NHS and Social Services separately. However, both must involve other interested stakeholders for effective budgetary management.

Theory into practice

Have a whole group discussion to explore what these points actually mean:

- for the commissioning of services
- to the patient who needs treatment.

The process of commissioning follows the outline given below:

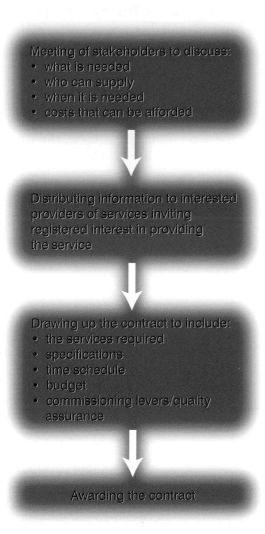

Meeting of stakeholders to discuss:
- what is needed
- who can supply
- when it is needed
- costs that can be afforded

Distributing information to interested providers of services inviting registered interest in providing the service

Drawing up the contract to include:
- the services required
- specifications
- time schedule
- budget
- commissioning levers/quality assurance

Awarding the contract

Social Service commissioning follows a similar pattern as does childcare.

Theory into practice

Invite a person from Social Services to the Centre. Ask them to talk to the group about how:

- local plans are drawn up
- to give an example of a standard set
- to give an example of the target for the standard
- to give examples of objectives for the target
- to explain the commissioning process
- Social Services works together with the health and childcare providers.

As a whole group discuss the outcomes from the information given by the speaker.

The process of monitoring and evaluating service provision

With the change in government policy towards foundation hospitals and 'meeting patient needs', a great deal of the monitoring and evaluation of the provision of services will be conducted by the Foundation Hospitals themselves. They will have the power to borrow money, to employ staff and to find resources.

Monitoring is seeking information about what is being done and recording the outcomes.

Evaluating is an investigative process to determine whether a process, item or action is cost effective or whether the objectives were achieved. Evaluation involves making judgements and drawing conclusions.

The monitoring and evaluation of the services provided by the Foundation Hospitals will be carried out by themselves and by the Strategic Health Authorities (StHAs). The structure of Health and Social Care Statutory services is currently (September 2006) as shown below:

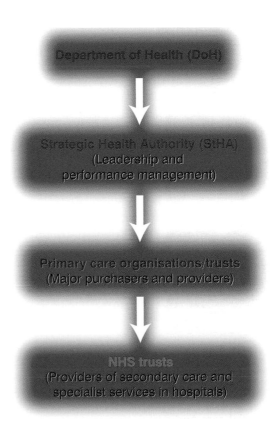

Department of Health (DoH)

Strategic Health Authority (StHA)
(Leadership and performance management)

Primary care organisations/trusts
(Major purchasers and providers)

NHS trusts
(Providers of secondary care and specialist services in hospitals)

Monitoring and evaluation is also carried out by the 'National Institute for Clinical Excellence' (NICE). The main purpose of NICE is to provide a rationale behind the use of resources. They will find out what is cost-effective and what is clinically effective, concentrating on what money should be spent on. NICE was set up in 1999 and is one of the main focus points for the government's modernisation agenda. NICE will carry out appraisals on new drugs that are available. Their guidance is intended to help **clinicians** to use treatments that work best for patients. Examples of appraisals conducted by NICE are:

- £10 million on drugs to treat cancers of the pancreas, lungs, brain and leukaemia, which has benefited approximately 10,000 people
- £76 million on drugs and interventions for people with coronary heart disease, which has advantaged over 70,000 patients.

(Source: *The Insiders Guide to the NHS:* Roy Lilley, Radcliffe).

Another source of monitoring and evaluation is the 'National Clinical Assessment Authority' (NCAA), which was put in place in April 2003.

The purpose of this organisation is to monitor the performance of individual doctors when PCOs/Trusts and Community Trusts have a problem with any individual. Their work involves:

- providing advice
- carrying out assessments of an individual's work.

The purpose of this group is to help employers, e.g. the Strategic Health Authority, to carry out an objective assessment relating to the quality of work provided by the individual concerned.

Methods that can be used for monitoring and evaluation can include:

- questionnaires
- interviews
- observation
- statistics.

Local Delivery Plans (LDPs) are monitored on a regular basis and evaluated to explore whether they are effective in meeting the needs of service users and stakeholders.

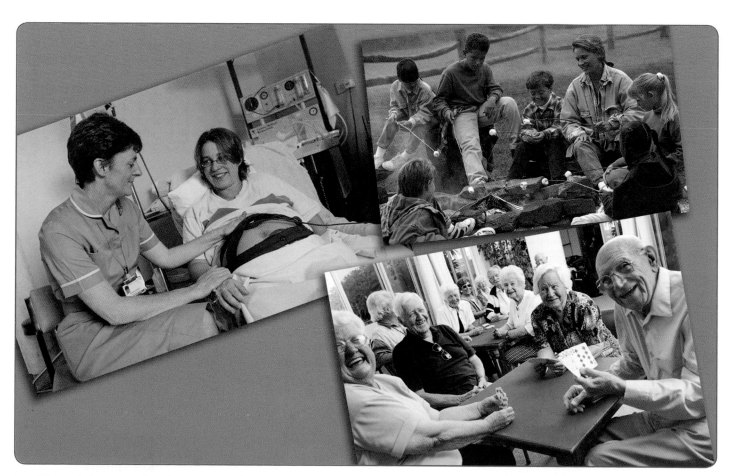

Health, social care and early years services

Services

Service users	Health care services	Social care services	Childcare services
Babies and children (including those with disabilities)	Hospital in-patient Hospital out-patient care GP Birthing/maternity services Mental-health care Speech therapy Dentistry Opticians	Foster care Adoption Child protection Residential care Child and family 　support groups Child psychologists Community services	Childminders Nursery schools Playgroups Family centres Crèches Toy libraries Parent and toddler 　support groups After-school clubs Holiday clubs
Adolescents (including adolescents with disabilities)	School medical services Hospital in-patient care Hospital out-patient care, e.g. physiotherapy GP Mental-health care Dentistry Opticians Health promotion Complementary approaches Community services, e.g. dietician Hospice	Youth workers Youth offending services Child protection Foster care Adoption Residential care Counselling Clinics (sexual health, 　smoking, alcohol, etc.)	Specialist education Training schemes
Adults (including people with disabilities)	Hospital in-patient Hospital out-patient, e.g. radiography GP Mental-health care Dentistry Opticians Health promotion Complementary approaches Day care centres Community services, e.g. district nurse Chiropody/podiatry Nursing homes Special services, e.g. dialysis Rehabilitation Hospice	Residential homes Day care centres Training/resource centres Psychologists Psychiatrists Luncheon club Home care services Community services Counselling Social Services, 　e.g. social worker Support groups	
Older adults (including those with disabilities)	Hospital in-patient Hospital out-patient, 　e.g. radiography/physiotherapy GP Mental-health care Dentistry Opticians Health promotion Complementary approaches Day care centres Community services, e.g. district nurse Chiropody/podiatry Nursing homes Special Services, e.g. dialysis Rehabilitation Hospice	Residential homes Day care centres Training/resource centres Psychologists Psychiatrists Luncheon clubs Meals on wheels (with voluntary sector) Home care services Community services Counselling Social Services, 　e.g. social worker Support groups	

Some services are delivered by private and **voluntary** groups. Examples of such services are:

Voluntary services	Meals on wheels	Red Cross	Cruse (bereavement counselling)
Private services	Hospitals	Shop mobility	Complementary approaches

Care Practice and Provision
10.2.1 Meeting the needs of service users at local level /
10.2.2 How services and practitioners meet individual needs

Assessment activity (AO1) Demographic characteristics and service provision

Maria and Martin   CASE STUDY

Maria and Martin are married. Maria is 35 years old and Martin is 40 years old. They have two children; Andre aged 13 and Alicia who is 8. Martin's mother, Petra, lives with the family as she is a widow and has mild Alzheimer's disease. Petra is 66 years of age.

The family live on the outskirts of a large city in an area where there are a large number of single parents and also a large population of older adults. There are also quite a lot of people with disability living in the area. Maria has a friend who has little mobility due to a stroke.

There is a great deal of unemployment in the community as a car factory closed down 18 months previously and many people living in the area lost their jobs and have been unable to find work since then.

1 Choose **one** service user from the case study.

2 For the service user chosen identify **two** demographic characteristics that exist in the area.

Explain how these would influence the planning of services for the area.

3 Explain how demographic characteristics are used to assess local need.

4 For **one** service user choose **two** services. Explain in detail each stage in the local planning procedure for each service, giving examples of:
- a standard
- targets
- objectives.

5 Explain in detail how the two plans are monitored and reviewed.

6 Explain why it is important to involve local stakeholders in the decision-making process.

7 Give a comprehensive and in-depth account of how health, social care and early years services are organised.

10.2.2 How services and practitioners meet individual needs

LOVE

FOOD

FULFILMENT

INTELLECTUAL STIMULATION

SHELTER AND SECURITY

BELONGING

We all have different needs

A professional carer must have the service user's needs as a central focus if they are to develop a working relationship with an individual that is effective. Look back at the beginning of this unit and remind yourself of the needs that individuals have.

In order to meet these needs the professional care worker will need to establish within the relationship with the service user:

Trust
The service user must feel that they can discuss issues without the professional care worker ridiculing them.

Confidence
Knowing only information that is on a 'need to know' basis will be passed to others and all else will be kept confidential.

Positive attitude
The service user will be provided with non-judgemental support by the care professional which does not label, stereotype or show prejudice.

Communication
Speaking in a way that does not patronise the service user and which presents the facts, allowing the service user to make decisions and choices.

Recognition of culture
Allowing the service user to express their views and to follow the traditions of their own religion or beliefs, for example providing a place for prayer.

Recognition of social values
Recognising that in some cultures care by a person of the same gender is preferred.

Competency in knowledge and skills
Carrying out tasks and skills with confidence.

Help the service user to feel valued
Promoting a positive self esteem by not putting a person down by ignoring them.

Help the service user to feel fulfilled
By giving mental stimulation and encouraging participation.

Isha   Activity 2

Isha has just moved into a nursing home as she is 82 years old and cannot look after herself any longer. She is the only Muslim living in the nursing home and staff are having to adjust to her needs. Isha has a hearing impairment and has severe mobility problems.

1 In small groups discuss how staff at the care setting could recognise and respond to the needs of Isha.

2 As a whole group discuss your findings.

3 Identify **two** different practitioners, from **two** different teams, who might be involved in caring for Isha, and show how they might work together to meet Isha's needs.

Prevention and treatment

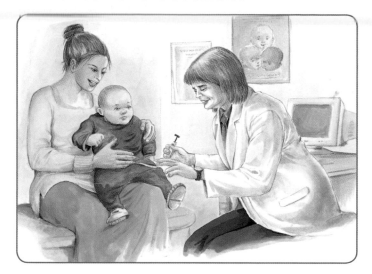

Prevention is better than cure!

Preventative approaches are those that aim to prevent illness and disease from occurring by encouraging good lifestyle choice or by means of vaccinations, immunisations or health screening.

Health promotion comprises prevention, health education and public health policy. Prevention is the foundation of 'good health' because many risk factors, such as smoking, obesity and alcohol, are alterable. By encouraging a healthy lifestyle, attempts can be made to reduce one or more factors that contribute to the burden of illness.

Traditional approaches are normally based on prevention of the onset of disease. **Interventions** can be on three levels:

- **Primary:** prevention of the onset of disease.
- **Secondary:** early detection and treatment of disease or conditions that are likely to lead to illness.
- **Tertiary:** minimising the illness/disability that cannot be cured so that the service user can, with some loss of function, continue to live as good a quality of life as possible.

Currently prevention of illness or conditions of ill health is one of the government's main standards as can be seen in 'Every Child Matters'. In this standard the government are trying to encourage parents to bring up children in a safe, secure environment making sure every child remains healthy and does not become obese. The government has many other standards which aim to protect people from all life stages and help to reduce the risk of ill health. These all require individuals to do something for themselves to promote their own good health.

All individuals are being encouraged to become more responsible for their own health by living a lifestyle that will reduce risks. Changes are being made in advertising, for example not having advertisements that encourage smoking, and also government regulations, for example road safety regulations. The general public is being encouraged through the media to eat differently and more healthily and to participate in more exercise in order to change attitudes and behaviour towards health.

Health screening

Health screening is finding out what could cause ill health in the body before a disease or condition reaches a point where surgery or severe forms of treatment are necessary. It is finding out about illness and disease before symptoms develop, to prevent unnecessary death. In some instances health screening is used, after symptoms have appeared, to examine the extent of the disease or condition and to know what treatments will be most suitable.

There are many forms of health screening available in today's society. The table on page 16 gives some examples of health screening methods used by today's practitioners.

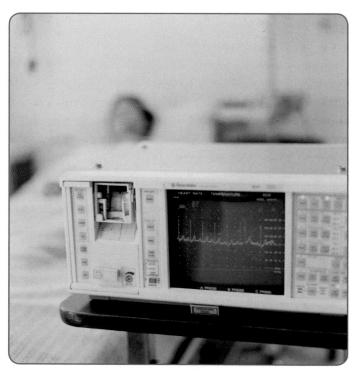

An ECG scanner

Screening	Method	Illness or conditions where used
ECG (Electrocardiogram)	Records electrical changes in the heart muscle and provides information about the condition of the heart and the way in which it is working. The results are displayed on paper.	Heart attacks Aneurysms
Ultrasound	Uses sound at a higher frequency than can be heard by the human ear. It is used to produce pictures of a baby in the uterus and gives information about a baby's size, age, sex and position. It also shows the position of the **placenta** and whether there is one baby, twins or more.	Checking the health condition of babies Used to check for deformities that may be part of a baby's growth
MRI scan	The service user lies inside a large cylinder-shaped magnet and radio waves are passed through the body. The scanner picks up the signals and a computer turns them into a picture. MRI stands for **magnetic resonance imaging.**	Strokes Abnormal growths Brain damage Heart dysfunction Joints Spleen Liver
CT scan	Uses x-rays to build up a picture from computerised **tomography** but is far more detailed than x-rays. Images are formed from two- or even three-dimensional images. They show, through the use of virtual images, what a surgeon would see only through surgery.	Abnormal growths Bleeding in the brain Aneurysms Lung disease Torn kidneys Spine injury
Angiogram	Tubes fed through the blood vessel in the groin at the top of the right leg. Longer tubes are then passed to the heart and a dye is carried into the blood vessels of the heart. This is shown up on an x-ray screen. The functions/dysfunctions can be seen.	Angina Narrowing arteries

Many private hospitals advertise 'Well woman' or 'Well man' health-screening clinics. These are proving to be very popular as service users can find out through a variety of scans or tests how well or fit they are. They are also given advice on how to maintain their health. Any dysfunction of body organs is immediately recommended for consultation and treatment, thus hopefully preventing the dysfunction from worsening.

Health screening is one method of reducing risks to service users. However, currently, debate has arisen in the media as to whether having an MRI health-screening test is putting service users more at risk.

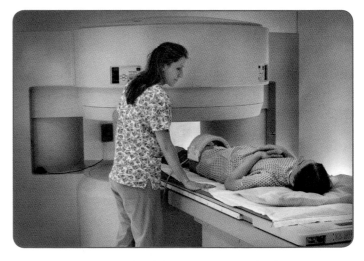

An MRI scanner is a health-screening method

Theory into practice

Discuss as a whole group whether MRI screening should be limited or made available to all. Why?

Angela | Activity 3

Angela had been having severe pains in her chest. She was convinced that the cause was overwork but she visited her GP just to have a check.

The GP was concerned so referred Angela to the hospital for an angiogram test. The health-screening process showed that there was no dysfunction of the heart and arteries. Unfortunately, however, as the tubes were being removed from the aorta, Angela had a stroke. She was blind and her speech was slurred. She was unable to think in sequence and could not be understood when she tried to speak.

The specialist arranged for Angela to have an MRI scan. The results of the scan showed a tiny clot had formed high up in the neck. This impaired sight and speech and caused confusion.

1 Carry out research to find out more about the angiograph method of health screening.

2 Explain how an MRI health-screening process would be carried out. Give the advantages and disadvantages.

3 Choose one other form of health screening and produce a case study to show:

- the method of delivery
- why it was used on the service user
- the results of the health screening method chosen.

Immunisation

What is immunisation? A person is given a **vaccine** that stimulates the immune system to produce **antibodies** against **antigens** in the vaccine. This is known as 'primary immune response'. After the immunisation the service user becomes infected with **pathogens** and as a result their immune system reacts faster and produces more antibodies, than it would have done before the immunisation. This is called 'secondary immune response'.

For some vaccines it is necessary to administer them in two or three doses with a time period between each. More and more antibodies are built up on each occasion. A 'booster dose' is sometimes given after a long period of time to maintain the immunity. Immunisation vaccine can involve using:

- pathogens that are dead and which have been killed by chemicals or heat, for example typhoid
- pathogens that are live but which have been altered so that they can no longer cause disease, for example measles and polio vaccines
- toxins that are in a harmless form but which produce diseases, for example tetanus.

Infants are often immunised to prevent them from having a disease later in life which can cause fatality or severe impairment. When individuals are going on holiday to an area where disease and illness, to which they are not immune, is

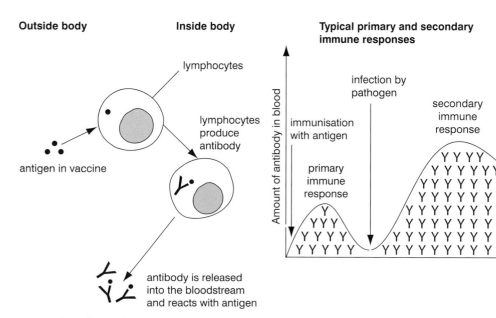

Outside body   **Inside body**

lymphocytes

antigen in vaccine

lymphocytes produce antibody

antibody is released into the bloodstream and reacts with antigen

Protection through immunisation

Typical primary and secondary immune responses

Amount of antibody in blood

immunisation with antigen

infection by pathogen

primary immune response

secondary immune response

present, they will visit their health practitioner to be immunised against diseases before they go. In this way service users are protected from disease and therefore the risk of illness is radically reduced. The table below gives some examples of immunisation:

Disease	Symptoms	Immunisation
Meningitis (bacterial)	Stiff neck, purple spots, drowsiness, fever	Three injections at monthly intervals from two months old
Measles (virus)	Fever, runny nose, cough, rash (after five days)	Combined measles, mumps and rubella vaccine (MMR) given to a child when one year old
Poliomyelitis (virus)	Headache, stiffness of neck and back with or without paralysis	Three doses of vaccine given by mouth at the same time as a DDT vaccine. Booster doses are given at later dates
Mumps (virus)	Painful swellings near the jaw	Rubella vaccines are provided for children who have not had rubella or MMR vaccine
Typhoid	Fever, constipation and dry cough	Two injections of vaccine with a month between each. A booster dose may be required
Rubella (virus)	Red rash and swollen glands	MMR vaccine offered

Theory into practice

Invite a health specialist who is involved in the immunisation process to the Centre to talk about the immunisation process. Find out their views about giving the MMR vaccine to children rather than having separate vaccines for each.

Have a class discussion to express views about why some parents may be opposed to the MMR vaccine.

The holistic approach

This approach to care means treating the whole person, not just the symptoms that occur. It is the 'social approach' to care which means including mental, emotional and social factors as well as any physical factors that occur. The holistic approach considers each of the P.I.E.S. separately but also considers their integration.

The holistic approach is very similar to the social model, which acknowledges that symptoms exist and have medical causes that require treatment but which identifies many of the problems facing people as being based in society. It recognises that attitudes within society, and the design of society, often prevent people from 'performing normally'. People who have only one good leg are likely to experience mobility problems. This is more likely to be due to a transport system that is not user friendly rather than having one good leg.

Factors in society are seen as barriers that help keep the individual in the **restrictive** medical model rather than enabling them to move to the empowering social model. Under the social model, the main solution lies with taking advantage of modern technology to enable people to overcome their difficulties, changing negative attitudes and creating a more equal society. The social model encourages an empowering approach and looks at ways of enabling people to fully participate in everyday life. A simple example is that of a gate which has a self-opening door, controlled by a remote control. This enables drivers, regardless of ability, to drive in and out through the gate without getting out of the car. It is beneficial to people who are small, concerned about personal security or have children in the car. The services this model promotes would be those that assist people in practical terms, but also that empower them.

The traditional model is the 'medical' model. Using the medical model a person tends to be seen as having a medical problem because part of the body is not working properly. The response is to try and cure or manage the problem, using medical means. This then becomes the responsibility of the medical and associated experts, e.g. doctors, physiotherapists, support workers, social workers and care staff.

Holistic health means considering the whole person:

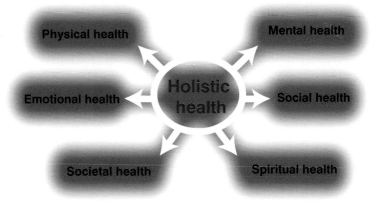

Considering these different aspects of health can be complex. Some activities which are conducted by human beings go across more than one component. For example, having a very close relationship with another person could involve all the components and could be interrelated.

The empowerment approach

The **empowerment** approach helps individuals to identify their personal issues and concerns and to gain the confidence and skills to deal with them. However, 'empowerment' can have two interpretations:

- **self empowerment** – helping service users to have more control over their lives
- **community empowerment** – gaining skills as a group to alter the community in which we live (social reality).

One method used in health and social care that illustrates the empowerment model is the development by medical staff and social care workers of **care plans** and assessment plans. These are developed jointly involving staff and service users. Staff work with service users, listening to their opinions and views. They provide information for the service user which allows the service user to make choices. The care plan or the **assessment** plan is drawn up as a result of working together as the service user has been empowered to make decisions and to take some responsibility. Similarly in childcare, teachers identify the needs of the children within their care, drawing up **individual education plans** which will help children to reach their full potential. Where possible the children are involved in the decision-making process and parents are consulted.

The empowerment model is time-consuming, but does enable the service user to take responsibility for their own care or learning.

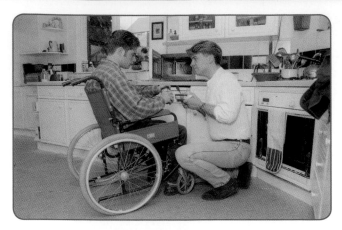

Making an assessment of the service user's need

Geoff   CASE STUDY

Geoff has been living in his own home but recently he has had several falls and the GP has requested an assessment of Geoff's needs by a social worker. The social worker arranges a time to visit with Geoff to make an assessment of his needs.

During the visit Geoff is given a range of information about services that could be provided in his own home that would provide support. He is also given information about residential homes and the social worker offers to arrange for someone to take him on a visit to several of these. With Geoff's consent the social worker observes Geoff making a cup of tea and washing his hands and face. He discusses his findings with Geoff after the observation.

Geoff   Activity 4

1   In pairs, role play the situation given in the case study, one person taking the role of Geoff and the other the role of the social worker. Use the empowerment approach to meet Geoff's needs.

Did you experience any difficulties?
What were these?

Did you find any disadvantages?
What were these?

2   Draw up another role play demonstrating the empowerment method for a teacher and child in a nursery school. The teacher is drawing up an individual learning plan for a nursery-aged child.

Did you experience any difficulties?
What were these?

Did you find any disadvantages?
What were these?

Theory into practice

Discuss as a group how the empowerment approach has been used by the social worker.

What are the advantages and disadvantages?

The behaviourist approach

In this approach service users are encouraged to adopt behaviours that improve health. One of the main disadvantages of this method is that an individual must be ready to take action, or the change is ineffective.

An advantage of the behaviourist approach is that individuals consider they have some ownership of it and that they are choosing to change and are willingly participating in the change to their care and lifestyle.

When using this approach care workers are involved in educating service users either as a small group or as individuals. For example, a person who has a heart attack and whose lifestyle involves eating a lot of fatty and junk food and who does not exercise and who smokes, can have their behaviour changed through the provision of information and one-to-one counselling by care workers. By providing this approach the service user is informed about the factors that have contributed to the heart attack and would probably be inclined to change his/her behaviour. The behaviour may not change drastically but it can be shaped and the service user could gradually change as improvement is seen.

Individual care and assessment plans

A practitioner drawing up an assessment or care plan will endeavour to use one or more of the approaches given above. The purpose of an assessment plan is to find out what the client is able to do or might be able to do if one of the approaches were used.

A care plan is drawn up after an assessment has been made in order to improve the quality of life for the service user.

Both assessment plans and care plans will be dealt with in more depth in the section that follows.

10.2.3 Ways in which practitioners in services work within multi-disciplinary teams

A multi-disciplinary team

Multi-disciplinary teams are not new but have currently become more common as they provide a **seamlessness of service** which is beneficial to the service user. Job roles, too, have changed, whichever sector an individual is working in, and one practitioner now has to be able to **multi-skill** in order to work effectively.

The initial assessment of needs and the care management cycle

The care management process is a system for assessing and organising the provision of care for an individual. Even when a service user appears to have the same condition as another their needs will be different because of their circumstances.

The stages involved in care management

The care management process is a cyclical process. There are seven main stages in the process. These include:

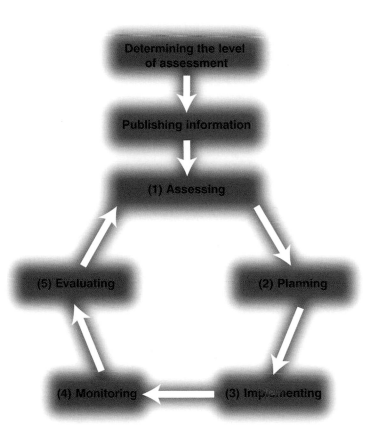

Publishing information

Care agencies provide information about the type of care they can offer, when they can offer it and a broad indication of costs. The care agencies clearly indicate, to both service user and to Social Services, the areas of care for which they are prepared to take responsibility. This is usually published as an information leaflet or in the form of a booklet or guide. Such services, if used, will have to be purchased, either by Social Services if they are to be provided free to the service user or by the service user themselves. The latter is usual if the service user has an income which is above that determined by the government for receiving free care.

Determining the level of assessment

A decision has to be made as to whether an assessment of need is of a simple or complex nature. The service user making an enquiry will indicate whether, for example, they need an assessment for one particular need or whether there are multiple needs that require assessment.

Stage 1: The assessment

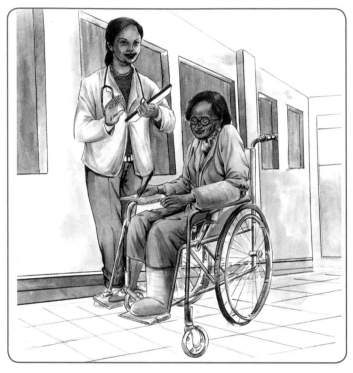

All needs must be considered when making an assessment

People should be referred to services according to their level of risk to independence that may occur if their needs are not met. When an assessment is sought, a referral will be made to the Social Services department. Such a referral could come from a GP, a hospital or another care professional. Once the enquiry is received it will be passed to the most appropriate department within Social Services to deal with. Within the department a person will be allocated to assess the service user's needs, for example a social worker or an occupational therapist. The person who carries out the assessment of needs must also, however, take into consideration the needs of the main carer who currently looks after the service user who is being assessed.

The order in which the assessment is carried out always follows the same pattern. That is:

- establishing the **scope** of the assessment
- deciding which location will be best for the assessment to take place
- making sure the service user is aware of the expectations
- ensuring the service user will participate in the assessment process
- making sure that a trusting relationship is established between the service user and the person undertaking the assessment
- assessing the needs of the service user
- making an agreement with the service user about the objectives
- recording the findings of the assessment
- forming a report about the results of the assessment.

During the initial assessment a practitioner will:

- talk with and listen to the service user
- talk with and listen to informal carers
- provide information about what is available
- (may) observe the service user carrying out a variety of tasks
- record information observed or discussed
- discuss with the service user their preferences regarding services that may be needed
- write a report about the outcomes of the assessment.

When undertaking an assessment it will be important to find out what is the least that it is necessary to know. The assessor (social worker) must, therefore, know how to target the relevant areas of need. If a complex assessment is to be carried out, a high level of skills will be needed to determine the scope of the assessment.

For example, in a complex situation it may be necessary to involve more than the assessor and the service user. An occupational therapist or a physiotherapist may also need to be involved. Assessment is between the assessor and the service user, being a two-way process that involves a great deal of trust. If other professionals are involved in the assessment, consent will need to be obtained from the service user for this to occur.

Discussion point

What other situation would be 'complex' involving the attendance of another person during assessment? Why would this be so?

An assessment, when it is carried out will:

Principle	What will this mean?
Be person centred	Consider the whole person not just the parts that are not functioning according to the norm
View the person to be assessed in the context of their family	Look at the needs of others in the family as well as those of the person
Apply the care values	Treat the person who is being assessed and their family with respect and dignity, making sure that their confidentiality is maintained and that equal opportunity, rights and beliefs are respected
Identify the service user's weaknesses as well as their strengths	Build on the strengths of the service user to assist with any weaknesses that exist
Take a multi-disciplinary approach to service provision	Linking health and social care services together to provide continuity and seamlessness of service
Be based on evidence-based knowledge	Using information gained through questioning and observation on which to base decisions
Will be clear	Will set out exactly what is to be assessed

The outcome of the assessment should be that the service user's strengths and weaknesses have been identified. It will then be possible to balance the two in order to achieve an holistic approach. Records of the assessment will be kept by the assessor. This could involve:

- a record of questions answered
- a tick box showing which tasks were accomplished successfully and which the service user was unable to complete
- an observation sheet indicating the skills demonstrated.

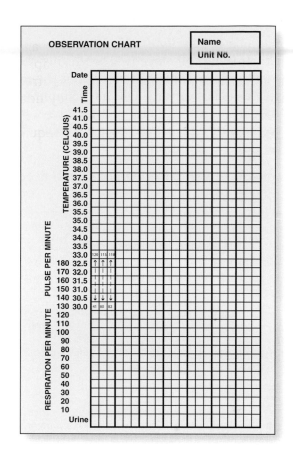

Needs	How needs are met	Action taken by
Personal Hygiene	Washing morning and evening	Care Assistant
	Bathing once every 2 days	Health Care Assistant
Domestic Tasks	Cleaning kitchen and sitting room each day	Care Assistant
	Cleaning bathroom/ bedroom twice each week	Care Assistant
	Shopping twice a week	Care Assistant
Nursing Needs	Dressing on leg to be changed daily	District Nurse
	Medication to be renewed	District Nurse
Personal Needs	Putting to bed – each day	Health Care Assistant
	Getting up – each day	Health Care Assistant
Social Needs	Visit to day care centre twice each week	Social Worker

Different records used to record the assessment process

Stage 2: Care planning

Care planning is identifying the most appropriate ways of achieving the objectives set during the assessment process. This will mean that the assessor (probably a social worker), will have identified the needs of the service user and will then have to link these to the best type of resources available. They will also have to set priorities.

When planning, the following points will need to be determined:

Explore the resources
What is available? Will they cost the service user or Social Services? Are they the best to meet the service user's needs?

Consider alternatives
What alternative services are on offer? Will they cost more or less than those first considered?

Establish preferences
Set the proposals with the alternatives to the service user and the main professional care workers. Discuss which are the most suitable.

Cost the care plan
How much will the individual services cost? Can the budget meet this need? What will the service user have to contribute from a financial perspective?

Agree with the provider the objectives that will be met
Finalise the arrangements with the service users and the providers, making sure the objectives are being met.

Co-ordinate the plan
Look at the whole plan to ensure that it is clear to all concerned.

Set the review date
The service user should be given the date set for the first review.

Identify any needs which have not been met
For what reason has a need not been met?

Record the agreements made
Clearly set out the actions that have been agreed.

Stage 3: Implementing the care plan/contributing to the provision of services

Responsibility for ensuring that the care plan is implemented at the correct pace will be that of the key worker. (Implementing means carrying out the plan or contributing the services.) The service user and the main carer(s) should be encouraged to contribute their ideas as much as possible, as the intention of any plan is to improve the quality of life for the service user and to ease the burden of caring on the main carer.

While the plan is being implemented, it is important to set out the arrangements for monitoring it. This is essential to make sure that the plan is still on course.

Stage 4: Monitoring the care plan

The services supplying care must be carefully monitored to ensure that:

- the expected quality of care is being provided
- the care being provided meets the objectives that were agreed
- the care being provided meets the cost agreed
- the timing of the service provision is suitable to the service user and the main carer
- any changes from the agreed plan and the reasons for such changes are recorded.
- a check is made whether there are any deficiencies within the plan.

Monitoring a care plan is important because it ensures that the service user's needs are continuing to be met. Monitoring involves:

Monitoring the objectives of the care plan
Is each agency delivering the service that was agreed?

Monitoring the co-ordination of services
Do the services complement one another? Is all information being shared? Are they being managed? Is there continuity of care?

Monitoring service delivery
Are all contributors fulfilling their commitment to the standards that were agreed?

Monitoring the quality of care
The quality of care that is delivered will be specified in the contracts agreed. Is the detail being met?

Monitoring the budget
Is the agreed amount of money being spent as agreed by each provider? Does this amount fall within the budget allocated?

Supporting service users
Is the service user satisfied with the care received?

Supporting informal carers
Is the care meeting expectations? Is it providing the desired help required?

Monitoring professional care workers
Resolving conflicts, checking on progress and chasing where there is a deficit.

Monitoring if needs are being met
Is fine tuning and change necessary to reflect the needs of the service user?

Where possible the person responsible for managing the care plan should also be responsible for monitoring, as this will ensure continuity of care. A variety of people will be involved in the monitoring process, for example:

- service users
- main informal carers
- service providers
- purchasing agencies
- inspection personnel
- managers/key workers.

Discussion point

Why is monitoring such an important part of the care management cycle?

Monitoring is to ensure that the objectives are being met and to ensure that care plans are adapted to meet the changing needs of service users. Monitoring could involve telephone calls, questionnaires, observation, home visits and interviews. It will be essential to establish exactly what has happened, what is happening and checking that this matches the needs of the service user and the intended outcome of the care pan.

Stage 5: Reviewing/evaluating the care plan

A review of a care plan must be made within the first six weeks of the starting date, according to 'The Department of Health Practice Guidance'. An evaluation or review must take place every year, or more frequently if it is considered necessary. Evaluation involves:

- looking at the objectives
- considering the nature of the interventions
- assessing the effectiveness of what has taken place
- considering if there is a need for improvement.

It is essential that a balanced view is taken when reviewing/evaluating. Those involved will need to reflect and to make informed judgements about what has taken place. They will need to analyse and to make critical judgements about whether aspects of the care plan could have been improved and whether the outcomes actually match with the objectives set.

Katrina Activity 5

Katrina is 81 years of age. She is recovering from a broken hip in hospital but is now ready to return to her own home. An assessment of her need is to be done in her own home before she finally leaves hospital.

1 Identify who is likely to attend Katrina's assessment. Explain the role of each.

2 Explain how the care management process will be applied to Katrina.

3 Describe **two** activities that are likely to take place at each stage of the care management process, identifying the professionals that will carry out the tasks.

4 Explain the difference between 'monitoring' and 'evaluating' the care plan.

Ensuring an integrated and seamless approach to service provision

Linking health and social care services together to provide continuity and seamlessness of service provides continuity for the service user. As a result the whole needs of the service user will be taken into consideration by the whole team rather than different individuals attending to their authorised portion.

Enabling early intervention and prevention

Because a range of professionals are dealing with the service user it is more likely that any conditions or potential symptoms of disease will be noticed fairly early. Such an approach will ensure that health screening can be conducted early and so possibly prevent any disease or condition from spreading without notice. This can also save the service user unnecessary pain and suffering.

Ensuring the co-ordination of services

All concerned with the care plan will be checking whether the services complement one another. They will ensure that all information is being shared so that no one is working 'in the dark'. Checking that the services are being managed correctly, so that:

- the service user receives the most effective care
- the plan is carried out according to the specifications
- the care provided does not exceed the cost

- that services are co-ordinated and that, for example, they do not attend the service user on the same day, will be extremely important for effectiveness.

Providing best value for the community and individuals

By constituting and implementing all stages of the care management process accurately both the individual and the community will benefit: the individual because the quality of their life has been improved; the community because the individual is able to contribute to a wider group – society.

A multi-disciplinary approach

A multi-disciplinary approach means that professionals from health and social services work together as a team rather than in isolation. Sometimes the voluntary sector will also be involved, depending on the type of care that is needed. There are advantages to this type of approach. For example:

- all will know what the targets are and will be working together to achieve these
- notes will be shared
- there will be discussion and agreement as to who will be responsible for each task
- timings will be co-ordinated to prevent overlap during visits
- discussion will take place with the whole team in order to achieve monitoring and evaluation
- costs will be shared.

The advantages of a multi-disciplinary approach are:

- carrying out observation – to see what is needed
- having regular meetings of the team – to check on what each is doing, to prevent duplication of activities
- all to be involved in drawing up the care plan so that each knows what the other's role is
- each to meet together to review the care plan so that they can evaluate the contribution each has made, to have an holistic approach, so that together future planning is meaningful
- leaving notes to say what the previous professional has done to keep each member of the team informed, to prevent duplication
- keeping a log – to see what has been done, to avoid duplication, to provide a record
- working out shared cost of care to keep within the budget, to save money, to save human resources, to save on material resources
- shared responsibility so decision making is not dependent on one person.

Care Practice and Provision

10.2.3 Ways in which practitioners in services work within multi-disciplinary teams /
10.2.4 How quality assurance is promoted by services

Assessment activity (AO2)

Maria and Martin CASE STUDY

Maria and Martin are married. Maria is 35 years old and Martin is 40 years old. They have two children; Andre aged 13 and Alicia who is 8. Martin's mother, Petra, lives with the family as she is a widow and has mild Alzheimer's disease. Petra is 66 years of age.

The family live on the outskirts of a large city in an area where there are a large number of single parents and also a large population of older adults. There are also quite a lot of people with disability living in the area. Maria has a friend who has little mobility due to a stroke.

There is a great deal of unemployment in the community as a car factory closed down 18 months previously and many people living in the area lost their jobs and have been unable to find work since then.

1. Choose **one** service user from the case study. This should be the same service user as used for Assessment activity (AO1).

2. Choose **two** services used by the service user. These can be one health and one social care or one health and one early years or one social care and one early years.

3. Describe in depth the approaches used by the practitioners in the two services used by the service user. Give examples to illustrate the points made.

4. Analyse how the practitioners in the two services chosen meet the needs of the service user.

5. Choose **one** service user from the case study. This should be the same service user as used for Assessment activity (AO1).

6. Choose **two** services used by the service user. These can be one health and one social care or one health and one early years or one social care and one early years. These should be the same as those used in Assessment activity (AO1).

7. Give an in-depth account of how practitioners from the two different services chosen work in multi-disciplinary teams to meet the needs of the service user chosen. Show how this method of working affects the care management cycle, explaining the benefits to the service user.

10.2.4 How quality assurance is promoted by services

What is quality assurance and how is quality care achieved?

The rights and responsibilities of service users and care workers are fundamental human rights which legislation safeguards. Professional care workers will need to know what rights service users have and about the laws that protect them. Quality care is achieved when care settings observe the rights of service users, follow legislation that protects both service users and care workers, and follow procedures that are in place within care settings to ensure the health and safety of all who live and work in them.

Quality care therefore encompasses:

Following safe working practices · Knowing our own attitudes · Not being prejudiced · Preventing barriers to access of services · Promoting quality care · Encouraging high self esteem · Applying the care values · Enabling fair and equal access to services · Knowing about relevant legislation

Improving information and consultation with service users

Making their own decisions or at least being involved in any decisions that concern them is a service user's right. All service users should be presented with options, not given solutions. Such options should be explained so the service user has a wide range of information to consider, from which they can make their decision. Whenever there are options, there are also risks. Care workers have a responsibility to present both sides of a situation so the service user can weigh up the advantages and disadvantages.

Sometimes it may seem hard for a service user to make a decision and on other occasions it may seem both quicker and easier for the care worker to make the decisions for the service user, particularly if the service user has difficulty in communicating. However difficult the situation, the professional care worker should not make the decisions for the service user. All must be done to ensure that the service user has their right to choose and to be consulted about the decisions that will affect them.

Providing service users with information, for example giving them 'Your Guide To The NHS' or providing them with a copy of the setting's 'Mission Statement' may help them to understand why some actions are necessary.

Participating in decision making can help a service user to:

- feel in control of their lives
- feel valued
- be independent.

Some service users may be restricted or limited in some way about the type of lifestyle they are able to have. They may need the help of an 'advocate' to help explain to them the options that are available, particularly if they have a learning disability.

The table below shows how quality assurance can be maintained:

Quality assurance	How quality assurance could be applied
Allowing the service user to express preferences	Examples of allowing service users to express preferences are: • about the GP they will have and deciding which services they may want • allowing them to choose what time they will go to bed or when they will have a bath.
To make choices	Options are possible when service users are given knowledge about the advantages and disadvantages of each option. They may wish to make choices about: • the treatment they have • whether they have traditional or alternative forms of treatment.

Quality assurance	How quality assurance could be applied
Enabling service users to develop their full potential	A service user may be a four year old attending a playgroup, an adult visiting a GP surgery or an older adult in a residential home. Whatever their ability or age the service user should always be encouraged to meet their full potential by: • having individualised action/learning plans • providing activities that are both challenging and stimulating • assisting the service user to reflect on and analyse the experience.
Allowing service users to make complex decisions	Making difficult decisions requires: • information about what is available • discussing options and looking at each from different **perspectives** • finding the best solution for the situation. Care workers must take the time to have discussions with the service user and to make sure they have understood the information presented.
To understand regardless of age and ability	Effective communication is essential. The care worker will need to use language the service user can understand, and speak at a pace that is appropriate.

Implementing quality service standards

In order to improve long-term care the 'National Service Framework' (NSFs) have been set in place. Their purpose is to improve specific areas of care by setting measurable goals which are to be achieved in specific time scales. The National Service Framework aims to:

- set national standards and to identify main interventions for a specific service or group, e.g. children or older people
- put in place strategies to support implementation

- establish ways to make sure progress is within an agreed time scale
- raise quality and decrease variations in services in 'a new and first class service' that is being provided.

The *NSFs* started in April 1998. They bring together health professionals, service users, carers, health service managers, partner agencies and others. The Department of Health provides support for the group and manages their overall process. The group known as *ERG (External Reference Group)* has a rolling programme. Examples of the areas it covers are:

- Coronary heart disease – 12 standards set for improved prevention, diagnosis and treatment. These are to be implemented over a 10-year period.
- Cancer – *The NHS Cancer Plan* was formed in 2000 and provides a programme for the reform of cancer services.
- Paediatric intensive care – to ensure a quality service for children who require intensive care.
- Mental health – concerned with how services for service users with mental-health needs will be planned, delivered and monitored until 2009.
- Older people – setting new national standards and service models across health and social care services for all older people whether they live in residential care or are being cared for in a hospital.
- Diabetes – to make sure that the 1.3 million people who suffer from diabetes receive an excellent standard of care.

There are other NSFs that cover other areas of ill health but all have at the heart of their function the values contained in the *NHS Plan*, that is, good service is the result of forming genuine partnerships between service user and provider. Establishing quality is of prime importance.

Theory into practice

In small groups carry out research into one aspect of the work of NSFs. Websites may help you find the information you need, e.g. www.dhl.gov.uk

Give a brief presentation to others about your work.

Using performance indicators

Performance indicators demonstrate how well a service within the NHS organisation is doing. An example of performance indicators could be found in 'Star Ratings' which gave an overview of:

- how good the Trust's service was to its patients
- how well it was run
- how good it was on reducing treatment waiting times.

Star ratings were awarded according to **performance indicators (PIs)** set by the *Health Commission* (also called *Commission for Health Care Audit and Inspection or CHAI*).

Performance indicators for trusts	Performance indicators for Primary Care Trusts/ Groups (PCTs/PCGs)
Key targets	Key targets
Patient focus	Access to quality services
Clinical focus	Improving health
Capacity and capability focus	Service provision

Training in performance measures — **Activity 6**

You have been asked to carry out a short training session to introduce new nursing trainees to Star Ratings or other performance indicators.

1 Carry out research based on the table above to find out what each performance indicator includes.

2 Prepare handouts to give to the trainees when you give a short presentation to them.

3 Prepare a presentation to explain the differences between the performance indicator for Trusts and the performance indicators for Primary Care Trusts/Groups.

4 Give a presentation to the group. Make sure you prepare speakers notes to accompany the presentation.

5 As a whole group discuss the effects that performance indicators are likely to have on service users.

Promoting quality assurance

Several other methods are being implemented by the NHS to improve quality assurance. These include:

Improving inspection procedures

Several inspection groups are in place, for example:

- CHIA – independent of the government and NHS (see earlier in this unit)
- Commission for Healthcare Audit and Inspection – public and private organisation responsibility
- Department of Health – a variety of inspection responsibilities.

Rewarding good practice

The Charter Mark is an example of providing a reward for good practice. It is given by the government when organisations are giving an excellent public service. Services have to show that they:

- set and meet clear performance indicators
- actively engage with service users
- are fair and accessible to everyone
- use resources effectively
- make a contribution to improving the quality of life in the community.

Evaluating the quality of services

The NHS Plan requires each NHS Trust to obtain feedback from service users. Surveys cover Acute Trusts, Primary Care Trusts, Mental-Health Trusts and others including National Service Frameworks for coronary heart disease, stroke and cancer. Listening to service users' views is considered essential to delivering the commitment given in the NHS Plan. The results of the survey are used in the annual performance indicators.

Questionnaires are used to obtain information when conducting a survey and each question will need to be analysed and evaluated.

Developing systems for complaints

Bodies dealing with complaints are:

- Patient Advice and Liaison Services
- Patient and Public Involvement (PPI) Forums
- Commission for Patient and Public Involvement in Health (CPPIH)
- Independent Complaints Advocacy Services
- The NHS Ombudsman.

Raising training levels within the sector

Council for Healthcare Regulatory Excellence (CHRE) aims to ensure greater consistency of standards and accountability across professional self regulation. It oversees individual NHS Health professionals' regulators, for example the General Medical Council, Health Professional Council and other similar bodies.

General Medical Council (GMC) protects patients, provides guidance for doctors and sets standards for medical education. It also maintains a register of medical practitioners and can suspend doctors when standards are not maintained.

Postgraduate Medical Training Board works closely with educational and regulatory bodies to raise standards of education and training process.

Note: Assessment for AO3 occurs at the end of the underpinning knowledge for 10.2.6

10.2.5 Effects of national policy and legislation on care practice and provision

The effects of legislation reflect on both service users and providers

Service users

All service users have rights. These rights are protected by laws and the application of values.

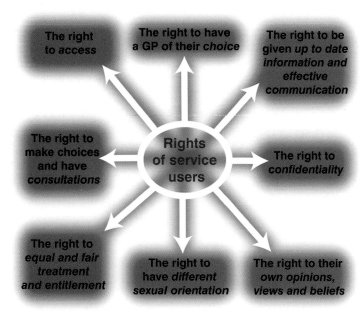

Examples of legislation that protects service users' rights in care settings are:

- Access to Health Records Act 1990
- Access to Personal Files Act 1987
- The Care Standards Act 2000
- The Children Act 1989
- Data Protection Act 1998
- Disability Discrimination Act 1976, 1995

- Mental Health Act 1983
- NHS and Community Health Care Act 1990
- Race Relations Act 1976

See also the following websites plus others in the Bibliography:

http://www.ingentaconnect.com/content/rcm/rcm/2003/00000006/00000009/art00005

http://www.dh.gov.uk/PolicyAndGuidance/OrganisationPolicy/FinanceAndPlanning/PlanningFramework/PrioritiesPlanningFrameworkArticle/fs/en?CONTENT_ID=4015852&chk=LDnu04

http://www.nhs.uk/england/AboutTheNhs/Default.cmsx

www.dh.gov.uk/PolicyAndGuidance/OrganisationPolicy/Commissioning/fs/en

Examples of policies that exist in settings that help to protect service users' rights are:

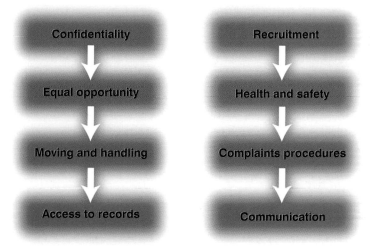

If service users are deprived of their rights it could lead to:

- not feeling valued
- behaviour problems
- low self esteem
- the service user feeling patronised
- the service user feeling they no longer have the right to be heard
- the service user feeling vulnerable.

Such effects can cause the service user to have ill health or go into **remission**. It is quality practice that ensures that procedures are in place within an organisation to make sure that service users do not feel that they are being discriminated against. Professional care workers should always challenge behaviour that does not value people.

Theory into practice

Choose one piece of legislation or one policy and carry out research to find out its aim and purpose. Explore how it affects one of the care settings you have chosen for assessment.

Services and/or practitioners

All care providers and practitioners are required to implement the standards set by government and regulatory bodies. Practitioners have the responsibility of making sure that legislation and policies are applied by themselves in the setting in which they work. They must make sure that the service user's best interests are the focus of all care and support that the service user receives. To enable this to happen services and practitioners need to understand how to apply the factors given below:

Roles and responsibilities
Understanding own role and how it relates to the role of others within the team of carers.

Accountability
Responding openly – recognising constructive criticism is intended to aid professional development and being answerable for one's own actions.

Working collaboratively
Being aware that caring for others means working as a team. This means valuing other services and practitioners, treating them with respect.

Being more responsive to service users' needs
Responding to the needs of service users rather than the practitioner thinking 'they know best'.

Changing existing provision
Services and practitioners will need to recognise that change is for the benefit of all not just one group. Change may be necessary because care needs alter.

Working with other services
Recognising information will need to be shared on a 'need to know' basis.

Joint funding
In multi-network teams responsibility will have to be shared for financial costs.

Make sure service users are empowered
Allowing service users to make decisions about things that affect them, e.g. treatment.

Carrying out a duty of care
Practitioners working wherever needed in a caring manner and without prejudice.

National and local care practice

It is the government's intention to improve the quality of both national and local provision. Its various pieces of legislation and regulation have had this intention at its heart. '*The NHS Plan*' which deals with the 'modernisation' agenda contributes towards this as well as '*Modernising Social Services*' and '*Our Healthier Nation*'.

Improving quality

Anti-discrimination is a way of making sure people are treated equally and with quality. Actions that support anti-discrimination are those that promote procedures and systems to ensure that discrimination does not, as far as is possible, occur.

Treating people equally does not mean treating everybody the same. It means treating service users

Care Practice and Provision

10.2.5 Effects of national policy and legislation on care practice and provision /
10.2.6 Conducting a survey relating to quality assurance

in a way that ensures they have equal access to all services they need. It is also making sure service users get equal benefits from services. Making sure that all service users feel valued is a way of promoting quality. This must be achieved through planning and delivering services.

Encouraging joined-up thinking

How can we best achieve this?

Multi-disciplinary approaches have been dealt with earlier in this unit. (Look back and remind yourself about these.) With the new emphasis of putting patients first, services will no longer be able to work in isolation as the new focus is to provide a continuum approach to care, which means working together is essential.

Changing the level and pattern of provision

The pattern of provision will be changed by the:

• standards set
• targets
• objectives

of any piece of legislation or policy introduced at government level. It will also be changed by the amount of funding allocated to the standard. 'Every Child Matters' reflects this for all its targets and objectives, an example of one being school meals. Certain foods can no longer be sold in school canteens, and other regulations have been introduced to ensure that healthy foods are introduced to children's meal time in schools.

Using funding to target national priorities

Funding to promote a piece of legislation or policy will help to ensure its success. This can be seen through a variety of government standards:

• *Every Child Matters*
  – money for healthy foods to be served
  – money to increase the standards of kitchens which are producing meals

• Reducing heart disease and strokes in men aged between 35 and 45
  – money for GP surgeries who provide basic diagnostic testing
  – money for hospitals who conduct more detailed testing on those who are referred by GPs.

National funding will result in more local services being provided.

10.2.6 Conducting a survey relating to quality assurance

How can we explore these issues?

Conducting a survey is a way of gathering information about a certain subject, in this case to find out how quality practice is achieved in care settings. The person conducting the survey will have to decide which data collecting tool(s) or method(s) will be used to get the information needed. There are advantages and disadvantages to all data collection tools.

A range of methods could be used for the collecting of information, for example:

- interviewing people
- using questionnaires
- observation of people or situations
- carrying out experiments.

Frequently more than one method is used to gather information for a survey, depending on the subjects that information is required about. For this survey, based on 'quality assurance mechanisms and practice in care settings', the focus of information gathering could be:

- through interviews
- by using questionnaires
- through observation.

Such methods will produce both **quantitative** data and **qualitative** data. Quantitative data is numerical and can be analysed using statistical methods. An example of a question that produces quantitative data would be, 'the number of complaints received in a six-month period'. Quantitative data can be displayed using graphs, charts and tables. If only a questionnaire was used to gather information about quality practice, the results could be very limited.

Qualitative data concerns attitudes and opinions and often cannot be produced in numerical form. The participants might talk about their feelings, for example, a service user may say, 'I feel I cannot complain as I don't know how'. Qualitative data is expressed in words and not in numbers.

Both qualitative and quantitative data can produce useful and meaningful results.

Look at the detail in Unit 16 to find out more about 'research techniques' before carrying on with your own questionnaire.

Devise questionnaires

A **self completed** questionnaire is one where the researcher hands out a questionnaire to the participants, who then answer the questions by filling in the answers in the spaces provided. The questionnaires are then collected by the researcher.

Survey – quality care practice

1   List the systems that are in place to maintain confidentiality:
       a) ....

       b) ....
       c) ....
       d) ....

2   Do you think these are effective?
       ....
       Why? ....
       ....

There are quite a number of questions to answer

This is a way of collecting qualitative data. The advantages of using questionnaires are that they are cheap, quick, anonymous and a way to collect information without interviewer bias. Participants can also take their time to answer the questions. The disadvantage is that there may be a poor response rate. For a survey that is investigating the quality care mechanisms in a care setting, a questionnaire could be the best option on its own.

When using a questionnaire:

- Use a short introduction that explains why the survey is being carried out and covers the issue of confidentiality.
- Begin with easy to answer closed questions and work towards questions which need more thought at the end.
- Ask factual response questions linked to demographic factors about the respondent such as age, sex, ethnicity, for example.

Remember:

- make sure the questions are easy to understand
- do not use questions which allow the respondent to repeat a previous answer
- do not assume the respondents have any previous knowledge of the topics
- thank the respondents for completing the questionnaire, once finished.

Ideas for the methods used for the survey could come from secondary research, for example from the work of others who have already completed similar research. Secondary sources can provide data that would be difficult to collect for oneself. For example, government papers, research papers and statistics completed after inspection reports may all help to make decisions about the methods that should be used for conducting the survey.

Research — **Activity 7**

You have been asked to collect information about how a care setting ensures quality practice.

1. Work in pairs to produce **four** research questions based on quality mechanisms that could be used by care settings if you were producing a self completed questionnaire.

2. Share your questions with another pair within the group and ask them to try answering the questions. Did you get the type of answers you were looking for? Rewrite any questions that were ambiguous or were not successful.

3. As a whole group discuss some of the issues that have arisen when producing the questions.

4. Work in a small group to think about qualitative data that you might want to collect about quality mechanisms. Work out the main topics.

5. Write **four** questions that could be used in an in-depth interview with a care worker or manager to find out about quality practice.

A plan provides a framework within which to work. Decisions will need to be made about:

- the aim of the survey, e.g. what is the overall purpose?
- the objectives, e.g. what are the steps within the aim to achieve the outcome?
- the time scales for the survey, e.g. start and completion times
- which care setting, e.g. residential home, day care centre, hospital – will you be able to obtain all the information you need?
- who is to be involved in the research, e.g. professional care worker or manager?
- the method(s) to be used, e.g. self completed questionnaire, structured interview or both?
- the type of questions, e.g. open and/or closed, follow-on questions?
- how the results are to be presented, e.g. graphs, charts?

If the survey is to be carried out through a questionnaire or an interview, the sequence of the questions cannot be decided until the questions themselves are written.

For this survey the main topics are:

- What mechanisms are in place to maintain quality practice?
- Which quality assurance mechanisms are used when dealing with complaints?
- Which quality assurance mechanisms are used when working in a multi-disciplinary team?
- How do legislation and policies contribute to providing quality care?
- How does the legislation/policy affect day-to-day living/staffing?

It must be remembered that the focus of the survey is on quality assurance mechanisms so questions must be focused on this. Make sure both open and closed questions are used and that follow-on questions are appropriately placed.

Collection of information

The researcher will need to prepare a document for recording the questions and a space to be able to write the answers given. This is an example of the type of document and questions that could be used in an interview:

Questions	Answers
1 Can you tell me what rights service users have?	
2 What systems are in place to maintain the right to choose?	
3 Do you have a policy to help maintain rights?	
4 Can you give me some ideas as to what is in the policy?	
5 What mechanism do you have to check quality assurance for efficiency?	
6 How are new staff made aware of the setting's quality assurance mechanisms?	
7 What monitoring methods do you have in place to ensure that rights are maintained?	
8 What would happen if a service user were denied their rights?	

An example of an open question in this recording document is:

'What systems are in place to maintain the right to choose?' Follow-on question, 'how are these effective?' These questions allow the person being interviewed to give their thoughts and feelings on the subject as well as being able to talk about the facts.

An example of a closed question in this recording document is:

'Do you have a policy on allowing service users to have rights?' The care worker can answer 'yes' or 'no' to this question.

Sometimes follow-on questions are required. For example, if the care worker says 'yes', the follow-on question would be 'can you tell me what is in the policy?' If the care worker says 'no' the follow-on question might be 'can you tell me why you do not have a policy relating to choice?'

When producing questions for the survey, it will be necessary to include some follow-on questions to obtain the whole picture of what is happening as far as quality care is concerned.

Before visiting the care setting with the questions and recording documents it is always a good idea to 'trial' the questions. This means trying them on another person to see if they are **unambiguous** and that they produce the type of answers that are needed. Giving the questions to other people in the group or to relatives or friends is a method that could be used when trialling. Being able to trial questions provides the opportunity to alter any questions that are not clear.

Find out how data from quality assurance responses is used

Data collected by the person who has conducted the survey will need to be examined. Examining the responses will help to analyse and interpret the information collected.

Quantitative information can be collated into a table of responses. This information can then be presented using a computer spreadsheet. The program will calculate statistics for you and enable you to create graphs or charts.

A frequency table and pie chart

Confidentiality is securely maintained in the care setting:

	No	%
Strongly agree	20	40
Agree	10	20
Neutral	6	12
Disagree	4	8
Strongly disagree	10	20
Total	50	100

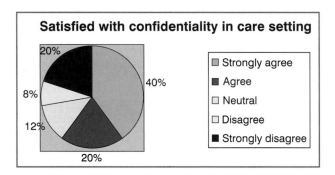

Qualitative data is more difficult to present and needs a word-based description of the findings. Written discussion of findings could include flow charts or diagrams to illustrate particular points. Where respondents give similar answers, these can be presented using graphs or charts as for the quantitative data.

Analysis of qualitative data is similar to writing a report. A summary will be required of comments made, trying to give an accurate account of what has been said. These should not be written word for word. Quotes can be given to clarify and confirm what the care worker or service user has said. It is important to keep referring back to the questions asked so that a meaningful picture is given.

Assessment activity (AO3)

Maria and Martin   CASE STUDY

Maria and Martin are married. Maria is 35 years old and Martin is 40 years old. They have two children; Andre aged 13 and Alicia who is 8. Martin's mother, Petra, lives with the family as she is a widow and has mild Alzheimer's disease. Petra is 66 years of age.

The family live on the outskirts of a large city in an area where there are a large number of single parents and also a large population of older adults. There are also quite a lot of people with disability living in the area. Maria has a friend who has little mobility due to a stroke.

There is a great deal of unemployment in the community as a car factory closed down 18 months previously and many people living in the area lost their jobs and have been unable to find work since then.

1 Choose **one** service user from the case study. This should be the same service user as used for Assessment activities (AO1) and (AO2).

2 Choose **two** services used by the service user. These can be one health and one social care or one health and one early years or one social care and one early years. These should be the same as those used in Assessment activities (AO1) and (AO2).

3 Using a range of research techniques, including primary and secondary sources, giving reasons for their use, comprehensively analyse the quality assurance mechanisms used by the two services chosen. For example, you could use questionnaire, interviews, surveys, observation and primary sources.

4 Keep a bibliography/source list of the sources used and give reasons for the use of each.

Remember to make reference to the Assessment Grid **AND** amplification found in the Unit Specifications which gives guidance about the depth and breadth of evidence required.

Evaluate the effects of one national policy or one piece of legislation on care practice and provision (AO4)

Look back at the previous section and select a piece of legislation or a policy that has had an effect on the two services you have chosen.

Theory into practice

In groups choose one from:

- NHS Plan
- Care Standards Act 2000
- Clinical Governance
- Our Healthier Nation
- Every Child Matters
- Any other that interests you

Discuss the effect of the legislation or policy on the settings chosen. Examine this from the perspective of the service users and the practitioners, as well as the effect it has had on the service.

The point of evaluation is analysing the results of the survey and drawing conclusions about the topics, for example the mechanisms used by two services to ensure quality care. Reflecting on the results of the analysis will be required, that is, to consider what you have found out and to draw conclusions based on your findings by making judgements.

It will be important to make sure the conclusions are supported by the data (information) collected. However, the information collected may show that some mechanisms are effective while others might not be. Whether rights are being partially met or fully met, the conclusions drawn must be supported by evidence from the data collected.

Example of drawing a conclusion supported by evidence from the data

'At Portside Trust Hospital I asked how the service users' views on quality assurance were collected and presented. I was told the service users were provided with a questionnaire which was completed at the end of their stay. At the end of each month the information was collated and conclusions were drawn against each question.'

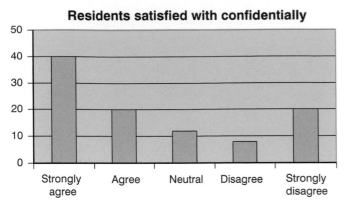

Residents satisfied with confidentially

Example bar graph of 'see at a glance' results from frequency table on page 36

'The results were issued to all involved with the patients' care for that month and at meetings these were discussed and viewed against the targets set and against the performance indicators. Ways of improving performance were also discussed with action points made for the future'.

From this evidence it is possible:

• to know the question that was asked
• to recognise that a conclusion has been drawn

• to see that conclusions drawn are supported by evidence, e.g. observation, written policies, answers to questions.

Using quality assurance to inform future action

Research is often based on a cyclical movement.

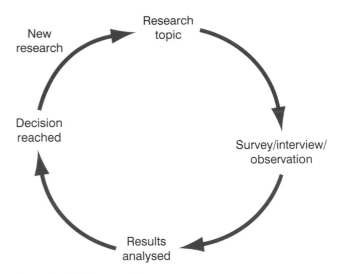

The wheel of research

Informing future practice is an important aspect of any research, giving purpose and improving standards.

Assessment activity (AO4)

Maria and Martin   CASE STUDY

You have conducted a survey to find out about the mechanisms used by **two** settings to provide quality assurance.

Write an in-depth evaluation making reasoned judgements and drawing valid conclusions about the effects of **one piece of legislation or policy** on care practice and provision of the service chosen. Evaluate how this has affected:

• the service user
• the practitioner
• the service.

Remember to make reference to the Assessment Grid **AND** amplification found in the Unit Specifications which give guidance about the depth and breadth of evidence required.

Unit 11 Understanding Human Behaviour

Contents

About this unit

Within this unit you will investigate:

- factors influencing human development
- theories relating to human development
- how to apply theories to aid understanding of human behaviour of individuals in care settings.

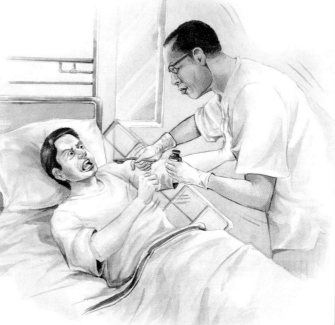

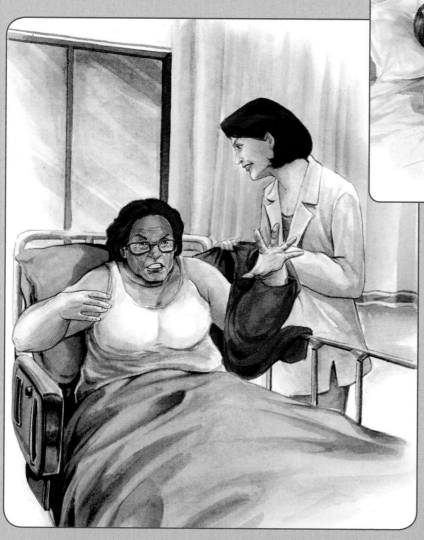

Working effectively with others means understanding the reasons why people behave as they do

Introducing this unit

Human behaviour in the caring sector, including early years, can be a fascinating subject. Often service users who need care do not act in a reasoned, logical way. Why might this be? There could be a number of answers to that question, but some of the main reasons are that the service users may feel threatened by the situation in which they find themselves; they may feel that they are no longer in control; they may feel fearful or they may not trust those who are caring for them. Those who require care are **vulnerable** and may behave very defensively.

Human behaviour is very complex and to understand why people behave in a particular way means that it is necessary to study the influences that have affected the development of an individual, such as inherited, social, economic, environmental and psychological influences. It is also necessary to consider some of the theories put forward to explain human behaviour, for example those of Freud, Erikson, Rogers, Vygotsky, Bandura and others. The views of such theorists can help to explain the behaviour of those for whom we are caring and help us to interpret why service users are behaving in a certain way.

Professional care workers need to be aware of how to manage challenging behaviour, in a manner that will provide support and which will promote a positive self concept. Having the ability to interpret the behaviour of service users, whether it is positive or negative, is an important aspect of the caring process and can be applied to settings whatever life stage the service user is in.

11.2.1 Factors influencing human development

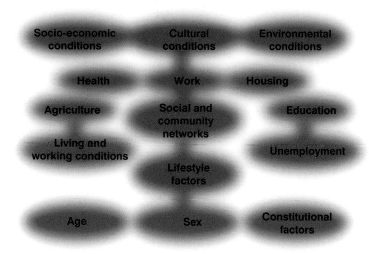

Factors that can affect development

Human development is affected by many factors which may have a positive or detrimental influence. Understanding the factors that influence human behaviour means that the **nature-nurture** debate must be considered. For example, which has the stronger influence – nature or nurture? Inherited factors such as inherited disability, known as the 'nature' factor, or the experiences an individual has, for example education, known as the 'nurture' factor. In other words are the skills that we possess **innate** or are they socially learned.

Inherited influences

Genetic inheritance is having a mixture of genes from our parents that instruct our bodies to make an enormous range of proteins. These make up the structures of our cells and tissues. They control all the chemical reactions going on in our body so determining what we look like and how our body works. They also control what diseases we are susceptible to and which we can fight off, as well as being involved directly, or indirectly, in all aspects of our metabolism. Early philosophers believed that much of our personality and intellect was determined by the genes inherited and could not be interfered with. We will certainly have some inherited influences from our parents but we also develop according to other external influences such as the friends we have, our culture, where we live, the amount of money available to us and the education we have.

Theory into practice

Discuss with another person the aspects of your own development that are a result of 'nature' and those which have been influenced by 'nurture'.

The rate at which we **mature** is genetically determined. Maturation is the rate of physical growth and starts at **conception**. All normal foetuses develop at approximately the same rate (the norm), and after birth we all learn to crawl, walk and run within approximately the same time scales. All people pass through the same stages of maturation in the same order. However, we don't all mature at *exactly* the same rate. For example, some children stand at six months, but others not until ten months. Children are not all the same, however, and this is because each person's combination of genes is different.

Maturation at an early age

Discussion point

Why are all children not the same?

Autism

Autism is a disorder which disrupts the development of social and communication skills. Autism is severely incapacitating and is a life-long disability that usually appears within the first three years of life. It is best described as a **neurological dysfunction** with 75% of those with autism also having accompanying learning difficulties.

An autistic child

Autism and its related disorders are estimated to occur in 1 in 500 individuals. The disorder is more common in boys than in girls and knows no racial or social boundaries. Autism is not a mental disorder and children who have the disorder are not simply children who choose not to behave in the accepted way. Some people think that MMR vaccines may cause autism but this has not been proved, in fact it is nearer to being disproved.

Some children who have this disorder are only affected mildly while others may be more severely affected. Areas affected by having autism could be:

Communication – language develops slowly or not at all, with speech developing much later than usual. When it does develop, language skills may not be normal, for example:

- the child may not be able to express themselves well
- they may not be able to make up their own words
- they may not use hand gestures when they speak
- they may not understand difficult commands
- they may not be able to understand facial expressions or tone of voice.

Behaviour – an autistic child may also display some other unusual behaviour, for example:

- anger if routines change
- they may hurt themselves when they are angry by banging their head to get the attention of their carer
- they may laugh or giggle at things which are not appropriate
- they may avoid eye contact
- they may have no fear of danger
- imaginative play is limited.

Parents who have an autistic child may feel angry or guilty with themselves, blaming themselves for their child's condition. They will require a lot of practical support and may find joining a support group helpful. Treatment for an autistic child will involve both physical and neurological examination. It may include specific diagnostic tests such as:

- Autism Diagnostic Observation Schedule (ADOS)
- Autism Diagnostic Interview-Revise (ADI-R)
- Gilliam Autism Rating Scale
- Childhood Autism Rating Scale (CARS).

Development of communication and language skills is a very important aspect of treatment and visual aids are often helpful with this process. Designing an individualised programme is also essential and will involve a combination of supporting therapies.

Theory into practice

Try to invite a specialist to the Centre to talk about autism. Try to find out about the symptoms and behaviour of children with autism and how a child can be encouraged to develop communication and language skills both at home and when they reach school age.

Dorrinda   CASE STUDY

Dorrinda is 4 years old and has autism. She lives with her two sisters and brother, all of whom are older than Dorrinda. Dorrinda's mother first noticed that she was not developing normally for her age when she was nine months old, as she was not doing the same things as other children of that age. Her mother took her to her GP who referred Dorrinda to a child psychologist. Eventually it was agreed that Dorrinda had autism and special help was organised.

1. Give the possible causes of Dorrinda's autism.

2. Explain how Dorrinda's intellectual, emotional and social patterns may not follow the norm for her age.

3. Explain how the family could help Dorrinda.

4. Explain the specialist professional help that could be available for Dorrinda and other children who may be autistic.

Tourette's syndrome

One of the winners of 'Big Brother' had Tourette's syndrome

This is a rare disorder that starts in childhood with repetitive grimaces and tics usually of the head and neck and sometimes of the arms and legs. It is accompanied by involuntary barks, grunts and other noises which may occur as the disease progresses. In many cases those who have the disease experience 'coprolalia', which means using foul language or swearing. This is uncontrollable and can be embarrassing for those with the condition. The syndrome is more common in males and is life-long.

Other genetic influences

Cystic fibrosis is a disease caused by a faulty gene that results in the body producing mucus that is much stickier than normal. This mucus, which would normally perform a protective or lubricating function, clogs up tubes in the lungs, pancreas and reproductive structures. Life expectancy is much better than it used to be and people with this condition, which is usually diagnosed in early childhood, live well into adulthood, leading near normal lives. This condition does, however, affect their ability at certain sports owing to impaired lung function and can lead to reduced growth rates owing to the effect on the digestive system. Regular physiotherapy is required and CF patients do tend to suffer frequently from severe lung infections that result in hospital stays. Emotional, social and cognitive development can all, therefore, be affected as schooling and social interaction is disrupted.

PKU (phenylketonuria) is also a genetic metabolic defect resulting in the build-up of a chemical derived from dietary protein call phenylalanine. This is tested for after birth and can be dealt with following a strict diet. If not detected, or if the diet is not adhered to, brain damage occurs, resulting in learning difficulties and behavioural changes.

Recent research in the United States shows that there is a gene that causes disruptive and aggressive behaviour. The studies carried out on twins show that some children will be badly behaved no matter what sort of environment they are brought up in. Their anti-social behaviour was directly related to the level of activity of the gene. Other research has identified four genes which make those with them more likely to indulge in criminal activity.

Genes will affect us physically by producing physical or metabolic differences that favour certain individuals in particular sports, for example making some more suited to short anaerobic bursts of activity like sprinting, whilst others would be better at long aerobic sports like marathons.

Susceptibility to certain diseases runs in families, whether it is high cholesterol levels leading to an increased likelihood of coronary heart disease, or carrying particular genes that increase the risk of breast cancer. Some women with such a family history choose to have both breasts removed before there is any chance of developing the cancer. Other families carry genes that affect the pumping of the heart and unless detected will result in impaired breathing as the lungs fill with fluid. Premature death is a possibility without treatment, which may involve a heart transplant.

The symptoms of Huntington's disease only start to show in people in their late 40s or early 50s causing loss of balance and jerky movements before progressing to dementia. There is a fifty percent chance that their children will have this condition.

Sometimes there is a large imbalance of genes which results in a pronounced effect on our development and behaviour. Here whole chromosomes containing hundreds of genes are either extra or missing. Conditions such as Down's syndrome with all its various effects on physical, behavioural and cognitive development is one such example of an extra chromosome, as is Kleifelter's syndrome, where men have an extra X chromosome. This may lead to abnormal development at puberty resulting in some feminine features such as breasts, soft skin and a higher or softer voice. Some learning difficulties may also be evident.

Genes therefore have a profound affect on all aspects of our development but these effects can obviously be further influenced by our environment.

Socio-economic influences

Socio-economic influences include both **primary** and **secondary** socialisation.

Family

The home is the first place where an individual is socialised. Socialisation is almost like having

Different types of family each provide primary socialisation of their children

The wider society that influences development

a series of lessons which prepares a child for its adult role. Whether the family is a **nuclear** unit where mother, father, brothers, sisters and extended family exist or whether it is a single parent family or commune, it is the family who are the main people who contribute to learned attitudes and beliefs. It is in this context that a child will learn the way of behaving according to the particular culture of the family in which he/she lives. The **values** and **norms** of the society in which the child is being brought up become the accepted way for the child. The family is responsible for primary socialisation. The family develops the 'conscience' of new members. Once a bond has been formed between a child and its parent or main carer, any threat to that bond will cause the child anxiety. Therefore, rather than losing the close association that it has with its parent or main carer, the child will adopt the norms and values taught by them.

This includes the young child's learning and experiences of prejudice, gender roles and the skills of language. For example, if the family has the attitude that some people are **inferior** to their own family, then the children in the family are likely to follow their example.

Other socio-economic influences are known as secondary socialisation. A child will learn from the '**wider society**', such as from the people it meets and the organisations with which it has contact. As the child meets more people and has contact with a number of organisations, some of the views and opinions previously accepted from the family are questioned. This process may begin when the child is at playgroup or attends nursery school and continues throughout school life and through experiences in adolescence, adulthood and later adulthood.

Secondary socialisation can include:

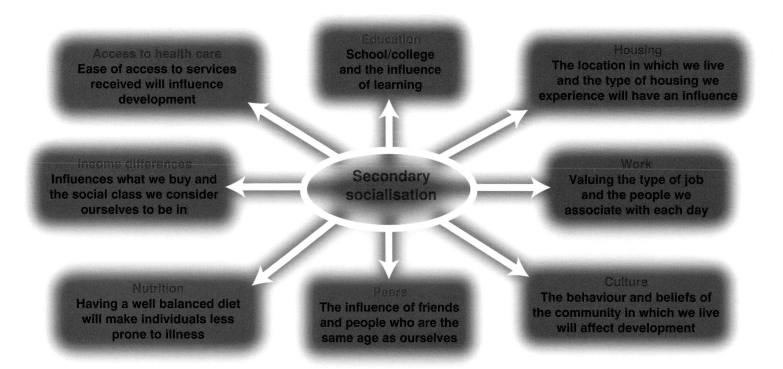

Education

Within the education system children have the opportunity to learn new skills, gather information and pass a number of national examinations. Such examinations are important as they allow the individual to access employment, which in turn can lead to a reasonable and consistent income. While in the education system, children learn about their past history, about the world around them and about different cultures and attitudes. It is through exposure to such topics and through the people met while being educated that secondary socialisation takes place. Attitudes and opinions can change quite drastically as a result.

Educational achievement can, however, be influenced by particular factors, some of which are **genetic** and others which are **environmental**. Intelligence is an inherited factor passed down from parents, while environmental factors are linked to where you live. Both genetic and environmental factors can affect educational success. One of the current debates is 'what causes underachievement' in education. Research has shown that gender, race and social class can affect educational success.

Discussion point

Why do you think working-class parents are encouraging their children to move on to higher education?

Secondary socialisation is also learnt from teachers and from peers. If you were to observe the same students with two different teachers, it is possible that behaviour changes would be apparent in each class. Some teachers allow the students to talk within class and to have more freedom. Others do not permit talking and demand one hundred percent concentration. Through this tolerant/non-tolerant approach children are being socialised, albeit in different ways.

Research indicates that low income can also influence educational success. Working-class children in particular are disadvantaged by this factor and are less likely to do well at school. Working-class parents are likely to encourage their children to leave school and get a job at the end of compulsory education. On the other hand, middle-class parents are more likely to encourage their children to do well at school and to stay on in higher education, which is likely to result in acquiring higher paid jobs which are far more fulfilling. Currently there is a slightly less obvious divide as more working-class parents are attempting to persuade their children to fulfil their full potential.

Discussion point

How can parental attitude influence achievement in the learning environment?

Housing

Different types of housing

Housing and the location where people live can strongly influence the development of people, particularly of children. For example, if a person lives in a rural area, this could determine the number of health, social care and early years services they are able to access, and the recreational activities they can join could be limited. Visiting friends and extended family members may be more difficult and they may have to travel to receive their education entitlement. However, living in a rural area could provide easier access to natural environments which can enhance learning and development.

Children and people living in an **urban** area could experience social deprivation as they could be more exposed to higher crime rates and vandalism and may be fearful of going out. Access to services may be easier when living in a town or city and there may be more activities in which to participate.

Housing in inner cities and towns may take the form of flats to which there are no outside gardens, whereas in rural areas, houses are more likely to be detached, semi-detached or terraced, having their own gardens. There is likely to be less traffic in a rural area and consequently pollution is likely to be less of a problem.

Cold and damp conditions within the home can aggravate chest conditions and conditions such as arthritis and rheumatism. Overcrowded housing conditions can also affect the spread of disease as where people live closely together, infection and disease can spread more quickly. Illnesses such as the common cold can easily be spread through families and in the past tuberculosis (TB), cholera and typhoid often reached epidemic proportions.

What are the effects on development likely to be?

Discussion point

You have been given the opportunity to decide where you will live, for example a rural or urban area. Which would you choose? Give advantages and disadvantages. What are the likely effects on development?

Culture

The family will live in a **society**. That is, it will live with groups of other people who all have a similar pattern of life. The society will have its own rules, traditions and organisations, with perhaps its main beliefs. This is known as culture, which is about the way we live. In today's society in this country we have a multi-cultural society. This is because people from a variety of different cultures have been born in this country and have grown up here. A child today would, therefore, probably be used to different patterns of living and different beliefs and so would be more accustomed to the approach.

Good cultural attitudes can be used as tools to help with shared thinking. Richard Dawkins, a biologist, calls this the **social evolution approach** as he believes that social learning is a shared process with the exchange of ideas and information between people. Every culture has its own way of doing things and new ideas are more acceptable in some cultures than others. Such societies that reflect this approach are known as **open societies** whereas those who are not so open are known as **closed societies**. Cultures can be rich in expressive arts and as a result the valuing of such traditions is well guarded. A family may have either conscious or subconscious prejudice which children will learn.

Effects of living in a rural area	Effects of living in an urban area
Promotes good health because of natural open areas	Illness treated quickly because services are easier to access
May be reserved as social activities may be restricted	Could be more comfortable in social situations and with people
May be physically fitter as open countryside enables walking, cycling, etc.	Could be less fit as there are fewer open spaces or these may be more difficult to reach
May be more economically aware as money is needed to reach urban areas for shopping, leisure activities, etc.	May be able to spend more money on wants as travelling costs do not have to be taken into account

Other factors that will have an influence on development are:

Socio-economic influence	Effect on development
Access to health services	A person who lives close to health, social care and early years services will be able to visit a GP, hospital, dentist or other services easily or when there is a need. Costs of transport will not have to be considered, nor time for travel. Therefore, a person is less likely to be prone to illness. Also, if a person knows or is aware of the services that are available, they will be able to access them when needed. If language is an issue, a person may not be able to access the service either because the language used to advertise the service is not that person's own or preferred language or because the person needs the help of an advocate to help them understand what is available and where.
Nutrition	If income is reasonable, fresh food could be purchased. This could lead to having a well-balanced diet which in turn could make an individual less prone to illness. Having some knowledge of nutrition will also influence the way an individual develops. For example, a person without knowledge could on a daily basis have foods that are rich in fat and carbohydrate. Additionally, they may take little exercise with the result that they: • become overweight • have mobility problems • have heart conditions • experience breathing problems • lack mental stimulation. All of which could lead to poor health.

Income differences

The work that people do will often lead to dividing people into layers or **strata**. Most societies tend to have some form of **stratification** system that distinguishes people as more or less important than others. In Britain the stratification system is known as the 'class system', the differences between the classes being in terms of educational success, the type of work that is being undertaken and the money earned. A person's occupation is therefore used to assess the importance of people. These differences are recorded in scales. For example, the Registrar-General's scale:

Class	Definition	Example
A or 1	Higher Professional & Higher Managerial	lawyer, accountant, doctor, minister, bank manager
B or 2	Lower Professional & Lower Managerial	nurse, teacher, farmer, school teacher, MP, police officer
C or 3	Skilled Manual and remainder of Non-manual Workers	plumber, shop assistant, typist, mechanic
D or 4	Semi-skilled Worker	lorry driver, assembly line worker, postman, bus conductor, agricultural worker
E or 5	Unskilled Worker	window cleaner, labourer, messenger, road sweeper, cleaner

C is often sub-divided into two, known as **C1** and **C2**.
Classes **1, 2 and 3**, are middle classes, **4** and **5** are working class.

The Registrar-General's scale

This scale is often considered to be 'top heavy', with more middle-class type occupations and working-class jobs. On the other hand, the 'Hall Jones scale' has seven categories rather than five and therefore is consider to be fairer by many people.

Class	Definition
1	Professional and high administrative
2	Managerial and executive
3	Inspectional, supervisory and other non-manual, higher grade
4	Inspectional, supervisory and other non-manual, lower grade
5	Skilled manual and routine grades of non-manual
6	Semi-skilled manual
7	Unskilled manual

The Hall Jones scale

It is generally believed that belonging to a social stratum in a system of stratification affects a person's chances in life. This means that it influences people's opportunities, for example education, leisure activities and work opportunities.

Environmental influences

Surroundings can affect the way a person feels and behaves. Research suggests the use of colour for different effects, for example yellow for learning, green for relaxing. The position of objects within a room will also influence behaviour.

Individuals who are attracted by **negative identity** may be attracted to an environment that is

A room that allows people to relax because of the positioning of furniture

without organisation or structure or may feel more comfortable in an area that is unsafe, whereas others will feel threatened or unsafe in such conditions.

Other environmental influences which can affect development are shown in the table below:

Environmental influences	Effect of environmental influences
Water pollution	Clean water is essential for healthy living. This particularly applies to drinking water, which is a need for all individuals. The main source of freshwater pollution is from the discharge of untreated waste and dumping of industrial **effluent**. Water-borne infectious diseases include hepatitis, cholera, dysentery and typhoid. Exposure to polluted water can cause diarrhoea, skin irritation and typhoid.
Air pollution	Conditions such as asthma, irritation to the eyes, bronchitis, pneumonia and other respiratory problems are likely to be activated when the air is polluted. This is because the pollutants in the air cause a reaction in the lungs, making smaller airways constrict. As a result breathing becomes more difficult. The effect on the individual can be: • poor health • low self esteem • social isolation • depression.
Noise pollution	Noise, above an acceptable level, that is experienced regularly can damage our health. It is not just the ears that are affected but the whole nervous system, including the brain. Noise pollution can be self inflicted through wearing headphones to listen to music at high volume or by attending discos where high volume music is being played. Living near a busy main road or near an airport where there is constant noise can also be irritating, making a person feel that they have no peace. This can cause: • bad temper • depression • low self esteem • social isolation • social and emotional ill health possibly leading to mental illness.

Stuart | Activity 1

Stuart lives with his parents and three brothers in a flat near a busy road and an airport. The flat is damp and in winter mould grows on the walls. Stuart shares a bedroom with his younger brother, has asthma and suffers from respiratory infections. The family eat a lot of fried beefburgers, chips and junk food.

1. What environmental conditions may affect Stuart's health?

2. How are the housing conditions likely to affect Stuart's development?

3. How is the family's diet likely to influence their development?

Psychological influences

Self concept is the individual as known to that person. It is understanding ourselves, having **self awareness** which leads to us forming an opinion about ourselves – our self concept. Our self concept involves:

- having knowledge about ourselves
- receiving feedback from other people.

From these two perspectives we will form an opinion of ourselves, so that we either have a high self concept/self esteem or a low self concept/self esteem. This is part of emotional and social development and can be influenced by the experiences we have, the life events we experience and the age or life stage we are in.

A high self esteem helps individuals to relate more easily to the people we meet, such as family, friends and colleagues. A person who has a high self concept will often view life very positively and value themselves as a person. If a person thinks they are valuable, they will expect others to value them.

An individual with a low self concept will not feel good about themselves. They will not like the image they have of themselves and as a consequence may not be able to relate well to others. They may feel that others do not value them and that they are unable to make a worthwhile contribution to society. The overall result will be that such people have a very low opinion of themselves and a poor self portrait.

Self esteem can be influenced by a number of factors, for example:

Factors that influence self esteem	Effect on self esteem
Age	If a person is treated harshly or abused as a child then they are more likely to grow up with a low self concept. On the other hand, if a person is really successful at work and has a good family relationship, they will feel they are making a positive contribution to society and are likely to have a high self concept.
Body shape	Both males and females become concerned about their body shape. If they are overweight, strategies for slimming are likely to be implemented. Some will go to extremes and eating disorders such as anorexia nervosa may develop. The result is likely to be a low self esteem.
Gender	Gender is not the same as sex. Gender is about the way society expects individuals of both sexes to behave. Gender affects self esteem because individuals have to learn how someone of their sex behaves. This is known as gender role. A person who does not conform to the role expected often suffers extreme emotional torment.
Appearance	Sometimes a person will not like the way they look, for example an adolescent who has acne. This can cause them to have a low self esteem and to become withdrawn. Facial expressions play a major role when interacting with others as our facial appearance often reflects our innermost feelings.

Concept of others

It is human nature to compare ourselves to other people and also for other people to compare themselves with us. Parts of our self concept will only make sense if it is considered in relation to other people. Social comparison theories consider that individuals evaluate features of themselves or their lives by comparing themselves to others. In this case people choose their own targets for comparison. Think about a group of mothers meeting together and discussing their child at the beginning of compulsory school. They will probably be comparing how they reacted to their first day, what they can do as far as making letters and reading is concerned or whether they have reached any developmental milestones and also how they are coping with the change to their lives. Some of these mothers will go away feeling quite proud that their offspring appear to be far more advanced than the youngsters of other mothers, whilst there will be some mothers that will start to have **anxiety** and **fear** that they or their child are somehow not demonstrating the same abilities. Some of these comparisons are not always healthy but they are necessary!

A child's self concept can be affected when their abilities are compared with another child.

I can play the guitar better than David can

For example, if one boy's musical skills are compared to another, such as when a group of adolescents were studied it was found that those with the highest self concept were those that came from a higher social class, performed well at school and who had been leaders at clubs. The results show that children who were able to compare themselves favourably to other people had a higher self concept/self esteem.

Sometimes a comparison can be made by considering the role that we have with the role of others. For example, we could compare the knowledge and skills of a nursery nurse or a care assistant with those of another nursery nurse or care assistant. We create a personal and social hierarchy of people we know, depending on the role they have and how we value them, fitting ourselves in to the role we see ourselves.

Discussion point

Who do you compare yourself with? Why?

Assessment activity 11.2.1

CASE STUDY

1. What is meant by the term 'emotional' development?

2. Explain the differences between 'cognitive development' and 'physical growth'.

3. Explain how the family can influence emotional development.

4. How can environmental influences shape an individual's development?

5. Discuss how 'nature-nurture' influences development.

6. What is meant by the term 'socio-economic' and how does this influence the development of individuals?

7. Mary-Ann is the youngest child in a family of four. She is very protected by her brothers who do everything for her. When Mary-Ann attends play group she stands and watches the other children. She has lots of toys to play with at home and prefers to play with these.

   Explain the influences on Mary-Ann's development.

11.2.2 Theories of human development

A. Erik Erikson (1902–1994)

B. Hans Eysenck (1916–1997)

C. Sigmund Freud (1856–1939)

D. Ivan Pavlov (1849–1936)

E. Jean Piaget (1896–1980)

F. Carl Rogers (1902–1987)

Theorists are individuals who have studied in detail human behaviour and who, having seen patterns and reasons for behavioural reactions, have analysed why this should occur. They have then put forward theories to back up the research they have done. Examples of theorists are:

Psychodynamic perspective

Psychodynamic theory emphasises the **interaction** of biological drives with the social environment. Psychodynamics refers to the broad theoretical model for explaining mental functioning. Psychoanalytical therapy involves exploring the impact of early experiences on the mental functioning of a person.

Freud

The founder of psychoanalysis is Sigmund Freud (1856–1939), followed by C G Jung, Wilhelm Reich, Melanie Klein, etc. Approaches put forward by Freud include transactional analysis and gestalt therapy.

What was Freud's perspective? Freud's theory considered:

- Our unconscious feelings direct the way we behave – we do not always know our feelings, therefore, we do not always know why we behave as we do in a particular situation. All actions have a cause.
- We are deeply influenced by our earliest childhood experiences, for example what we believe and how we feel as adults.
- Individuals go through psychosexual stages of development, e.g. oral, anal, phallic, latency and genital.

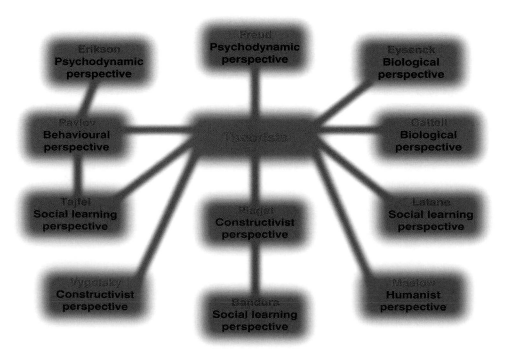

Freud thought that people have:

- an **id** – which makes 'I want' demands
- an **ego** – which tries to resolve conflicts between id and the super ego
- a **superego** – which represents the demands made by parents and society about how to behave.

If a person listens more to the 'id' than the 'superego', the person concerned is **egocentric** which means they are self seeking and selfish. When an individual listens to the 'superego' more than the 'id', the person is seen as a '**conformist**', which means self denying. When the 'id' is well balanced with the needs of the 'superego' that person is considered to be a 'well-grounded person' that is balanced.

Theory into practice

In groups carry out further research about the theories of Sigmund Feud. Prepare materials for a short presentation about his work showing how it could be used to interpret the behaviour of:

- a child in an early years setting

OR

- an older person in a day care centre

OR

- a person receiving health care in a hospital

Erikson

Erik Erikson worked in the tradition of Freud, but developed his own theories and ideas. This is known as neo-Freudian. Erikson believed that personality continues to develop throughout life. He thought that development:

- had a biological basis, e.g. that the stages are genetic and universal
- was influenced by our interaction with our environment, enabling us to pass through the stages of development
- was part of **psychosocial** development.

Erikson suggested that all human beings pass through eight stages of development and that each stage is characterised by a psychosocial crisis. He considered that human beings never fully resolve these crises, but instead retain an element of both the **adaptive** (positive) and the **maladaptive** (negative) features of each stage. Healthy development of self involves the positive (adaptive) quality outweighing the negative (maladaptive) quality. Unsatisfactory experiences can be compensated for in later life, although it becomes increasingly difficult to do so. Likewise, positive early experiences can be reversed by later bad experience.

Erikson's eight life stages are:

Stage	Crisis	Significant relationships	Outcomes
0–1 yrs	Trust vs. mistrust	Mother	Trust in people, or mistrust of others
2 yrs	Autonomy vs. shame and doubt	Parents	Self control vs. fear
3–5 yrs	Initiative vs. guilt	Family	High or low self esteem
6–11 yrs	Industry vs. inferiority	Friends	Success or failure
Adolescence	Identity vs. role confusion	Peer groups	Sense of identity or lack of identity
Early adulthood	Intimacy vs. isolation	Same and opposite sex relationships and friendships	Ability to have deep relationships or failure to love others
Middle age	Generativity vs. stagnation	Marriage	Wider interests and personal growth or self concern
Old age	Integrity vs. despair	All people	Sense of fulfilment or lack of fulfilment with life

Erikson considered adolescence to be the key time to form self identity. At this age, the inability to integrate the self into a coherent whole means individuals suffer role confusion and low self esteem. As we grow older, so our self concept becomes more positive, according to Erikson's model.

From the table on the previous page it can be seen that children from the age of 0–11 pass through four stages of development, each stage having a significant person who acts as the main role model with each stage having a specific outcome.

Feni — Activity 2

Feni is 10 years of age. She attends the local primary school but will soon be moving to a much larger comprehensive school. Her teachers are very worried about how she will manage this situation.

Feni has only been in England for the last three years. She has not yet mastered English and gets very angry when she cannot do an activity that has been set by the teacher. When she thinks someone is not looking, she will punch the person sitting next to her or throw her work across the room.

At break times the other children try to involve Feni in their games but she always wants to be first to 'have a go' and sulks if anyone criticises what she has done.

1. Explain how Erikson would interpret this behaviour.

2. Compare the similarities and differences between Freud's and Erikson's theories drawing logical conclusions.

3. How can the theories of Freud and Erikson be used to explain sudden violence from an adult who is normally quiet?

4. In pairs, produce a case study based on the behaviour of an older adult who behaves badly at the dining table of a residential home.

5. Exchange case studies with another pair within the group and discuss how Freud and Erikson would interpret their behaviour.

Biological perspective

From the biological perspective, theorists, such as Eysenck and Cattell, believe that people are genetically programmed as far as their personalities go. People are born with their personalities and there is nothing they can do to change their nature. Genetic differences can help to explain why some people are predisposed to be sad and pessimistic while other people put in the same circumstances are not.

Eysenck

Hans Eysenck (1967) explained that personality is dependent on a person's brain which has inherited physiological tendencies. His theory could be traced back to Galen (AD 129–199). Galen's theory had stated that people were influenced by the four bodily fluids – phlegm, blood, yellow bile and black bile.

Although this fluid theory of Galen had been dismissed by medicine, Eysenck argued that Galen's observations could be related to his four types of personality:

(1) extroversion – (2) introversion – this refers to a person's tendency to seek stimulation – a person who is highly extroverted is more likely to take risks, to have lots of friends and to be outgoing, than someone who is introverted. Most people fall between the two types. An introverted person is keen to avoid risks or excitement.

(3) neuroticism (instability) – (4) stability – this refers to a person's tendency to become emotionally upset. A neurotic person can be moody and restless whereas a stable person is usually calm.

Eysenck believed these four types of personality are heavily influenced by biology. In particular, he thought that extroverted people had higher thresholds for stimulation than introverted people. Introverts were likely to be over-stimulated by kinds of activity that extroverts find most comfortable.

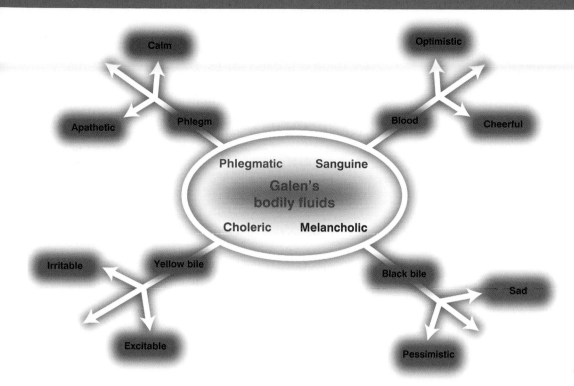

Galen's four bodily fluids

Cattell

Raymond Cattell (1965) identified sixteen factors of personality (each a continuum from one extreme to another) and developed a questionnaire that could be used to measure each of these factors in an individual or in a group. The questionnaire was known as 16PF (16 Personality Factors). However, Cattell recognised the uniqueness of each person and he suggested that a personal profile accompanied each 16PF showing the individual's unique traits.

1. sociable – unsociable
2. intelligent – unintelligent
3. emotionally stable – emotionally unstable
4. dominant – submissive
5. cheerful – brooding
6. conscientious – undependable
7. bold – timid
8. sensitive – insensitive
9. suspicious – trusting
10. imaginative – practical
11. shrewd – naïve
12. self assured – apprehensive
13. radical – conservative
14. self sufficient – group adherence
15. self discipline – uncontrolled
16. tense – relaxed

Cattell's 16 Personality factors   Activity 3

Using Cattell's personality factors (16PF), decide where you should be placed. Ask a close friend to carry out the same exercise on you.

1. Where were the similarities and the differences?
2. Did you both come to a similar overall conclusion about you?
3. Repeat the exercise on your friend.

Humanist perspective

Humanistic theorists believe that it is the way that we as individuals have come to understand our own self concept that is important, not our early experiences or our conditioning. We are free to control our own destiny, which is the issue of a free will versus **determinism**. A primary motivational approach is the force that leads to growth and **self actualisation**.

Maslow

Abraham Maslow put forward his psychological theories of human motivation in 1954. Maslow was extremely interested in 'why' people never seemed to be satisfied with what they had. He noticed that people were often dissatisfied with their situation and wanted something more. However, when individuals got what they wanted it was not long before they wanted something else. Maslow suggested that human motivation should be considered in terms of a 'hierarchy of needs'.

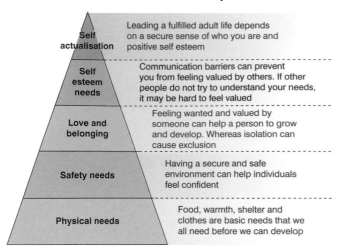

Maslow's hierarchy of needs

Some needs are basic to us all for physiological survival, for example warmth, shelter, food and water. These needs completely motivate behaviour, with all our actions aimed at getting the food, water and shelter that we need. There is little time for anything else. However, once basic needs are satisfied, a different level of need in the hierarchy becomes important. For example, individuals may now have shelter but then try to strive for conditions of safety and security. Again, once safety and security have been achieved, according to Maslow, social needs become of **paramount** importance. Human beings need to feel that they belong with other people and to be accepted.

At the top of the hierarchy Maslow placed 'self actualisation'. This means being able to use our talents and abilities to the full. Maslow sees this as '**ultimate** achievement' and suggests that it is only obtainable by a relatively few people. There are some weaknesses in Maslow's theory, however. One example is that some individuals find that the higher need, that is self actualisation, is more important than having shelter and regular meals. An example that illustrates this point is that of a dedicated playwright or an artist, who denies security and who will sometimes go hungry in order to fulfil needs of creativity.

Another weakness in Maslow's theory of motivation is that his way of looking at motivation is very specific to Western culture. In some cultures people see their identity as being firmly located within their own village community and the idea of accumulating personal wealth is completely alien.

It is a fact that we all operate on different levels at the same time. Sometimes we will do things because

they are approved by our social group, but also because we want to achieve them personally and we think it is good for us. By observing the many different types of motives which people have for their behaviours, it is possible to identify some of the influences which might be working in any one example of human behaviour at a given time.

Davina CASE STUDY

Davina is 60 years old and during her working life was a teacher. She has lived on her own for many years, at first looking after her parents but when they died she was completely alone. When she retired from teaching she joined some of her friends and colleagues for holidays and outings, but gradually the number of these reduced and she never went anywhere or saw anyone unless she went to the shops. She communicated with only a few people.

Davina's bungalow started falling into a state of disrepair, not because she could not afford to pay for any work to be done but because she could not be bothered. Her neighbour tried to talk to her regularly over the garden wall. She noticed that Davina was losing weight, was wearing clothes that were dirty and that she seemed to be getting very little sleep. One day Davina revealed to the neighbour that a man had pushed his way into the bungalow and had taken her pension book and her money. Davina called the police and they in turn involved Social Services.

Davina eventually agreed to move into a residential home. After a few weeks her neighbour went to visit her. She was surprised to find Davina looking well-fed, with colour in her cheeks and looking very happy. She was enjoying being involved in a creative activity with others. Davina confided to her neighbour that 'she was very happy and didn't want to return to the bungalow ever'.

1 How would Maslow interpret Davina's behaviour prior to her being admitted to residential care?

2 How would Maslow interpret Davina's behaviour after being admitted to residential care?

3 Write a case study based on the behaviour of an adolescent. Provide separately an answer to show how Maslow would interpret the behaviour of the adolescent.

4 Exchange the case study with another person in the group and write an answer to show how Maslow would interpret the behaviour shown by the adolescent.

5 Discuss the points that you and your partner have made.

Rogers

Carl Rogers was a humanist psychologist. This means that he believed that all individuals are able to 'self direct' and have the ability to shape and direct their own lives. As a result of his beliefs Rogers developed a 'person-centred' approach, believing that the best expert on any individual was that individual themselves, not others.

Humanists believe that all people are born with a sense of direction on self actualisation. This is a desire to achieve one's spiritual and actual potential. To be able to do this very much depends on the development of one's self. The main focus of Rogers' theory is our individual view of self, which in Rogers' opinion is 'the organised and consistent set of beliefs about ourselves'. Rogers thinks that there are two main sources of beliefs about ourselves. These are:

- personal experience   AND
- evaluation of self by others.

All children need to experience positive regard from their parents. That is, they need to feel valued by their parents, not to be continually told they are wrong or displeasing in some way. They also have the need for positive **self regard**. That is that they feel that their behaviour and values are approved by significant others – people who matter to them and who provide a role model for them. This is known as **congruence** and is an indicator of having high self esteem.

Sometimes, however, the evaluation of self by others can damage a child's self concept. For example, Rogers believed that children learn that in order to obtain love and approval by others, particularly their parents, they have to behave in a certain way. As a result of this thinking children know that love and praise will be withheld until they achieve certain standards of behaviour. Rogers calls this **conditional positive regard**. A child who learns to behave in ways that are approved by parents and significant others will gain approval. This is known as self worth. For example, a child who is given a reward, such as sweets or a toy, every time they stop having a temper tantrum in a supermarket, will soon learn that he/she is positively thought of by the parent and will not continue with poor behaviour.

Conditions of worth are **internalised** and if they match with the child's experiences and values, then the child will have a positive self concept. If they do not match, the child will try to suppress their own feelings to ensure that they meet approval from others. This can lead to a poor self esteem and a low concept of self worth. Rogers believes that a child needs to experience **unconditional positive regard**. In other words a child should experience total acceptance and support for whatever they do in a non-judgemental way. As a result positive self regard will develop independently. A child, therefore, is not criticised for doing wrong, but the behaviour that is wrong is identified. A child who is continually told that they are a nuisance or stupid will experience incongruence for the rest of their lives, no matter how successful they are in the future.

Theory into practice

Try to observe a child either in their own home or in a care and education setting for 15 minutes. Record what they do. How would Rogers interpret their behaviour?

Constructivist perspective: Piaget and Vygotsky

Piaget and Vygotsky were two famous theorists who developed the constructivist approach. Constructivists believe that children develop their knowledge by constructing their own understanding and adapting it to the world around them.

Piaget

Piaget did not believe that a child's intelligence was fixed at birth. He believed that a child takes in information from the environment which is stored in the brain and as this information is processed then the child's behaviour changes as a result of this.

Piaget was interested in how a child understands the world. He believed that a child goes through different stages of cognitive development depending on their age. He called their patterns of learning, **schemas**. These schemas are what a child constructs in their mind in order to understand what is happening around them. He thought that a child's actions and exploration of their environment were important to help them learn.

According to Piaget, developing theories or schemas about the world involves four processes:

1. Accommodation – this is where the child has to fit new knowledge into existing schemas.
2. Assimilation – this is where a child has to change schemas, ideas or thoughts when new information is received.

3. Equilibrium – this is where the child has to balance their new knowledge with their previous knowledge and make sense of it. For example, a child might look at black and white cows in a field and think that all cows are black and white. However, the next time she goes into the country she sees some white cows and some brown cows. She recognises them as cows and now realises that cows can be all different colours.

4. Adaptation – the child changes its thoughts and behaviour due to assimilation and accommodation.

Cows can be all different colours

Piaget also thought that a child passes through four stages of cognitive development.

Age	Stage	Description
0–2 years	Sensori-motor	Senses and physical activity help the child to experience the environment.
2–7 years	Pre-operational	Gradual development as the child learns through their experiences with environment. Words and images (i.e., symbols) help the child to make sense of environment.
7–11 years	Concrete operational	Child continues to learn through their environment, accessing more information to make sense of the wider environment.
11–adult	Formal operational	Child learns more advanced thinking skills, which develop in the adult, to be able to problem solve abstractly.

Piaget's stages of cognitive development

Vygotsky

Lev Vygotsky was a social constructivist in that he believed that people were as important in influencing a child's development as was the environment. According to Vygotsky, social relationships played a key role in helping a child to learn. Interaction with the environment could help a child to learn but if an adult helped then the child could learn so much more than if they were on their own. Like Piaget, Vygotsky was concerned with cognitive development, but whereas Piaget thought too much adult interference could be harmful, Vygotsky thought that the adult's role was very important. According to him, adults had a crucial role to play in advancing a child's cognitive development. With adult help a child could be helped to acquire necessary knowledge, understanding and skills beyond what they could learn on their own. Vygotsky called this the zone of proximal development (ZPD). Explained simply, this means the difference between what a child could learn on their own and what they could learn with the help of an adult or a more competent peer. Vygotsky stressed the importance of knowing when to offer help or support and when the help or support is no longer needed. The child should be challenged on to the next stage but not challenged so far ahead of their development that they are completely bewildered and out of their depth.

Vygotsky   Activity 4

1. According to Vygotsky what is the zone of proximal development?

2. Compare Piaget's and Vygotsky's theories of cognitive development.

Behavioural perspective

Behaviourists such as Pavlov and Skinner believed that studying human behaviour could give them the answers to why people behave the way they do. This meant that they had to watch and listen to what people say and do. Feelings, thoughts and emotions do not come into this as behaviourists only study what they can see. Behaviourists believed that people develop skills and abilities related to their learning experiences.

Pavlov

Ivan Pavlov put forward the theory of **classical conditioning** in 1906. Pavlov was a Russian physiologist who was studying the digestion of dogs. He noticed that the older dogs started to salivate as soon as the dog handler entered the laboratory with their meal, even before it was put down in front of them. Pavlov worked out that the dogs associated the dog handler with being given a meal. Pavlov experimented further and rang a bell just before the food arrived for the dogs. Soon the dogs associated the ringing of the bell with feeding and if a bell was rung they started to salivate in preparation for a meal. Even if they could not see the food, once the bell rang the dogs salivated. Pavlov said the dogs had become conditioned to salivate when they heard the bell.

Before the introduction of the bell, the dogs had made an unconditional response (salivating) to an unconditioned stimulus (seeing food). This was an automatic biological response which dogs do not learn – they are genetically programmed to do so. However, later into the experiment the dogs could salivate at the sound of the bell because it became linked to feeding in the dogs' brains. Pavlov called the bell a conditioned stimulus and the dogs' salivation a conditioned response. This was because the dogs had become used to associating the bell with food. When an unconditioned stimulus (e.g., the dogs seeing the food) is replaced by a conditioned stimulus (e.g., the dogs hearing the bell) this is known as a classical conditioning (or association).

People are sometimes conditioned to avoid some foods. This is usually caused by the person feeling ill after eating some type of food. They may then think they will feel ill if they eat that food again so they always avoid that food. They have learned this by association or conditioning.

Desai — Activity 5

Desai is five years old. One day he does not feel well but his grandmother persuades him to eat some vegetable soup. A short while later Desai is sick. He blames the soup as it is the first time he had eaten it.

1 Explain why Desai might not want to eat vegetable soup again.

However, conditioning can also apply to good experiences as well as unpleasant ones. For example, a person might wear a new suit to an interview and get the job. They may then want to wear the interview suit again as they associate this suit with a pleasant experience.

Skinner

Burrhus Frieberic Skinner developed the behavioural learning theory beyond the simple associative learning. He stated that rewards or reinforcements are the most important element in learning. Skinner worked with animals, mainly rats, and developed the Skinner box for the purpose of testing animals. A rat would be placed in the box and would run around examining the box and looking for a way out. Purely by accident the rat would step on a lever which released a pellet of food. Very quickly the rat would learn to deliberately step on the lever to get some food. In this way Skinner carried out many different experiments to find out which were the most effective negative and positive reinforcements.

A positive reinforcement is something that makes a person want to repeat the behaviour again because the results are pleasant. People change their behaviour if they are given a reward after they have given the required response. Behaviour that is reinforced tends to be repeated and behaviour that is not reinforced tends to die out. Reinforce simply means to strengthen, therefore behaviour which is strengthened is often repeated. For example, if people are paid a bonus for doing a job well, they are very likely to have a reason to repeat the job.

A negative reinforcement is something that is rewarding when it is stopped. An example of this was when Skinner applied an electric shock to the rat which could only be avoided if the rat jumped into a shuttle box. This is a learned response or operant conditioning.

Khalid and Nadia — Activity 6

Khalid is five years old. He lives with his parents who always praise his achievements and his good behaviour. He always gets a hug from both his mother and his father when he tidies away his toys.

Nadia is six years old. She lives with her parents. She is a tidy girl but her parents never acknowledge when she puts her toys away – they expect good behaviour and tidiness.

1 According to Skinner, who is most likely to maintain their good behaviour – Khalid or Nadia? Explain why.

Mindi
Activity 7

Mindi is eighteen months old. She has a pet dog at home. The dog is very friendly and Mindi plays with the dog – she pulls the dog's ears and tail, takes the ball away from it and the dog licks her. She has started to develop a schema about dogs.

Out shopping with her mother she pulls another dog's tail. The dog snarls and goes to bite her and she gets a shock and bursts into tears. She assimilates that the dog bites (assimilation). Her existing schema is that dogs are friendly and do not bite. She now has to adjust her schema to include the fact that dogs can be friendly or unfriendly (accommodation). When Mindi next sees a dog she does not touch it. She has adapted her behaviour as she knows dogs can bite.

This scenario has been described from a constructivist's perspective, i.e. Piaget.

1 How would a behaviourist, e.g. Pavlow or Skinner, explain Mindi's change of behaviour?

Social learning perspective

The social learning approach is closely linked with the behavioural approach. Social learning theorists believe that behaviour is the result of continuous interaction between an individual and their environment.

Tajfel

Henri Tajfel is a social identity theorist who has provided a very useful way of understanding many important aspects about how and why human beings act in a particular way. Within his work Tajfel pointed out how the social groups to which we belong vary in terms of:

- how powerful they are
- how widely they are known
- how much prestige they have.

Most people are aware of these differences. For example, a person who belongs to an athletic club that provided coaching for young people would realise that in the local area that athletic club would be well respected because of what they were trying to achieve with their members. The club also provides a social interactive opportunity. Trainers and young people would be proud of belonging to such a group.

Belonging to a particular social group is part of an individual's identity, part of who they are. Sometimes an individual would be involved in speaking up for the group or would take the opportunity of giving a member's point of view. At other times a different social identity would be more relevant. For example, an argument between two people about who should do the cleaning in the home could begin as just a discussion between two partners, but if one of the partners makes a remark about gender the discussion can rapidly change to a confrontation about jobs that 'men' and 'women' should or should not do. Each person could argue as a representative of their gender group rather than the perspective of their individual self.

As individuals, we all have a number of social identities. Tajfel considers that social identities come from a basic human tendency to sort things into different categories. As human beings, we also categorise other people, for example as a typical person who lives in a particular area or does a particular thing.

It is very important for an individual to feel good about the groups to which they belong. If the group does not have a very high status, the individual may redefine it so that it is seen as more important than it actually is. If this is not possible they may choose to leave the group. This is a matter of being able to keep a positive self esteem.

Who we are and how we see ourselves is very closely linked with the ways that we interact with other people. We all have our own personalities, but we also exist in a network of social interaction. Other people's reactions matter to us and they influence how we act in life. Our cultural background also shapes how we see ourselves and so do our social identities. Tajfel considers that none of us are totally patterned by these social influences and we are not totally dependent on them as everyone is different.

Theory into practice

Discuss as a whole group how Tajfel's theory of social learning perspective could be interpreted through the social groups to which members have belonged and how the development of individuals could have been influenced.

Examples of other theorists who support the social learning perspective are:

Latane

Bibb Latane, working with John Darley in the 1960s, developed the Social Impact Theory. Their work looked into 'bystander apathy'. Their research involved conducting a series of experiments on helping behaviour in emergencies. During their experiments the researchers found that as the number of people increased, the likelihood that any of them would help decreased. It appeared that people help others more often and more quickly when they are alone. This phenomenon is often called the bystander effect. It has two sociological explanations:

1. The more bystanders present the more likely people will assume that someone else will help. If alone, people realise that they are 100% responsible for taking action. The more bystanders there are, the less obligated the individual feels to intervene and help.
2. People look to others to define what is going on – if others are calm the person takes their cue from them and may decide that whatever is happening it does not require their help. People look to others for information, waiting for someone else to define the situation and act. Because everyone is waiting for someone else to act it could be that no one does anything.

Bandura

Albert Bandura considers that a major part of what a person learns occurs through imitation or modelling. He considers that learning takes place in the context of social situations. During a social interaction an individual is likely to model their behaviour on how others in the group are responding. Bandura thought in a similar way to Skinner, the main difference being that Bandura considers that not all learning takes place as the result of direct reinforcement of responses, but that individuals learn by imitating the behaviour of other people. Bandura suggests that children can learn new responses simply by observing the behaviour of others.

In one of his experiments Bandura subjected a group of children, between the ages of three and six, to watching adult models punching, kicking and yelling at a large inflated Bobo doll. When later the same children were allowed to play with a Bobo doll they displayed twice as many aggressive responses as a group of children who had not witnessed the spectacle of the adults' behaviour.

Examples of children showing aggression after seeing Bandura's Bobo doll experiment

As a result of Bandura's theory parents and teachers are probably the most important model in a child's environment. Conditions of learning are therefore established not only by what the parent or teacher says but also by what they do.

The behaviour of students or service users can be changed by behaviour modification techniques. In order to do this the person who is the leader, for example the teacher or supervisor, must *define clearly* what it is the student or service user should learn and *how* the individual is to show that the learning has taken place. The stages that take place in this type of learning are:

• setting the goal
• establishing the student's operant level (what do they need to learn)

Understanding Human Behaviour
11.2.2 Theories of human development /
11.2.3 The application of theories to aid the understanding of human behaviour of individuals in care settings

- using reinforcement to strengthen or *condition* some student behaviour
- withhold reinforcement or *extinguish* other individual behaviour.

It should be noted that Bandura considered that *reinforcement* always increased response rates. When a student is given rewards for their learning, for example by the giving of 'gold stars' for good work, positive reinforcement has occurred. Negative reinforcement occurs by taking away the positive reinforcer.

The key to successful reinforcement behaviour modification techniques is *consistency*. It is necessary for the teacher or supervisor to follow through on the established reinforcement schedule without exception. Reinforcement must follow not precede the student's response. People who work with young children are therefore very important status figures for the child's social learning. The main problem with this approach is that it does not see children experimenting with *different* ways of doing things. The method suggests that children only copy what they see.

Theory into practice

Arrange with your tutor to visit an early years setting to observe children playing and/or learning. Take a recording document to record your findings.

Discuss as a whole group how Bandura would interpret the behaviour observed.

Assessment activity 11.2.2

CASE STUDY

1. Using theory from the humanist perspective assess ways in which an individual's social and emotional perspective could be influenced.

2. How could an individual's personality be shaped by the biological perspective?

3. Use the theories from the psychodynamic perspective to help explain why obsessive behaviour of a service user in a residential home is occurring.

4. Explain how the social learning perspective could be used to condition a child who demonstrated poor behaviour and lack of learning in a primary school.

5. Outline the constructivists' behavioural perspective giving examples applied to service users.

11.2.3 The application of theories to aid the understanding of human behaviour of individuals in care settings

Human behaviour is usually interpreted by different psychological perspectives.

Major theories can be used in care settings to interpret a service user's behaviour. These theories should help care workers to cope with a range of different behaviours whilst treating the service user with respect and understanding. Service users using care services are often vulnerable for a variety of reasons. Children may be vulnerable because they do not know enough about themselves. Older adults may feel vulnerable through illness, loss of their home or partner and the fear of a changing world which they no longer understand. This vulnerability can make people angry or depressed and they may lash out at carers.

Childcare and education settings

These include any setting where young children are looked after, including pre-schools, nurseries and childminding services. It is essential for any adult who is working with young children to have an understanding of cognitive development, as this will help the adult to provide the optimum learning experience for the child.

The main theories which apply to early years are:

- psychodynamic perspective
- constructivist perspective
- behavioural perspective
- social learning perspective.

Psychodynamic perspective

Psychodynamic theories have influenced the way childcare practitioners help children to deal with stressful events in their lives. Both Freud and Erikson thought that unresolved issues in the early stages of development could affect a person's ability to cope in later life. This means that anyone involved in early years has a very important role to play, as their treatment of the child could affect that child for the rest of their life. For example, if a young child is with a childminder or nursery nurse who does not meet their needs adequately, then the child may develop a feeling of mistrust which could last throughout their life. Similarly, toddlers need to be allowed to

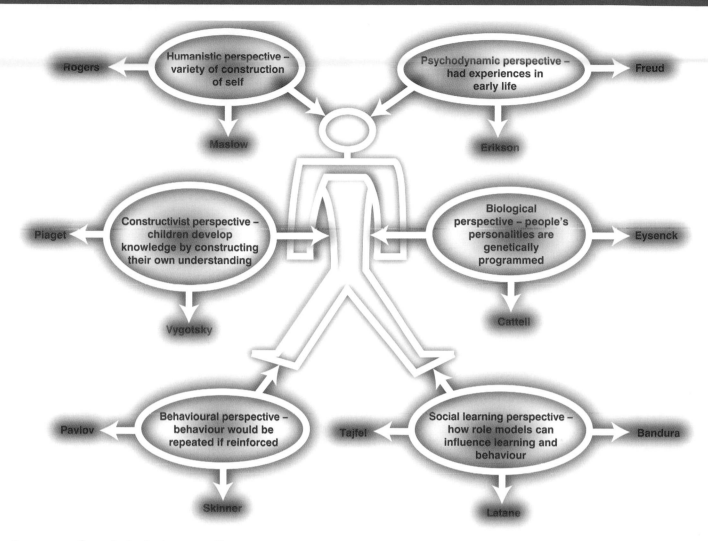

Summary of psychological perspectives

Awareness of cognitive development effects

do things for themselves; if not, they could develop feelings of self doubt or inadequacy. At infant school children need to be encouraged to be active and take the initiative otherwise they find, in later life, that they have little sense of purpose.

Psychodynamic theories have led to childcare practitioners encouraging children to 'act out' and use creative activities to pour out feelings that they might otherwise not be able to express; for example, sadness and worry if daddy has to go into hospital for a serious operation. Books and toys help to prepare children for big events in their lives, for example going into hospital or going on a long-distance flight.

A book can help a child talk about their fears

Toby — CASE STUDY

Sarah is a nursery nurse. She is concerned about Toby who is 3 years 2 months old. Her concern comes from Toby's mother, who seems to be very protective of her son. She is an older mother and Toby was a much wanted child, born after his parents had given up hope of ever having a child. Toby's mother is reluctant to leave him in the morning and spends a lot of time cuddling him and saying her goodbyes. Toby is very clingy and cries after his mother leaves. He does not mix well with the other children, is reluctant to try anything new and lacks confidence. His grandfather died recently but his mother has told nursery staff that Toby does not know about this as he will be too upset.

1 Using the psychodynamic perspective, explain how and why Toby could have problems in later life.

According to the psychodynamic perspective Toby is being let down by his mother because he is not being allowed to do anything for himself. This means that when he is faced with the other children and any activities, at his nursery school, he feels inadequate and lacks confidence.

Toby's mother should have told him about his grandfather having died otherwise she is not

Continued... — CASE STUDY

taking Toby's needs into account. Toby could develop feeling of mistrust of people which could be with him for the rest of his life.

2 If you were Sarah (and you were asked for it) what advice would you give to Toby's mother?

His mother should allow Toby to do things for himself which will help him to build up his confidence. She should not encourage Toby to cling to her.

Sarah could advise Toby's mother to tell him about his grandfather's death even if she has to use toys and books to help her to explain.

Constructivist perspective

Constructivists such as Piaget and Vygotsky have had a great impact on the way childcare practitioners view a child's learning and the way they are taught, particularly in pre-schools and nurseries. In order to learn fully, children must be given the opportunity to explore their environment using their senses. Childcare practitioners will need to allow children plenty of scope for different experiences. They should facilitate opportunities for children and adults to mix and spend time together as social constructivists emphasise the importance of the role of social influence on children's learning. They need social interactions for intellectual growth and development. Children must be given the opportunity to relate to other children as well as adults. Childcare practitioners must allow children the chance to resolve any conflicts they may have themselves. For example, whose turn it is to use the pram. If the children cannot sort it out themselves then the adult should step in to intervene but not before allowing the children to try to solve it.

Adults can move a child onto the next stage of learning and help them reach their full potential. The key message from constructivists for childcare practitioners is that they need to support and promote learning. Children do learn by themselves but they learn more when they receive help and encouragement from a skilled adult.

Discussion point   Everyone remembers a good teacher

Remember the advertisement on television which said that everyone remembers a good teacher? As a group discuss if this is true and why.

Amir — CASE STUDY

Amir is 3 years 4 months old and has just started at the nursery unit at the local primary school. He attends nursery five mornings every week. On Mondays and Wednesdays he works with a nursery teacher who is very keen to show Amir what to do. For the rest of the week he is with a different nursery teacher who believes in leaving the children to learn independently. The nursery is well equipped. It has 32 regular under-4 year olds, one nursery teacher and five nursery nurses at every session.

1 Discuss Amir's likely cognitive development according to the constructivist perspective.

Constructivists would say that perhaps both nursery teachers do not best meet Amir's needs. One teacher is keen to show him everything perhaps not allowing him to explore his environment for himself. The other teacher lets Amir get on with it himself! However, the best situation would be if he were allowed to explore by himself with help and encouragement from the teacher, as children need support to promote learning. He should also be encouraged to socialise with other children.

Behavioural perspective

Pavlov and Skinner believed that if behaviour was rewarded (reinforced) then that behaviour would probably be repeated. This model has been widely used in all types of education and childcare from birth to Year 13. The idea is that positive reinforcement of any type, for example praise, smiles, house points, merit stickers, etc., will encourage a child to change their behaviour. The thought that a person will receive reward for good behaviour is sometimes enough to encourage them to behave. Behaviour that is rewarded tends to be repeated but any behaviour that is not rewarded or produces unpleasant results usually will not be repeated. Children need an appropriate reward for good behaviour, e.g. for tidying the toys away. Every time the child behaves in an appropriate way then they should be rewarded. This will establish an appropriate behaviour pattern. Once the behaviour is established, however, it should be reinforced occasionally. Childcare practitioners must be careful that they do not encourage a child's inappropriate behaviour by using partial reinforcement. For example, if a child has a temper tantrum to get what they want and the adult gives in, then this will reinforce the child's behaviour. But if the adult

is consistent and never gives in, then the child will realise that temper tantrums do not work and so will stop them.

Reinforcing inappropriate behaviour

Gail and Andrea — CASE STUDY

Gail and Andrea are four-year-old twins. They love going to the supermarket with their grandparents who usually buy them sweets or chocolate. Their mother, Debbie, who is pregnant, has recently given up work so Gail and Andrea are not with their grandparents during the day. When Debbie takes them to the supermarket the girls ask her for a bar of chocolate. She tells them they cannot have one and is shocked when Andrea has a temper tantrum in the middle of the store. Debbie is embarrassed and she felt she had no choice but to give in to the girls' demands. Next time she goes shopping she again gives in but decides that from now on she will be strict and not give in. However, after several weeks of tantrums she gives in and buys the girls their sweets. She now dreads taken them shopping.

Using the behavioural perspective:

1 Explain how the girls' behaviour was reinforced.

Gail and Andrea's behaviour was reinforced when his mother rewarded their behaviour by giving in to their demands and giving them chocolate. If their behaviour had not been rewarded they would probably not have repeated their inappropriate behaviour.

Continued...   CASE STUDY

2 How did their mother strengthen their behaviour?

To Gail and Andrea their bad behaviour – a tantrum – was rewarded with chocolate.

3 How could Debbie get the girls out of this inappropriate behaviour cycle?

Their mother must be consistent and never give in to their demands. They will know that their tantrums do not work and will not repeat them.

Social learning perspective

This theory is based on the idea that children copy the behaviour of others. Childcare practitioners are often role models for the children in their care, therefore, they need to lead by example. It is no good telling children to wash their hands after going to the toilet if the childcare practitioner does not do it! Children will take notice of how the childcare practitioner speaks and behaves towards other people. Children learn social skills in this way; for example, if a child sees a childcare practitioner talking with their mouth full then the child is likely to copy this behaviour. They also learn how to behave and how to resolve conflict.

If a child observes another child being rewarded for good behaviour then the observing child may be motivated to change their inappropriate behaviour, as they want to be rewarded too.

Children are heavily influenced by the adults who look after them. It is good practice for the childcare practitioner to praise a child who is behaving well so that all the other children see and hear the child being praised. This is positive reinforcement and the other children could copy the behaviour; this is their motivation to imitate the good behaviour.

Michael   CASE STUDY

Michael is four years old. He attends his local nursery. Nursery staff have noticed that Michael is aggressive and if he cannot get what he wants he pushes other children out of his way or hits out at them. He is particularly aggressive towards girls and never wants to play with them. When this is mentioned to his mother she admits that Michael's father is abusive and violent towards her.

Staff have noticed, too, that Michael gets attention from staff when he is aggressive.

1 Use the social learning perspective to explain a possible reason why Michael is aggressive towards girls.

Continued...   CASE STUDY

Michael's aggressive behaviour is learned behaviour as he has observed his father hitting his mother. Michael thinks this is normal acceptable behaviour and has copied it.

2 How can the nursery staff encourage Michael to behave appropriately?

The nursery staff could praise the other children when they are good so Michael will want to copy them so that he too is praised.

The following theories relate to day care settings, residential and nursing homes for older service users.

Day care settings for older people

This includes any day care setting as shown in the diagram below.

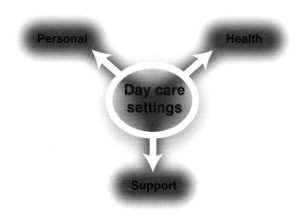

Types of day care settings for older people

Some of these day care settings are found within a residential or nursing home setting.

Older people who use day care centres and residential or nursing homes may exhibit challenging behaviour due to their fear of an unknown situation. They may feel disorientated and unhappy about their situation and it could mean that the care worker has to be patient and skilled in the way they communicate with the person. The main perspectives which apply to older service users, whether having day care or living in residential or nursing homes, are:

- psychodynamic perspective
- biological perspective
- humanist perspective
- behavioural perspective.

Psychodynamic perspective

This theory would put forward the view that the person who was aggressive was agitated or disturbed. The way the carer behaved towards the service user could remind the service user of someone from their past who caused them stress and unhappiness. The service user transfers their negative, aggressive feelings from the past to the current situation and so could lash out at the carer. Many emotional problems of adult life stem from an insecure or unhappy childhood. The care worker would need to recognise this and not take the aggression personally. Carers have to be careful not to make assumptions about people. They need to be aware of the importance of the older person's previous life experiences and the ways in which they have been affected by them. However, it is also important that the care worker also takes into account the culture and social systems of the service user. This theory is limited by the fact that it relies heavily on the internal workings of the service user's mind and psychodynamic theorists would recommend psychoanalytical therapy which would try to explore the subconscious motivations within the service user's mind.

Mimi   CASE STUDY

Mimi is a 78-year-old woman who lives in her own home. She is becoming increasingly frail and finds it difficult to manage on her own. She goes to a day care centre three times a week. Here she has a bath, two goods meals, her nails are cut, etc. Mimi is challenging to the staff who take her to the centre and also to staff within the centre. She frequently attacks them both verbally and physically. Mimi never married and stayed at home to look after her father after her mother died 59 years ago. Her father was very strict and had set ideas about how girls should behave. Mimi had no friends and did not leave the house very often. She and her father lived very frugally. Her father died last year at the age of 104. Mimi seems lost and confused at times although her brain is healthy.

1. Explain why Mimi displays challenging behaviour.

   Mimi could be displaying challenging behaviour as she is transferring her negative, aggressive feelings she had for her father onto her current situation therefore causing her to lash out at the carers.

Continued...   CASE STUDY

2. How could staff deal with this challenging behaviour?

   Staff should be aware of Mimi's past situation and should not take the aggression personally. They should treat her with kindness and respect and try to calm her down.

Biological perspective

This perspective would state that a person has the physiological tendency of aggression already in their personality. In this instance the care worker could not change the person's characteristics but could try to calm them down, if they were agitated, by removing whatever the person found threatening, although this is not always possible.

Care workers realise that it is dangerous to label people and remember that anyone can be aggressive depending on the circumstances.

Care workers could try to manage a person with a predisposition to anger by reinforcing positive social behaviour and not reinforcing aggression.

Herbie   CASE STUDY

Herbie is 86 and lives in a residential home. He has lived there for three years and tends to keep to his own room where he reads a lot of books. Staff think he's grumpy and try to avoid him if possible. When he does appear at mealtimes he often doesn't answer when spoken to and sometimes he shouts and waves his stick around. This adds to his bad-tempered label.

Recently Herbie had a minor fall in the home and the doctor was brought in to examine him. In the course of the examination the doctor found Herbie was very hard of hearing. Since he has had a hearing aid fitted Herbie is a different person – full of jokes and good humour.

1. Do you think the residential home used the biological perspective on Herbie?

   Yes, staff had already decided that Herbie has a physiological tendency to aggression. They had him labelled as bad tempered.

2. How could they have helped Herbie's behaviour to be more acceptable?

   They could have helped Herbie by not labelling him as grumpy. They could have tried to have more social interaction with him and reinforced any of his positive social behaviour.

Humanist perspective

Any care worker using the humanistic approach would try to understand the service user's aggression. Service users would be encouraged to talk about their needs and worries. The care worker would recognise that healthy personal development, whatever the person's age, comes from the love and respect of others. So to put that into practice the care worker would ensure that the service user was treated the way they would treat someone they loved and respected regardless of their behaviour. This would be unconditional affection – not dependent on how good or bad their behaviour.

Maslow's hierarchy of needs is useful in helping care workers to understand what service users' needs are. It also encourages care workers to see service users as individuals who are striving to meet their various needs. Careful assessment and care planning can help service users to meet these needs. Care workers would provide a safe, supportive relationship for service users where they could discuss any issues. Within this non-confrontational atmosphere both service users and carers could build self esteem needs. Care values dictate that carers respect the self concept of the service user.

The Orchids   CASE STUDY

The Orchids is a newly opened residential home which houses 42 older service users. The food is excellent but the home is in the middle of a busy street where there are several take-aways, public houses and night clubs. Residents often lose sleep over noisy disturbances. During the day there are few organised activities as staff are kept to a minimum to keep down costs.

1. Use Maslow's hierarchy of needs to explain why the residents of the Orchids are unlikely to reach self actualisation.

   Residents are unlikely to reach self actualisation as there are few activities for them at the home; therefore they will be bored and will not lead a fulfilling adult life. Also the noisy disturbances during the night do not lead to a secure and safe environment for the residents. They will not be confident that they are safe in their home and so will not be relaxed.

Behavioural perspective

This perspective helps carers to understand aggressive behaviour and helps them to be able to manage it. Any care worker using this theory to manage aggressive behaviour will try to seek calmness and co-operation from the service user. If the service user responds to the care worker this should be acknowledged with praise and thanks. The care worker must be assertive but not aggressive and must not reinforce aggressive behaviour with anger of their own.

The care worker, in this situation, would be using reinforcement to help manage the situation. If the service user feels happy with the outcome following their co-operative behaviour, then their aggressive behaviour may eventually disappear to be replaced by co-operation.

Hilda   CASE STUDY

Hilda lives in a residential home. Usually she is fairly calm and even tempered. However, one day she appears in the lounge shouting that someone has taken her watch. She approaches another resident and accuses her of taking it. A care worker intervened and asked Hilda to calm down. Hilda is very angry by now and screams back at the care worker. Another resident joins in the argument and Hilda goes to slap her. The care worker screams at her to calm down. Hilda yells back, slaps the other resident and slams out of the home banging the door.

1. Was this situation well managed by the care worker?

   No, the aggressive behaviour was not well managed by the care worker.

2. Write out an alternative transcript for the care worker.

   The care worker should have tried to calm down Hilda. Once calmed Hilda should have been praised and thanked for her cooperation. By remaining calm the care worker would be using reinforcement to help manage the situation.

Social learning perspective

This perspective can help care workers to realise that service users can feel nervous and worried if they feel they do not fit in or do not relate to any of the other residents in their care setting and this could cause aggressive behaviour. Care workers can make the transition into residential care a much happier experience for service users if they remember this. Service users could be made to feel welcome in their new surroundings if they were encouraged to bring some of their own items of furniture to use in their own room. Being introduced to some like-minded people would also help them feel at home.

Carers must also ensure that residents are aware that staff expect them to carry out certain achievable personal tasks. This will help to prevent learned helplessness where residents effectively give up doing anything for themselves. Service users can also withdraw and give up if they feel they cannot influence the way they are treated. Carers should consult with service users in order to prevent this happening.

Hedy   CASE STUDY

Following a mild stroke, Hedy has had to go into a nursing home. Hedy is 86 and prior to her stroke had managed quite well in her own home. After her stroke Hedy did not go back to her house but went straight into the residential home as it was felt that there was no one to look after her. Her son and daughter live abroad – one in Canada and the other in Australia. Both flew in to see her after her stroke and were pleased to see her progress.

Three months later her daughter comes to visit Hedy in the nursing home. She is shocked by her appearance; Hedy was sitting in an armchair making no attempt to choose her food or to feed herself. Staff do not encourage Hedy as they find it easier to do everything for her. They put this helplessness down to her age and her stroke. Her daughter is very unhappy about the situation. At the time of her stroke the plan was that Hedy would go back to her own house once

Continued...   CASE STUDY

she regained her strength. Her daughter now feels this would not be possible.

1 What has happened to Hedy?

Hedy has learned helplessness since she has given up doing anything for herself, as staff do not encourage Hedy to do anything since it makes their job easier. She has withdrawn from the situation, as she felt she had no influence on how she would be treated.

2 According to the social learning perspective how could the nursing home have helped Hedy to cope with her new circumstances?

She could have been encouraged to bring some of her furniture into the home. She could have been introduced to like-minded residents.

More importantly she should have been aware that staff expected her to carry out any tasks that she could.

The theories applied to the day care settings for older people also apply to residential and nursing homes as is demonstrated by the use of residential/nursing home case studies.

Assessment activity 11.2.3

John   CASE STUDY

John is a 35-year-old man who is in a nursing home. He has a genetic condition which results in cerebral palsy. One morning the care assistant is helping him to dress himself when he lashes out and starts to swear. It is not possible to tell why he has become angry and aggressive.

1 Using at least **two** different psychological theories interpret John's behaviour.

Contents

About this unit

Within this unit you will investigate the:

- respiratory system
- cardio-vascular system
- digestive system
- reproductive system
- renal system
- musculo-skeletal system.

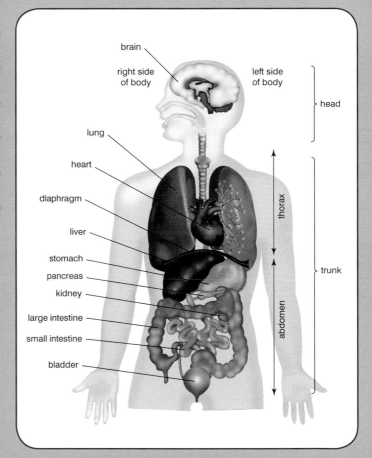

The interrelationship of human body systems

Introducing this unit

Understanding the gross structure, basic micro-anatomy and the functions of important human body systems will help to understand and to explain some of the range of diseases and dysfunctions that cause ill health.

How diagnostic tests can contribute to improving health and well being by providing health specialists with more specific knowledge about dysfunctions will also be considered.

Special note for this unit

It should be noted that words marked in green are either explicit range items or words that are implicitly associated with the range. They have been highlighted in green to make them easily identifiable to the reader.

12.2.1 Respiratory system

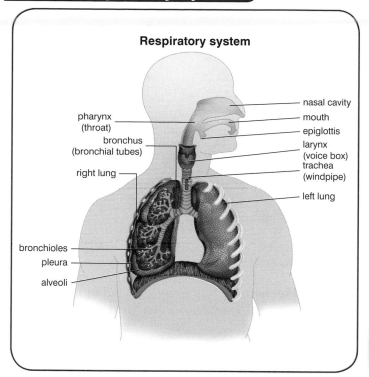

Respiratory system

- pharynx (throat)
- bronchus (bronchial tubes)
- right lung
- bronchioles
- pleura
- alveoli
- nasal cavity
- mouth
- epiglottis
- larynx (voice box)
- trachea (windpipe)
- left lung

Human respiratory system

Structure of the respiratory system

The respiratory tract starts at the nose and mouth. The nose helps filter out larger particles of foreign matter.

- The **trachea** (windpipe) extends from the neck into the thorax and divides into the right and left main bronchi. These enter the right and left lungs, where they divide into smaller **bronchi and bronchioles**. They finally become small air sacs called **alveoli** and it is here that **gaseous exchange** occurs.
- The left lung is smaller than the right, to accommodate the heart.
- Each lung is divided into lobes, three lobes in the right lung and two in the left.
- The pulmonary arteries and veins move blood through the lungs. Their primary function is to supply oxygen and to remove carbon dioxide.

Function of the respiratory system

The gaseous exchange that occurs in the alveoli relies on simple **diffusion**. In order to provide sufficient oxygen and to get rid of carbon dioxide there must be:

- a large surface area for gaseous exchange
- a short diffusion path between alveolar air and blood
- concentration gradients for oxygen and carbon dioxide between alveolar air and blood.

Haemoglobin in the blood continually binds with oxygen that diffuses across the alveoli membrane, forming oxyhaemoglobin. Carbon dioxide that is dissolved in the blood plasma is released back across the membrane. This is known as gaseous exchange.

The temperature and humidity of inspired air increase as it travels toward the alveoli. The respiratory tract is lined with a moist mucosa at body temperature. This moistening of the air increases diffusion efficiency.

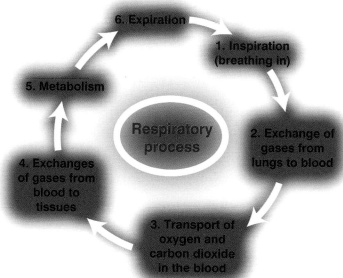

6. Expiration
1. Inspiration (breathing in)
5. Metabolism
Respiratory process
2. Exchange of gases from lungs to blood
4. Exchanges of gases from blood to tissues
3. Transport of oxygen and carbon dioxide in the blood

Dysfunctions of the respiratory system

Asthma is a chronic disease of the lungs that currently affects about 5 million people in the UK. For reasons that have not been established, the number of sufferers is increasing. Asthma causes difficulty in breathing when the airways become inflamed, narrow and constricted. This condition is indicated with symptoms of episodic wheezing and breathlessness. The attacks can vary in severity in short periods of time. The action of 'breathing out' causes most distress. The patient may experience sweating, rapid heart beat and extreme anxiety. Cyanosis (blue discoloration) of the lips and face may occur in severe attacks.

The exact **causes of asthma** are unknown, but asthma and allergies are more prevalent in some families through **genetic factors**. It is also closely associated with hay fever and eczema. Other family members may have asthma, hay fever, or eczema, or combinations of these. Asthma may be inherited, but is activated by outside factors.

People who have positive allergy tests to one or more common airborne allergens are more likely to develop clinical asthma. Allergy is only one of many external triggers affecting chronic asthmatics. Other non-allergic triggers include stress and being overweight.

Certain aspects of **lifestyle** will affect the asthmatic's condition. Being overweight can often increase the incidence of attacks, due to the extra **exertion** required when carrying additional weight. Living in dusty and polluted environments does not help the condition, with fungal spores often being a contributory factor. Other **pollutants** or triggers include:

• house dust mite, cat/dog fur, horses, pollen
• chemical irritants, e.g. cigarette/tobacco smoke, pollutants from factories and car exhausts, household cleaners and sprays, perfumes and other aerosol cosmetics
• low temperatures
• exercise.

Diagnostic techniques

Every sufferer with asthma should have a 'care plan' agreed with his/her doctor. The severity of the symptoms needs to be measured carefully and this may involve measuring the airflow in and out of the lungs with a '**peak flow meter**'.

Diagnostic imaging techniques such as x-rays or scans may also be of use to assess the condition of the lungs. **Blood tests** may be used to analyse information on cells, proteins, chemicals, antigens, antibodies and gases present in the blood. Antigens are chemicals, for example on the surface of bacteria, that cause the body to produce special proteins called antibodies that help the body to destroy the foreign organism or substance.

Treatment for asthma

Although there is no cure for asthma, many attacks can be prevented with good management. Tests to discover which particular allergens may trigger an attack can help the patient to avoid contact, e.g. allergic reactions to house mite dust may be alleviated by appropriate care of mattresses, pillows and carpets.

Antibiotic drugs are prescribed when there is infection present and accompanied by a temperature. If the antibiotics fail to reduce the inflammation, then a course of **steroids** may be prescribed over a course of five days. Steroids help to open up the tubes of the lungs to increase air flow. They also reduce the production of mucus.

Most GP practices employ a specialist nurse who regularly monitors the patients who are diagnosed with asthma. She is also able to advise on possible

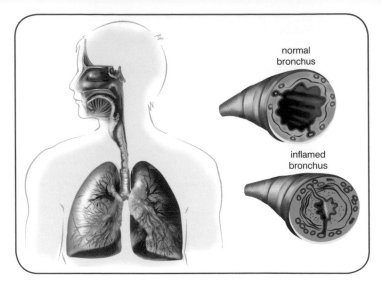

Diagram of respiratory tubes

lifestyle changes such as smoking cessation, improved exercise and weight management programmes.

| **Asthma** | **Activity 1** |

Invite a local 'asthma nurse' to offer the group a seminar on the subject of asthma.

Bronchitis

Bronchitis is an inflammation of the air passages between the nose and the lungs. It affects the trachea (windpipe) and the bronchi. The bronchi are air tubes through which air flows into and out of the lungs. The mucosal linings of the bronchi become swollen and congested and pus is formed.

Bronchitis can be either **acute** (of brief duration), or **chronic** (long lasting). Acute bronchitis is usually caused by a viral or bacterial infection. It usually resolves fairly quickly without complications. Chronic bronchitis is a sign of more serious lung disease and is more common in smokers, babies and older people. It can often be slowed, but it cannot be cured.

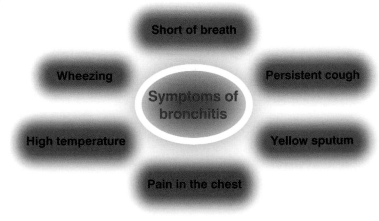

Causes of bronchitis

Bronchitis is usually caused as a complication following a viral infection, such as a cold or influenza, but may also be the result of air pollutants. Attacks are more common in winter. Smoking is the main cause of chronic bronchitis. It stimulates the production of mucus in the lining of the bronchi and thickens the muscular walls and those of the **bronchioles**, resulting in the narrowing of the air passages. **Chronic obstructive pulmonary disease (COPD)** is a combination of chronic bronchitis and **emphysema** and is more common in the UK than anywhere else in the world. Emphysema is a condition almost entirely caused by smoking. Chemicals and particles in the smoke cause the alveoli of the lungs to disintegrate so reducing the surface area for gaseous exchange. About 3 million persons in the UK suffer from the disease.

Diagnosis and treatment of bronchitis

It may be necessary to investigate the severity of the chest problems by undertaking chest x-rays, blood tests, sputum analysis and lung function tests. If the person is breathless, a **bronchodilator** drug may be prescribed to widen and relax the bronchi. Oxygen may help to relieve some symptoms and antibiotics may be administered to prevent a bacterial lung infection.

The most important preventative measure is for people to stop or to never start smoking. Improved exercise tolerance and diet and weight control will also help to reduce further risks to health.

The single most important thing a person can do to improve health is to stop (or never start) smoking

Cystic fibrosis (CF)

Cystic fibrosis is a chronic, **progressive** condition that has a range of symptoms. Cystic fibrosis causes certain organs to make thick, sticky mucus. The organs most affected are the lungs and the pancreas.

In the lungs, thick mucus causes breathing difficulties and can lead to chronic lung infections. Over time, this can lead to loss of lung function. Most often, cystic fibrosis develops in childhood and leads to long-term complications. The condition usually gets progressively worse with age. Occasionally, cystic fibrosis develops in adulthood, with less severe symptoms. In some cases the condition is obvious soon after birth. In a typical case, a child passes a pale unformed, foul smelling stool and shows signs of failing to thrive. Growth is stunted and the child suffers from recurrent upper respiratory chest infections, causing coughing and breathlessness.

Causes

Cystic fibrosis is inherited and is present from birth, due to a defect in a gene on chromosome 7. The protein produced by this gene results in mucus secreting cells making a sticky form of mucus instead of the normal runny type.

Diagnosis and treatment

Early diagnosis is essential, because the sooner intensive physiotherapy and appropriate antibiotics are started, the less lung damage will occur by repeated infections.

The diagnosis is assisted by **radio-diagnostic imaging**. The chest x-ray is one of the most widely used imaging techniques. X-rays can show any changes in lung structure due to dysfunction or disease process.

Computerised axial tomography (CAT) uses x-rays to produce a 3D picture and is useful in showing chest changes. It can measure the size and extent of any change and also differentiate between solids, liquid and gas. A sweat test is also used as individuals with cystic fibrosis produce sweat with abnormally high levels of salt.

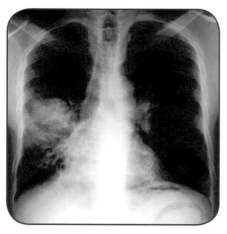

Diagnostic imaging is still one of the best ways to diagnose lung dysfunction

A **peak flow meter** will measure how fast a person can breathe out (or exhale) air. The test is commonly used to diagnose and monitor lung diseases such as asthma, chronic obstructive pulmonary disease, emphysema or chronic bronchitis. Monitoring can be used to measure the effect of treatments, or indicate if a condition is not improving.

Peak flow meter – inexpensive and accurate

Cystic fibrosis can de diagnosed by a genetic test of **DNA**. The DNA sample is obtained either by:

- collecting cheek cells using a swab or
- obtaining a blood sample.

Steroid medication can improve the symptoms of cystic fibrosis, but it does not slow down the progression of the disease. Long-term oral steroid treatment also carries the risk of side-effects, such as:

- osteoporosis
- diabetes
- infections
- weakening the skin, making it easy to bruise and tear.

Antibiotics may be used to treat infections caused by bacteria.

An extreme form of intervention is a lung transplant. This usually involves a combined heart/lung transplant as it makes the surgery more straightforward.

A new form of treatment is gene therapy. This is where a manufactured artificial gene for the correct protein is introduced into lung cells by a modified virus using a nasal spray. The virus takes over the cells and they now produce the normal mucus. Patients treated this way notice a huge

transformation in their lives. However, the treatment has to be regularly repeated and is very expensive.

Lifestyle changes can improve a person's overall condition. Smoking is a major problem affecting all respiratory dysfunctions. It paralyses the cilia that line the lungs, leading to a build up of mucus that can eventually become infected.

Pollution can often trigger asthma attacks. Fresh, clean air is well known to be beneficial to lung disease sufferers. Being overweight can put more stress on the respiratory system, leading to increased chest complaints. If a person tries to keep healthy, by exercise and eating a well balanced diet, they should be able to improve and maintain their health.

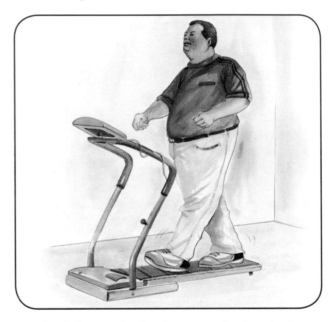

Exercise helps respiration by strengthening the lungs and helping to maintain optimum weight

Angela   CASE STUDY

Angela has always had chest problems, mainly due to her lifestyle. Her health has always been affected by the following:

- damp old Victorian house
- draughty rooms
- poor heating
- a lack of vitamins and minerals.
- the effect of the hairs from her pets.

1 Explain why the factors given could cause Angela to have chest problems, especially in winter.

2 How could this situation affect Angela's chest?

3 How could Angela reduce the effects on her health?

Assessment activity 12.2.1

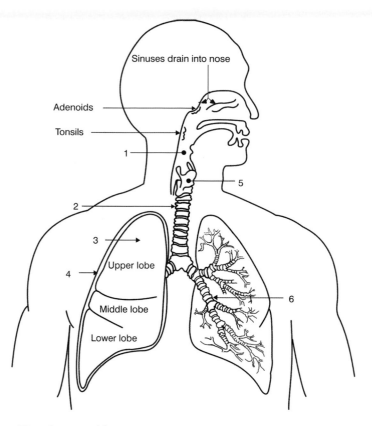

The chest and lungs

George — CASE STUDY

George has chronic obstructive pulmonary disease and does not understand his condition. Use the following questions to help George understand his dysfunction.

1. Label the structures 1 to 6.

2. Explain how oxygen gets from the lungs to the blood and how carbon dioxide is released back into the lungs.

3. Describe **one** dysfunction of the respiratory system in detail, giving its
   • possible causes
   • methods of diagnosis
   • treatments.

4. How can the dysfunction described affect an individual's health and well being?

5. Explain the physiological effects of smoking on the lungs.

6. What are the effects of long-term steroid treatment?

12.2.2 Cardio-vascular system

Heart

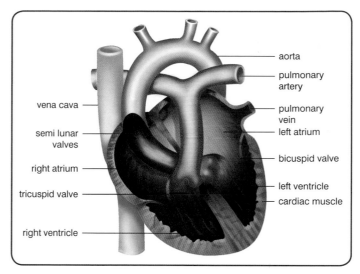

The structure of the heart and the main vessels

The heart is a little larger than a clenched fist and is located between the lungs. Its primary purpose is to pump blood at 60 to 80 times per minute to deliver oxygen and nutrients to all body cells. Each day the average heart beats 100,000 times and pumps about 2,000 gallons of blood. It is divided into four separate compartments known as **atria** and **ventricles**.

The circulatory system is a network of veins and arteries that carries oxygen and nutrients to all parts of the body. Arteries, arterioles (small arteries) and capillaries (minute blood vessels) carry oxygenated blood. Venules (small veins) and veins carry deoxygenated blood back to the heart. Laid end-to-end, the system would extend for about 60,000 miles.

Structure, type and general function of blood

Blood normally accounts for 7–8% of bodyweight and consists of red cells, white cells and **platelets**, contained in watery fluid called **plasma**. The plasma contains dissolved proteins, sugars, fats, salts and minerals. The functions of blood include transporting oxygen and nutrients to body cells and getting rid of carbon dioxide and other waste products. It plays a vital role in helping to fight infection and in maintaining body temperature and **homeostasis**. Homeostasis is how the body maintains constant conditions such as body temperature, blood pressure, concentration and Ph of the blood and cells.

	Structure	Function
Arteries	The walls (outer structure) of arteries contain smooth muscle fibres that contract and relax under the instructions of the sympathetic nervous system. They do not have valves (except for the semi-lunar valves of the pulmonary artery and the aorta).	To transport blood *away* from the heart; they transport oxygenated blood only (*except in the case of the pulmonary artery*).
Arterioles	Arterioles are tiny branches of arteries that lead to capillaries. These are also under the control of the sympathetic nervous system, and constrict and dilate, to regulate blood flow.	To transport blood from arteries to capillaries. Arterioles are the main regulators of blood flow and pressure.
Capillaries	Capillaries are tiny (extremely narrow) blood vessels, of approximately 5–20 micrometres diameter. There are networks of capillaries in most of the organs and tissues of the body. These capillaries are supplied with blood by arterioles and drained by venules. Capillary walls are only one cell thick, which permits exchanges of material between the contents of the capillary and the surrounding tissue.	The function is to supply tissues with essential components carried by the blood, and also to remove waste from the surrounding cells. In this process there is an exchange of oxygen, carbon dioxide, water, salts, etc., between the blood and the surrounding body tissues.
Veins	The walls of veins consist of layers of tissues that are thinner and less elastic than the corresponding layers of arteries. Veins include valves that aid the return of blood to the heart by preventing blood from flowing in the reverse direction.	To transport blood *towards* the heart. Veins transport deoxygenated blood only (*except in the case of the pulmonary vein*).
Venules	Venules are minute vessels that drain blood from capillaries and into veins. Many venules unite to form a vein.	To drain blood from capillaries into veins, for return to the heart.

Structure and function of blood vessels

Red cells, or **erythrocytes**, are relatively large cells without nuclei; they make up 40–50% of the total blood volume and transport oxygen (attached to the haemoglobin from the lungs), to all living tissues. The red cells are produced continuously in bone marrow from stem cells, at about two million cells per second. Each red cell has about 270,000,000 iron-rich haemoglobin molecules. People who are anaemic generally have a deficiency in red cells.

White cells, or **leukocytes**, vary in numbers and types and make up only about 1% of the blood's volume. Leukocytes are not restricted to the blood system and occur elsewhere in the body. They are found in the spleen, liver, and lymph glands. Most are produced in our bone marrow from the same kind of stem cells that produce red blood cells. Others are produced in the thymus gland, which is at the base of the neck in children. White cells are the first to respond when the immune system detects a problem. They seek out, identify, and bind to foreign proteins on bacteria, viruses and fungi, so that they can be destroyed.

Platelets, or **thrombocytes**, clump together to block holes in blood vessels and are essential to arrest bleeding and repair damaged blood vessels.

Various types of blood cells

Blood group compatibility					
		Donor blood group			
		A	B	AB	O
Recipient blood group	A	✓	✗	✗	✓
	B	✓	✓	✗	✓
	AB	✓	✓	✓	✓
	O	✗	✗	✗	✓

Key   ✓ = Compatible   ✗ = Incompatible

Blood groups/types and their classification are essential for safe blood transfusion.

ABO groups: In 1900, two types of antigens were discovered on the surface of red blood cells, which are called A and B. According to whether the person's blood contains one or other antigen, both or neither, the blood is classified as 'Type A, B, AB or O'. The fluid part of the blood contains antibodies against other antigens, anti-A, and/or anti-B that react with these antigens. A person cannot be safely transfused with blood of a group containing antigens to which he or she has antibodies. In the UK, the most common of the ABO groups is A, then O, then B and finally AB. (see table above)

Rhesus factors is another group system discovered in 1940 during experiments on Rhesus monkeys. This identifies several antigens, the most important being factor D. This is found in 85% of people and called Rhesus (Rh) positive, while 15% lack this factor and are called Rh negative. Individuals are therefore classed as, for example, 'O positive' or 'B negative' on the basis of their ABO and Rh groups.

Function of the cardiovascular system

- **Deoxygenated** blood from the body is pumped through the right atrium and the right ventricle to the lungs where it is oxygenated. It is then pumped through the left atrium and the left ventricle and around the body. It is essential that blood flows in the correct direction through the heart, so the structure of the heart includes a series of valves.
- The **tricuspid valve** separates the right atrium from the right ventricle.

- The **pulmonic/pulmonary valve** separates the right ventricle from the pulmonary artery.
- The **mitral or bicuspid valve** separates the left atrium from the left ventricle.
- The aortic valve separates the right ventricle from the ascending aorta.

Heart contractions arise from the heart's natural pacemaker, the sino-atrial (SA) node, which is in the right atrium. The sino-atrial node sends out regular electrical impulses causing the atria to contract and to pump blood into the bottom chambers (ventricles). The electrical impulse then passes to the ventricles through the atrio-ventricular node. This electrical impulse spreads into the ventricles, causing the muscle to contract and to pump blood to the lungs and the body.

Dysfunctions of the cardio-vascular system

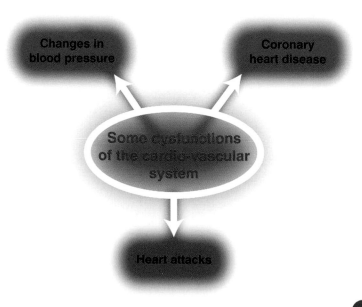

Changes in blood pressure

Coronary heart disease

Some dysfunctions of the cardio-vascular system

Heart attacks

Changes in blood pressure

The heart circulates five litres of blood around the body every minute and the smaller blood vessels produce a resistance to blood flow. The pumping of the heart against this resistance pressurises the system and allows return flow. Circulation of blood is essential for nutrition of the major organs, providing the vital oxygen and nutrients necessary.

When the heart contracts, the highest pressure it produces is called the systolic pressure; when it relaxes, the lowest pressure is called the diastolic pressure. Both of these pressures can be measured and can indicate the risk of **heart attack** and stroke. The normal blood pressure in a young person might be around 130/80. This indicates a systolic pressure of 130 and a diastolic pressure of 80. A person is considered to have high blood pressure or **hypertension** when readings are above the 160/100 thresholds.

Coronary artery disease (CAD)

Coronary artery disease (coronary heart disease) is when one or more of the coronary arteries becomes narrowed or totally blocked by a gradual build-up of fatty deposits (**plaques**). The coronary arteries are blood vessels that take food and oxygen directly to the heart muscle. This narrowing therefore causes a reduction in the oxygenated blood flow to the heart muscle. As a result, the heart muscle begins to die and this is known as an infarction.

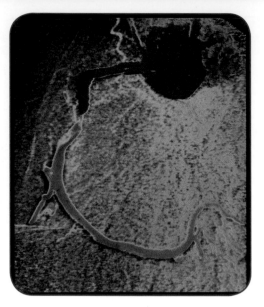

Coronary arteries can be blocked at any point

Heart attacks

The term 'heart attack' is used to describe the events that follow a blockage in one or more coronary arteries. It is also known as **myocardial infarction (MI)** or coronary thrombosis. A heart attack happens when the blood flow in the arteries is reduced so much that part of the heart muscle dies.

Layers (plaques) of cholesterol build up inside the coronary arteries (atherosclerosis). These plaques can rupture, and when a blood clot forms over the rupture, it can block the blood supply and trigger a heart attack. A heart attack can also occur when the heart muscle demands more oxygen than the blood supply can provide.

Fact: Approximately 300,000 people in the UK have a heart attack each year and nearly half die.

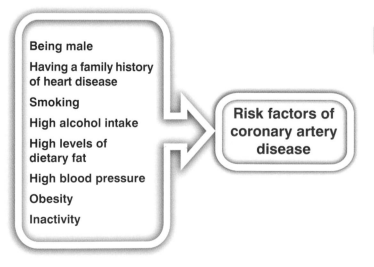

Being male

Having a family history of heart disease

Smoking

High alcohol intake

High levels of dietary fat

High blood pressure

Obesity

Inactivity

→ Risk factors of coronary artery disease

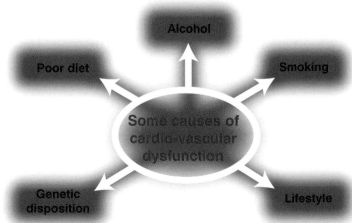

Alcohol

Poor diet

Smoking

Some causes of cardio-vascular dysfunction

Genetic disposition

Lifestyle

Diet has major effects on all of the body systems, especially the cardio-vascular system. High levels of salt and saturated fats are common causes of CAD and **hypertension**, both of which can lead to heart attacks. Too much salt (more than 2,400mg) can lead to the development of hypertension.

Too much saturated fat means that the body starts to deposit the increased cholesterol in important arteries. Overall, too many calories increases bodyweight and this also puts a strain on the cardio-vascular system.

Alcohol can be a friend or an enemy in respect of developing heart disease and high blood pressure. Effects depend on:

• how much alcohol you drink
• drinking pattern
• age.

A small amount of alcohol gives protection against heart disease, at least in middle-aged men (over 40) and in women who have gone through the menopause. Red wine contains antioxidants, which are good for the heart, but there is no clear evidence that any one type of drink gives more protection than any other. The protective effects of light drinking are possibly due to:

• an increase in the level of **HDL-cholesterol** (There are two forms of cholesterol: LDL-cholesterol, which is a harmful type responsible for the formation of plaque, and HDL-cholesterol, which is a good form that actively removes plaque.)
• a decrease in the tendency of the blood to become 'sticky' and form clots.

Alcohol is also a toxin and too much on a regular basis can damage the heart.

Health professionals advise keeping within these sensible limits.

Women:	No more than 3 units daily (maximum 21 units per week).
Men:	No more than 4 units daily (maximum 28 units per week).

A unit of alcohol is 10 ml of pure alcohol. The number of units in any alcoholic drink varies according to the strength and volume of the drink. A pint of medium strength bitter, cider or lager would be rated at 2 units whereas stronger varieties are 3 units. A glass of wine is about 2 units. Spirits range from 1 to 2 units according to the type and measure. An 'Alcopop' is 1.5 units.

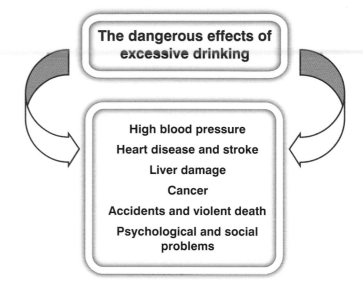

The dangerous effects of excessive drinking

High blood pressure
Heart disease and stroke
Liver damage
Cancer
Accidents and violent death
Psychological and social problems

Smoking is the biggest killer and up to 18 in every 100 deaths are from heart disease associated with smoking. People who smoke cigarettes have twice the risk of a heart attack. If a person is under 50 and a smoker, the risk of heart disease is ten times greater than for a non-smoker of the same age. The more a person smokes and the younger they started, the greater the risk.

Passive smoking also increases the development of heart and lung disease. About 70% of smokers want to quit and there are now many support services and **pharmacological** preparations on the market to help people.

The biggest killers on the planet

Genetic disposition

Early coronary heart disease can be caused by a single gene defect. However, most people with a genetic risk of heart disease have inherited several genes, each of which slightly increases their risk. Some of these gene variants are only a risk when other environmental factors are present.

Multiple genes are thought to be involved in susceptibility to hypertension. The estimate of the genetic contribution ranges from 30 to 50 per cent, but the risk contributed by any single gene is usually small. There are a number of rare inherited forms of hypertension for which single genes are known to be involved, e.g. Liddle's syndrome (a rare hereditary disorder of the kidney).

A lifestyle that includes becoming more active and improving diet can greatly benefit the heart. Taking more exercise helps reduce blood pressure, improves cholesterol levels and boosts metabolism, thus reducing the risk of CAD.

Stress has long been linked to ill health. A study of 10,000 civil servants found a link between stress and metabolic syndrome, which involves obesity and high blood pressure. Factors such as social class, smoking, high alcohol consumption and lack of exercise were all recorded as part of the study.

Heart dysfunction	Activity 2

Dysfunctions of the heart can occur in many forms.

1. Choose **one** heart dysfunction and carry out research to show the causes, the effects and diagnostic treatment.

2. Give a presentation to the rest of the group using your findings. Include speaker notes.

Diagnosis

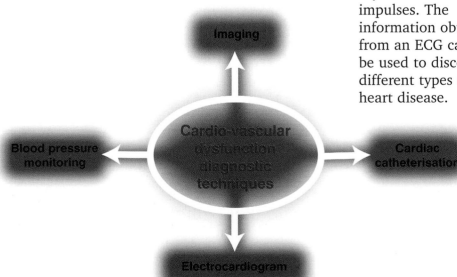

Imaging

The diagnosis of heart disease is assisted by **radio-diagnostic imaging** in a variety of forms. The chest x-ray is one of the most widely used imaging techniques. X-rays can give a good outline picture of any changes in heart size and shape due to dysfunction or disease.

One form of diagnostic imaging is the use of angiograms. Here a dye that absorbs x-rays is injected into the blood and is used to locate sites of blockage.

Theory into practice

Carry out primary or secondary research to find out how radio-diagnostic imaging actually works.

Blood pressure monitoring

Monitoring blood pressure is an essential way of checking for hypertension. It is currently commonplace for people to have their own monitor at home as they are now inexpensive, non-invasive and simple to use.

ECG

ECG (electrocardiogram) is a test that measures the electrical activity of the heart. The signals that make the heart's muscle fibres contract come from the sino-atrial node, which is the natural pacemaker of the heart. In an ECG, the electrical impulses made while the heart is beating are recorded on a piece of paper. This is known as an electrocardiogram and records any problems with the heart's rhythm and electrical impulses. The information obtained from an ECG can be used to discover different types of heart disease.

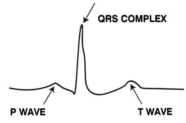

A typical ECG trace is made up of three waves. The P wave shows the contraction of the atria; the QRS wave, the contraction of the ventricles; and the T wave, the relaxation of the ventricles.

Abnormal patterns will show differences in the rate of the heartbeat and whether

Atrial flutter/fibrillation

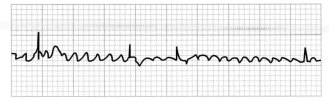

Ventricular tachycardia

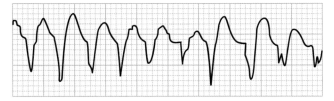

Ventricular fibrillation

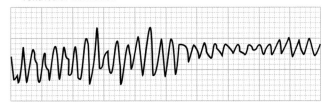

damage to the heart has resulted in the atria and ventricles contracting on their own rather than being co-ordinated by the pacemaker.

The test can show evidence of disease in the coronary arteries and can also be used to assess if the patient has had a heart attack, or evidence of a previous heart attack. An ECG can be used in various ways, such as to:

- monitor the effect of medicines used for coronary artery disease
- reveal rhythm problems such as the cause of a slow or fast heart beat
- demonstrate thickening of a heart muscle (left ventricular hypertrophy), possibly due to long-standing high blood pressure
- see if there are too few minerals in the blood.

It is also useful for seeing how well the patient is responding to treatment. An ECG may appear normal even in the presence of significant heart disease.

Cardiac catheterisation

Cardiac catheterisation is carried out to confirm the exact nature of a heart defect if other tests have not given enough information. The procedure can also be used to treat some conditions, for instance:

- to close small holes
- to stretch a narrow blood vessel
- to replace a valve, avoiding the need for open heart surgery

- in cardiac catheterisation, a **catheter** is inserted through a special needle (cannula) into the femoral artery, through a small incision in the groin. The **cardiologist** then guides the catheter into the heart, using x-ray screening to monitor its progress.

The **catheter** can be used to measure the pressures within each chamber and in the arteries. Blood samples can be taken to check the oxygen levels in the different parts of the heart. An angiogram, using a contrast medium injected through the catheter, can demonstrate the heart chambers and blood vessels. These images are recorded for the cardiac team to review later when planning treatment.

Treatments

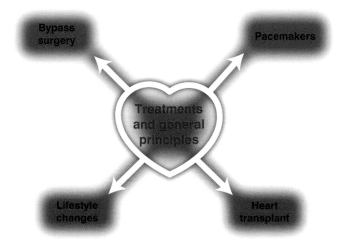

Heart bypass surgery

The operation, also known as a **coronary artery bypass graft (CABG)**, involves rerouting the blood flow around the obstructed part of the artery, by using a portion of a blood vessel taken from another part of the body (usually an artery from the chest). One end of the replacement is attached to the far side of the narrowed or blocked coronary artery and the other end is attached directly to the aorta. The blockage is therefore by-passed and the blood supply restored.

Heart pacemakers

A pacemaker is a small, battery-operated electronic device which stimulates the heart into beating regularly and at an appropriate rate. The generator contains the battery and the information to regulate the heartbeat. The leads go from the generator through the **subclavian** vein to the heart, where the wires rest against the heart wall. The generator sends the electrical impulses to the heart to maintain the beat. A pacemaker can usually sense if the heartbeat changes, at which point it will either automatically turn on or off to maintain the correct pace of beat.

Heart transplant surgery and prevention of rejection

Rejection of organ transplants is a complicated process whereby the recipient's immune system recognises the donated organ as foreign tissue and sets out to destroy it. This involves special white blood cells called T-lymphocytes producing antibodies. Matching the recipient and donor as closely as possible and the use of drugs called immuno-suppressants will reduce the severity of any rejection. The drugs will be taken for life and at high doses will make the recipient more likely to catch infections and develop certain cancers as their immune system is being shut down. After the first few months, the risk of acute rejection decreases and the amount of anti-rejection medication that patients need to take can be reduced. Chronic rejection occurs later, progressing slowly to cause eventual destruction of the transplanted organ. It is not well understood and is untreatable.

To reduce the risk of organ rejection, donor organs are only used if they are suitable for the patient. The blood is screened for **antibodies**, and the size and weight of the organs must be similar to those of the patient.

The success rate of this type of transplant has improved a lot in recent years. The survival rate is now around 85% after one year.

Lifestyle changes

After the treatments mentioned, most people can return to a relatively normal life. By this time they will be aware of the major factors that caused their problem (possibly smoking, drinking and stress), and should avoid these in future.

Assessment activity 12.2.2

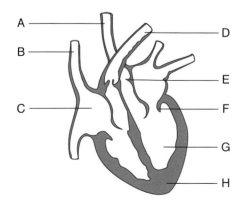

CASE STUDY

1. Identify each of the structures labelled A–H in the diagram and describe their function.

2. Describe the flow of blood through the heart, starting at the vena cava and finishing at the aorta, naming the valves and structures that the blood passes through.

3. Describe the information provided by an ECG and explain its value to a cardiologist when assessing the function of a patient's heart.

4. Explain to the group the different types of dysfunction that can affect the cardio-vascular system. Describe to them how the conditions are diagnosed and treated.

12.2.3 Digestive system

The gross structure and functions of the organs and glands of the alimentary tract (gut)

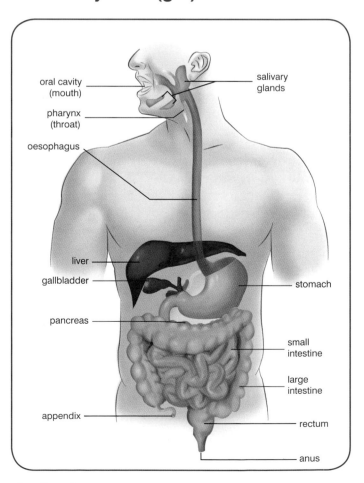

The digestive system

The digestive system may also be referred to as the **alimentary tract** or **alimentary canal**. This tract or canal extends from the mouth to the anus. There are associated accessory organs that are part of the digestive tract which are located outside the tract itself, but **secrete** fluids into it. The parts of the digestive tract consist of:

- the mouth or oral cavity, with the salivary glands as accessory organs
- the throat or pharynx
- the oesophagus (gullet)
- the stomach
- the small intestine, consisting of the duodenum, jejunum and ileum, with the liver, gallbladder and pancreas as accessory organs
- the large intestine, including the caecum, colon, rectum and anal canal.

The mouth or oral cavity

The mouth or oral cavity is also referred to as the **buccal** cavity. It is bounded by the lips in front, the throat opening into the pharynx at the back, the cheeks at the sides and the soft palate above. The floor of the oral cavity is mainly formed by the tongue and muscles. The tongue has specialised cells that are sensitive to taste, known as taste buds.

Surrounding the palate and the tongue are the teeth, which are set in the tissue of the gums. A normal adult has 32 permanent or secondary teeth, which replace the first (or milk) teeth that develop in early childhood.

The lips, cheeks and tongue contain food in the mouth, whose lining consists of **mucous membrane**, lubricated by saliva produced by three pairs of salivary glands. The tongue is a large muscular organ attached at the back, while the front of the tongue is relatively free.

In the mouth, food is broken down mechanically by chewing and saliva is added as a lubricant. Saliva also contains amylase, an enzyme that digests starch.

The **pharynx** connects the back of the mouth and nose to the oesophagus. It is lined with mucous membrane and forms part of both the respiratory and digestive systems. A fold of tissue called the **epiglottis** covers the opening to the larynx (airway) to prevent food and drink entering into the larynx during the swallowing action.

During the first stage of swallowing, food is shaped into a **bolus** and is moved from the oral cavity to the **oesophagus** along the pharynx.

The **oesophagus** is also referred to as the **gullet**. It is about 23 centimetres long and extends from the pharynx above, to the stomach. At either end of the oesophagus there are two **sphincters**, or rings of muscle, that act as regulating valves to control the passage of food.

The main function of the oesophagus is to propel food and fluids from the pharynx into the stomach. **Peristaltic** (involuntary wave-like) **contractions** move the bolus of food from the pharynx along its distance and into the stomach. Numerous glands in the wall of the oesophagus produce mucus, which provides lubrication and also helps to protect the lining from any acid secretions that may escape from the stomach at the lower end.

The **stomach** is situated in the left upper section of the abdomen just beneath the diaphragm. It is shaped like a bag and can hold approximately 1.5 litres, although its overall shape and size varies from person to person and depends on the contents. There are two openings in the stomach, each surrounded by a sphincter. The upper opening, from the oesophagus, is called the **gastro-oesophageal** opening; the lower opening is called the **pyloric orifice** or **pylorus,** situated where the stomach narrows to form the **pyloric canal**, just before connecting into the first part of the small intestine. The lining of the stomach has large folds known as rugae (wrinkles), which are present when the stomach is empty. These folds become less as the stomach fills with food.

The stomach fluid is very acidic, stopping the action of salivary amylase. It is harmful to bacteria, reducing the chance of infection. Food remains in the stomach for 1–4 hours, during which time the stomach wall continually mixes the food with gastric juice. Secretions are produced by the gastric glands of the stomach wall.

Gastric juice comprises:

- water
- hydrochloric acid
- **proteases** (protein-digesting enzymes)
- mucus.

The mucus provides a protective layer for the stomach that limits acid damage. The final mixture of partially digested food is called **chyme**.

The small intestine, consisting of the duodenum, jejunum and ileum, is a 7-metre long muscular tube that breaks down food using enzymes released by the pancreas and bile from the liver. The duodenum is largely responsible for absorption of nutrients into the bloodstream. The walls of the intestine have small finger-like **villi**, which greatly increase the surface area, allowing much greater absorption of nutrients into the blood stream.

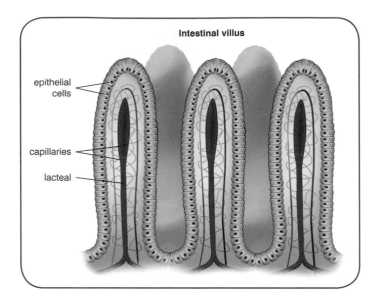

Intestinal villus

epithelial cells

capillaries

lacteal

The contents of the small intestine start out as semi-solid and end as a liquid. Water, bile, enzymes, and mucus contribute to the change in consistency. Once the nutrients have been absorbed, the flow moves on to the large intestine.

The main function within the digestive system is to process the nutrients absorbed from the small intestine. To assist in this process, **bile from the liver** is secreted into the small intestine and plays an important role in digesting fat. Additionally, the liver, as the body's chemical 'factory', takes the raw materials absorbed by the intestine and makes the various chemicals the body needs to function. The liver also **detoxifies** potentially harmful chemicals absorbed, such as alcohol. The gallbladder stores and concentrates bile, and then releases it into the duodenum to help absorb and digest fats.

The pancreas secretes digestive enzymes into the duodenum that break down protein, fats, and carbohydrates. The pancreas also secretes insulin directly into the bloodstream, where it promotes the uptake of glucose by cells especially in the liver and in muscles.

The **large intestine (colon)** is a 2-metre long muscular tube that connects the small intestine to the rectum.

The **large intestine** is a highly specialised organ that is responsible for absorbing the remaining excess water, processing waste and forming faeces.

The rectum is a 20 cm chamber connecting the colon to the anus. It is the rectum's job to receive **stools** from the colon. It lets the person know that there is stool to be evacuated and holds the stool until evacuation happens.

The anus is the last part of the digestive tract. It is a 5 cm long canal consisting of the pelvic floor muscles and the two anal **sphincters**. The lining is specialised to detect rectal contents. It informs the individual whether the contents are liquid, gas, or solid.

Basic functions and processes

The basic functions of the digestive system are the process of digestion and the absorption of food including the main digestive enzymes.

The digestive system is a food processing system that breaks down **macromolecules** of protein, fat and starch, which cannot be absorbed intact. It does this by turning them into smaller molecules, amino acids, fatty acids and glucose. They can then be absorbed into the circulatory system, for use by the body.

The table below highlights the functions of some of the main digestive enzymes and digestive chemicals.

Enzyme	Action
Salivary amylase	Starts digestion on starch
Pepsin	Catalyses the splitting of amino acid bonds in proteins
Trypsin	Breaks amino acid bonds forming peptide fragments
Carboxypeptidase	Splits amino acids
Lipase	Splits amino acids
Amylase	Splits polysaccharides

Hydrochloric acid is required to activate the protease enzyme in the stomach.

Bile from the gallbladder contains salts that break fats into smaller droplets so allowing the fat-digesting enzymes to work.

<table>
<tr><td colspan="2">**The digestive process**</td><td>**Activity 3**</td></tr>
</table>

The digestive process	**Activity 3**
Describe the process of digestion in the stomach and duodenum.	

Dysfunctions of the digestive system

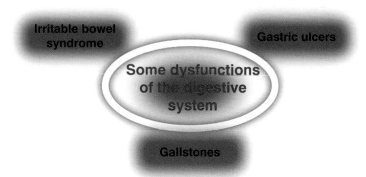

Irritable bowel syndrome (IBS) is a chronic disorder of the gut. Sufferers have either constipation or diarrhoea and sometimes the two alternate. They may experience abdominal pain, bloating or general discomfort and a change in bowel habit, without an obvious cause. Nevertheless, this painful and distressing condition seriously affects quality of life.

IBS frequently begins in early adulthood and comes and goes over the course of many years. It appears that:

- women are twice as likely as men to suffer from IBS

- it is more common in emotional and stressed people
- at some time or other, around one third of the population may be affected.

IBS is characterised by a range of interrelated symptoms; the most common are:

Abdominal pain	Mostly occurring on the right-hand side and varying from mild to severe. These cramp-like pains come and go and are often relieved by a bowel movement.
Bloating	A feeling of fullness in the abdomen, particularly after meals.
Constipation	Less frequent movements, straining during a bowel movement, hard, painful stools and feelings of incomplete evacuation. Often alternating with **diarrhoea**.
Diarrhoea	Frequent, hard-to-control bowel movements and loose, watery stools. Often alternating with constipation.

IBS is the most common disorder of the digestive tract, affecting 10–20% of adults. Usually beginning in early adulthood, some sufferers may find that their condition can be aggravated by certain foods, although the cause of IBS is not fully understood.

Anxiety is thought by some doctors to be the main contributory factor and **emotional stress** certainly exacerbates the condition.

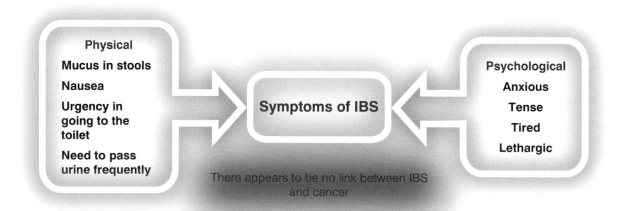

Diagnosis and treatment for irritable bowel syndrome

The two traditional steps to forming a diagnosis are:

1. a careful history of the onset of the illness
2. a physical examination.

Worry can be the biggest problem in IBS and the stress that develops can increase and exacerbate the symptoms, causing even more distress, pain and discomfort. One common effect of IBS is associated weight loss, due to the frequent attacks of diarrhoea. In most digestive dysfunction, individuals tend to limit their diet to reduce symptoms and this gives rise to weight loss.

If the digestive process is being compromised by the effects of the dysfunction, then nutrients will not be absorbed. **Malabsorption** is therefore always a risk with many types of digestive dysfunction.

With IBS, the structure of the digestive tract usually shows no abnormality and diagnosis is made on the patient's symptoms; however, an examination of the patient's faeces, a barium meal and a sigmoidoscopy (examination of the rectum and colon) may be undertaken. This is to eliminate other possible conditions such as bowel cancer.

Treatment usually includes a high-fibre diet plus medication to ease the symptoms, such as diarrhoea and any possible muscular spasms. These treatments tend to ease the symptoms but not to cure the problem. Patients often find that although the symptoms ease, from time to time the condition recurs throughout life.

A gastric or peptic ulcer is a break in the lining of the stomach and is usually non-malignant. About 4% of gastric ulcers are caused by a **malignant** tumour, however, which is why ulcers of the stomach are always treated seriously.

Gastric ulcers can be **caused by several factors**:

- Infection with a bacterium, **Helicobacter pylori**, which lives in the lining of the stomach. This can be found in about 80% of patients with gastric ulcers.
- Overuse of non-steroidal anti-inflammatory drugs (NSAIDs) or aspirin-containing drugs.
- Other drugs, for example drugs used to treat osteoporosis.

The most common symptom is indigestion, which can include **pain, discomfort** or a burning sensation in the upper abdomen. Other symptoms include:

- frequent vomiting
- vomiting blood
- passing tarry, black stools (**malena**)
- significant weight loss.

Diagnosis and treatment for gastric ulcers

A clear history of the patient's symptoms is vital in reaching an early and correct diagnosis. The patient's lifestyle is analysed, with advice given on possible changes, such as a more appropriate diet, and reduction in alcohol and smoking. Subsequent monitoring is usually undertaken, in conjunction with weight management and possibly training in relaxation techniques. Any symptoms of pain in relation to foods, meal times and emotional stress should be noted. A physical examination by a medical doctor is also a vital part of the diagnostic procedures.

The conventional way to treat ulcers is by using medications that lower acid production in the stomach, including drugs such as:

- **proton pump inhibitors (PPI)**
- **histamine H_2-receptor blockers.**

Helicobacter treatment consists of a PPI taken together with two antibiotics. Treatment is aimed at healing the ulcer and preventing recurrence. If aspirin is the cause, these drugs are often stopped.

X-rays are used to diagnose ulcers that do not respond to the conventional treatment. This involves swallowing barium sulphate solution, which outlines the stomach and can be visualised on the x-rays. Barium sulphate can also be introduced through the anus to outline the large bowel.

An endoscopy is another diagnostic test, where a flexible fibre-optic tube is passed through the mouth into the oesophagus and the stomach. This has a micro-camera at its end allowing images of the gut to be seen. This may also be referred to as a gastroscopy. The specialist can then see any abnormality and take a **biopsy** if necessary. A biopsy is when a sample of tissue is removed, usually using micro tools at the end of the endoscope. The sample will then be examined in the laboratory.

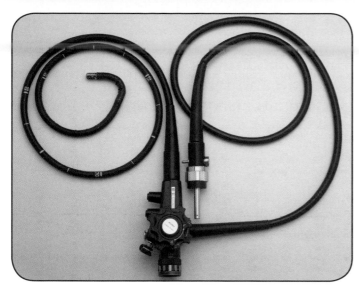

Imagine having to swallow this!

Gallstones are caused when the gallbladder absorbs water from the bile, causing it to thicken. Tiny crystals, formed from the cholesterol and pigments, grow gradually until one or several gallstones develop. Middle-aged women are particularly affected, but anyone, at any age and under certain conditions, can develop these stones.

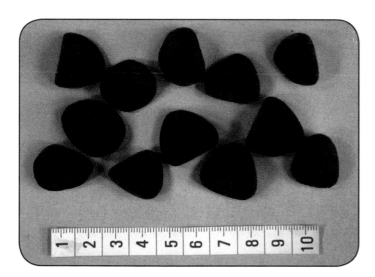

Something so small can cause so much pain

Many people with gallstones never experience symptoms, but may experience the following:

- colicky pain after meals when the gallbladder contracts
- stones irritating the gallbladder, causing acute inflammation.

Gallstones may block the main bile duct, stopping the flow and causing jaundice to develop. This is characterised by:

- the skin turning yellow
- dark urine
- white stools (steatorrhoea).

Gallstones are frequently blamed for:

- indigestion
- nausea
- intolerance to fatty foods.

Diagnosis and treatments for gallstones

Ultrasound scanning uses high frequency sound and can detect 95% of gallstones and is therefore the first test to be performed. In this test, sound waves are beamed into the gallbladder. If hard stones are present, the wave is reflected, giving a visual image. This method also allows the operator to measure anatomical structures.

Those with gallstones have to avoid fatty foods in their diet, so that the contractions do not give rise to **colic** and also try to avoid acidic food that might raise the acidity in the stomach.

Drugs are now available that dissolve cholesterol gallstones, which can take from six months to two years.

General surgery

In laparoscopic surgery, a tiny incision is made through the navel. A micro-video tube is then inserted, with three other needle-like instruments and the gallbladder is removed through the small incision. With general surgery, an 8–15 cm **incision** is made in the right-upper abdomen for gallstones and a larger incision toward the mid-line for gastric ulcers. Each of the procedures will be followed by a 3–6 day hospital stay.

Another technique called lithotripsy makes use of high energy shock waves to break the stones up into small fragments which are then expelled from the body.

Assessment activity 12.2.3

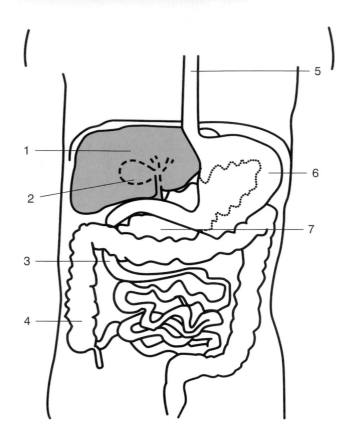

Dorothea | CASE STUDY

Dorothea's health is quite poor. She is suffering from gallstones and a gastric ulcer. Her husband is worried and requires help to understand her clinical problems. Use the questions below to help him develop an understanding of what is happening.

1 Identify each of the structures labelled 1–7 in the diagram.

2 Describe **one** function of each part of the digestive system given below:
- oesophagus
- stomach
- small intestine
- large intestine
- gallbladder
- pancreas.

3 Dorothea has to go into hospital for diagnostic tests. Explain to Dorothea what tests she might have to have and how they will use these to decide on her treatment. How do you think that this will affect her health and well being?

12.2.4 Reproductive system

The gross structure and function of the male and female reproductive systems, testes and ovaries

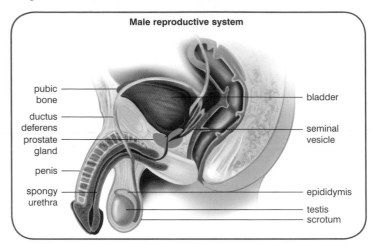

Male reproductive system

Male reproductive system

There are two **testes** in the male which lie in the scrotal sac. The development of sperm requires a temperature lower than that of the body, which is why the testes lie outside the main body cavity. At the upper end of each testis is a spermatic cord which contains the blood vessels. Leading from the end of the testes is a narrow coiled tube called the epididymis. Sperm produced in the testes are stored temporarily in an inactive form in the epididymis before they enter the sperm duct or vas deferens (ductus deferens).

Both vas deferens pass into the abdominal cavity. They loop over the ureter from each side and finally open into the urethra just above the prostate gland. Another gland called the seminal vesicle opens into each vas deferens. At the base of the urinary bladder is the Cowper's gland. The seminal vesicle, the prostate and the Cowper's gland secrete a nutrient fluid containing nutrients and enzymes. This nourishes the sperm and activates them; this fluid is collectively called semen. The seminal vesicles also store sperm temporarily before ejaculation.

The urethra passes through the centre of the penis, but does not allow semen and urine to pass through the urethra at the same time. This is done by a circular band of muscle called the sphincter muscle at the base of the urinary bladder. This muscle can be controlled at will and prevents urine from coming out of the bladder during ejaculation.

In the female there are two **ovaries** in the lower abdominal cavity, just below the kidneys. The **ova**

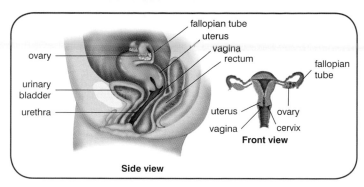

Female reproductive system

(eggs) develop inside the ovaries and it is believed that about 70,000 potential cells are already present at birth. Only 500 will ever become mature and they are released from puberty to menopause. Usually only one egg is released alternately from each ovary every month.

There are two **fallopian tubes** or oviducts which are narrow and muscular, each leading from the ovary to the **uterus**. Where the tube meets the ovary it has a funnel-like end to assist the transfer of the egg.

The **uterus** is a pear-shaped structure with muscular walls that are well supplied with blood vessels in the inner endometrial lining. If the egg is fertilised, it will implant into the lining and start to develop into a **foetus**.

At the lower narrow end of the uterus is a circular ring of muscle called the **cervix**. This leads to a muscular canal called the vagina.

Basic functions of the reproductive system – menstrual cycle

The menstrual cycle occurs regularly over approximately 28 days. Most women have cycles with an interval that lasts from 21 to 35 days. During adolescence, cycles are frequently unusually short or long.

The menstrual phase (days 1 to 6)

During this phase the **endometrium** is shed along with some bleeding. Problems that can occur at this time include:

- dysmenorrhoea (painful periods)
- menorrhagia (unusually heavy periods).

The follicular/proliferate phase

During this phase the pituitary gland of the brain produces a hormone called

follicle-stimulating hormone (FSH). Follicle-stimulating hormone promotes the growth of a follicle (egg sac) within the ovary. An ovum matures in the follicle during this phase. FSH also stimulates the ovary to produce increasing amounts of oestrogen. The oestrogen causes endometrial lining to build up.

The midpoint of the menstrual cycle (approximately day 14)

The build up of oestrogen causes the brain to reduce the levels of FSH. Instead the pituitary gland now produces another hormone called luteinising hormone (LH). This causes the release of the ovum about midway through the menstrual cycle. This is known as ovulation. The ovum then travels from the ovary down the fallopian tube, and into the uterus.

The luteal/secretory phase

Once the ovum has been released, the follicle becomes a sac known as the corpus luteum. Luteinising hormone (LH) then causes the corpus luteum to grow and to secrete progesterone.

During the secretory phase, progesterone makes the endometrial lining stronger and spongy in texture. Progesterone also stimulates glands in the

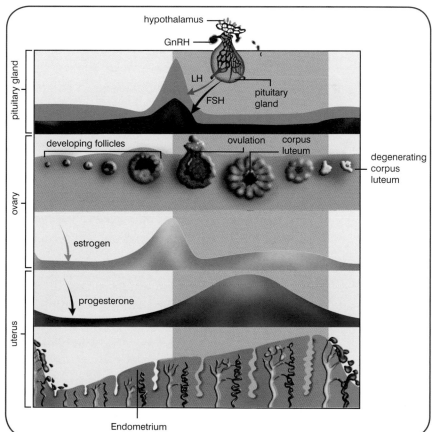

Menstrual cycle

endometrium that produce uterine fluid. Its purpose is to support embryonic development if fertilisation has occurred.

If pregnancy does not occur, the level of progesterone peaks about a week after ovulation and then begins to drop along with the oestrogen level. The flow of blood to the endometrium decreases, and its upper portion is broken down and shed during menstruation. At the same time, the corpus luteum withers and the drop in oestrogen then re-triggers the cycle.

Fertilisation occurs when the head of a sperm penetrates a mature ovum in the fallopian tube.

The newly fertilised ovum is now called a zygote and passes into the uterus where it becomes implanted in the prepared lining and will develop into a **foetus**.

As the zygote travels to the uterus and implants, it produces a hormone known as HCG. This hormone over-rides the control of the menstrual cycle and ensures that progesterone continues to be produced and that menstruation does not occur.

Pregnancy

There are three different stages of pregnancy, commonly known as trimesters.

Week 0–2		Sperm and ovum join. The cell is smaller than a grain of salt, but has all 46 chromosomes, a complete genetic blueprint.
	Days 3–4	Fertilised egg travels towards the uterus through the fallopian tube.
	Days 5–9	Implantation takes place.
		Upon implantation, complex connections between the mother and embryo develop to form the placenta.
	Days 10–14	Embryo releases chemicals and hormones that prevent the mother from menstruating.
Week 2–4	Day 20	Foundations of the brain, spinal cord and central nervous system are already established.
	Day 21	Heart begins to beat.
	Day 28	Limbs and muscles begin to show. The spine starts forming.
Week 6–9		Embryo is about 5 mm in length. A primitive heart is beating. Head, mouth, liver, and intestines begin to take shape.
	Week 6	Brain waves are detectable and recordable.
		Liver now controls the production of blood cells and the brain has begun to control muscles and organs.
	Week 7	Embryo can now move. The jaw forms.
	Week 8	It is now termed a foetus. It contains everything that a fully grown human being has, including digestive juices and forty muscle sets. The foetus is touch-sensitive.
	Week 9	Foetus has fingerprints and can move its hands.
Week 10–13	Week 10	Embryo is now about 5 cm in length. Facial features, limbs, hands, feet, fingers and toes become apparent. The nervous system is responsive and many of the internal organs begin to function. The foetus can squint, swallow and wrinkle its forehead.
	Week 11	Foetus can now urinate and make facial expressions.
	Week 12	Foetus sleeps and awakens and moves its muscles.
	Week 13	Hair has begun to grow and sexual differentiation is apparent.

First trimester

Week 14	Foetus is now 8 cm long and weighs almost 28 g. The muscles begin to develop and sex organs form. Eyelids, fingernails, and toenails also form. Spontaneous movements can be observed.
	Foetus can hear.
Week 18	Foetus is now about 13 cm long. The child blinks, grasps, and moves mouth. Hair grows on the head and body.
	Foetus responds to sound and the mother can feel movement.
Week 22	Foetus now weighs approximately 350 g and spans about 25 cm from head to toe. Sweat glands develop, and the external skin has turned from transparent to opaque. Oil and sweat glands are functioning.

Second trimester

Week 26	Foetus can now inhale, exhale and even cry. Eyes have completely formed, and the tongue has developed taste buds. Under intensive medical care the foetus has a greater than 50% chance of surviving outside the womb. The baby can use four of its five senses and can recognise its mother's voice.
Week 30	Foetus is usually capable of living outside the womb and would be considered premature at birth. The skin thickens and fat is stored underneath it.
Week 40	This marks the end of the normal gestational period. The child is now ready to live outside the mother's womb. Birth usually occurs between 266 and 294 days.

Third trimester

Birth

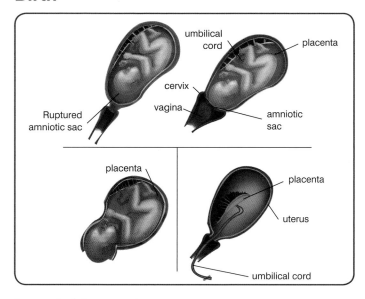

A wonderful moment

Giving birth is usually known as **labour** and is divided into stages.

The first stage of uterine contractions lasts for 40 or 50 seconds every 10 minutes. At the end, each contraction will last longer than a minute, and there will be a gap of no more than a minute between each one. Each contraction helps the uterus push the baby out and at the same time the cervix gradually opens up until the cervix is fully dilated. When mother is dilated 5–6 cm, the contractions become longer and stronger and labour begins to progress more quickly.

During second stage there is a very powerful need to push downwards and this is known as 'bearing down'. The mother usually needs to push about three times in each contraction. As the head stretches the birth canal and the **perineum**, a powerful, burning sensation is experienced. When the head becomes completely visible it is said to be 'crowning'. With the next contraction or two the baby's head emerges, and then baby is born.

Fertilisation — Activity 4

Describe how fertilisation happens and create a diary of major events through the first 20 weeks of pregnancy.

Dysfunctions of the reproductive system

These include:

- infertility
- ectopic pregnancy
- impotence.

Infertility affects approximately 15% of couples. Under normal circumstances, the chances of pregnancy occurring as a result of unprotected intercourse during the fertile time of the cycle are about 25% per month. After 12 months of trying, approximately 80% of couples will have conceived.

Problems with ovulation may occur as a result of hormonal imbalance. Other common causes include:

- stress
- weight loss
- weight gain
- excessive **prolactin** production
- polycystic ovarian disease.

Damage to the fallopian tubes may impede the pick-up or transport of the egg, thereby preventing fertilisation. Blocked fallopian tubes can be treated by micro-surgical techniques, but in other cases pregnancy can only be achieved with IVF.

Hostile mucus may affect sperm travelling at all times other than during ovulation. Hormonally induced changes in the mucus obstruct the free passage of sperm. Some women have antibodies against sperm within their mucus and sperm are often unable to pass through the cervical canal.

Causes of male infertility can be divided into two categories:

- physical abnormalities of the male reproductive tract, such as obstruction or impaired sperm production
- abnormalities of the sperm themselves.

Male fertility is assessed by semen analysis. A normal assessment should show:

- sperm count of more than 20 million sperm per millilitre
- 50% of the sperm actively moving
- 30% of the sperm must have normal shape
- sperm should survive for 24–48 hours.

Common male infertility problems are due to the following:

Defective sperm production and may be associated with infections, surgery or excessive drinking. Certain drugs, radiation and **radiotherapy** can also affect the production of sperm.

Azoospermia refers to the absence of sperm in the ejaculate. This may be due to:

- obstruction of the vas deferens
- the vas deferens being missing
- a hormonal problem stopping sperm from being produced.

Antibodies may attach to sperm and impair their motility and their ability to penetrate and fertilise an egg.

Ectopic pregnancy is when the fertilised egg implants itself outside of the uterus, usually in the fallopian tubes. An ectopic pregnancy is not usually capable of surviving and in most instances it will spontaneously miscarry. Almost all women diagnosed with an ectopic pregnancy will have to be operated on or treated with medication.

Impotence is another word for 'erectile dysfunction'. It is the inability of a man to achieve or maintain an erection sufficient for his sexual needs or the needs of his partner. Most men experience dysfunction at some point in their lives, usually by age 40, but it has now been established that impotence affects younger men too. The cause is often circulation-related, resulting from prescription drug use, smoking, drinking or diabetes.

Many men suffer a combination of physical and psychological reasons. It is very easy for a man with impotence to become stressed and depressed about his situation and this makes matters worse.

Diagnostic techniques and treatments

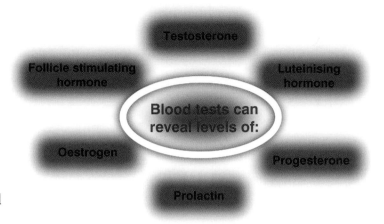

Blood tests can reveal reasons for the absence of ovulation, provide information on the endocrine system and may also be used to assess the individual's potential to become pregnant. This is done by measuring the hormone levels in the body to detect any differences or dysfunctions.

Women can be given different types of fertility drugs. These are often ovulation induction drugs, which trigger egg production in the body if it is not producing and releasing an egg each month.

The aim of **in vitro fertilisation (IVF)** is to stimulate the ovaries to produce several follicles, so that more than one egg can be retrieved, thus increasing the chances of a successful pregnancy. The eggs are collected and placed in special culture medium and prepared sperm is added for fertilisation to take place. The embryos are transferred to the uterus approximately two days after collection.

Ultrasound is used to examine the structure and function of the ovaries. In many cases it can show problems such as:

- polycystic ovaries
- **fibroids**
- endometriosis.

High-intensity sound waves are used to create visual images that can be recorded to assist treatment.

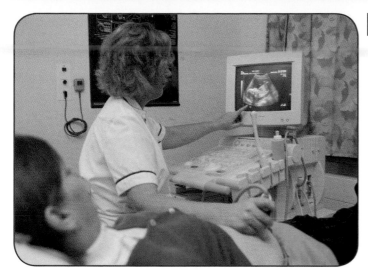

A clear picture to the trained eye

Assessment activity 12.2.4

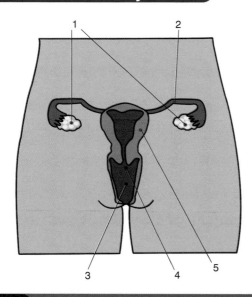

Erica   CASE STUDY

1 Identify each of the structures labelled 1–5 in the diagram and describe their function.

2 Erica has difficulty in becoming pregnant. Describe to Erica one dysfunction of the female reproductive system that could prevent a successful pregnancy.

3 Erica will have tests to find the cause of her infertility. Identify a diagnostic technique that could be used to diagnose the dysfunction that you have explained.

4 Describe the different types of treatment that would be available to help Erica become pregnant. How could this improve her emotional well being?

12.2.5 Renal system

Gross structure and function of the renal system

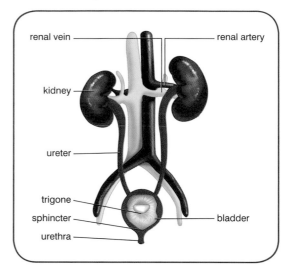

The renal system

Kidneys

There are two kidneys, each about the size of a fist, located on either side of the spine on the posterior abdominal wall at the lowest level of the rib cage. One million microscopic filters, each one called a glomerulus are found in each kidney. The glomeruli are each joined to small tubules which make up nephrons.

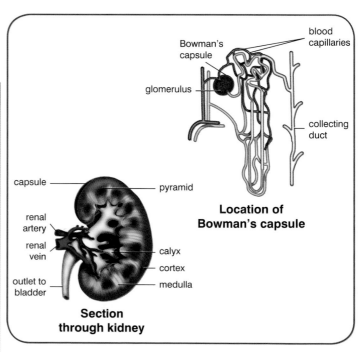

Location of Bowman's capsule

Section through kidney

Bowman's capsule: part of the filtering system in the kidneys

95

Each nephron is a tube-like structure with an enlarged end called the 'Bowman's capsule'.

Each kidney is joined to the aorta by a renal artery and the kidneys receive 20% of normal blood flow leaving the heart.

Functions of the renal system

The two main functions are:

- urine production
- homeostasis.

Urine production

The kidneys perform the function of filtering and returning to the bloodstream about 200 litres of fluid every 24 hours. About two litres are removed from the body in the form of urine and excreted to the outside. It may be stored in the bladder for anything from 1 to 8 hours.

The high pressure of blood entering the kidney tubules causes fluid to leak from the small capillaries of the glomerulus. This fluid passes into the tubule via the Bowman's capsule. Blood cells and large blood proteins do not normally pass through. The fluid in the tubule contains both useful substances, such as glucose, water and salts, as well as waste materials, such as a poison called urea that is made in the liver from amino acids, we don't need. As the fluid passes down the tubule special cells take the useful substances back into the blood leaving behind the urea, some salts and a variable amount of water. This is known as urine.

Homeostasis

The kidneys play an important role in maintaining the correct water content of the body and the correct salt composition of extracellular fluids. External changes which lead to excessive fluid loss initiate feedback mechanisms to maintain the body's fluid content and the kidneys act to limit water loss via excretion. The pituitary gland produces the anti-diuretic hormone (ADH). This regulates the levels of water in the blood by causing the tubules to reabsorb more water. The following table illustrates the body's reactions:

Thirsty or dehydrated	Too much fluid in the body
More ADH produced	Less ADH produced
More water reabsorbed	Less water reabsorbed
Urine is concentrated as it contains less water	Urine is dilute as it contains more water

Ureters

The ureters are narrow, thick-walled ducts, about 25–30 cm long and 4–5 mm in diameter that transport urine from the kidneys to the urinary bladder. The ureters enter the bladder at an angle to prevent reflux (back flow) of the urine when the bladder contracts.

Bladder

The urinary bladder is a hollow muscular organ, forming the main urinary reservoir. The shape and size of the bladder varies according to the amount of urine it contains. The urethra carries urine from the bladder to the outside. A ring of muscle known as the 'urethral sphincter' normally keeps the opening from the bladder tightly closed.

Prostate

This is a chestnut-shaped reproductive organ, located directly beneath the bladder in the male, and surrounds the first part of the urethra. Its function is to provide secretions that are part of the fluid for carrying sperm. At birth this gland is quite small and becomes larger during puberty. Its growth stops at about 20, when it weighs approximately 20 grams. In later life the gland may enlarge and affect urine flow.

Dysfunctions of the renal system

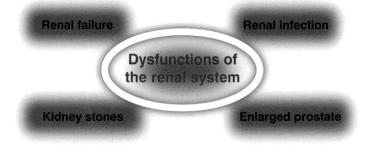

Renal failure is the term used when the kidneys fail to function and urine output stops. Renal failure can be life-threatening, because the blood becomes overloaded with waste products such as urea. This can cause **uraemia** and requires immediate **dialysis**.

Other causes of renal failure include:

Acute	Chronic
Shock	Hypertension
Injury	Diabetes
Illness	Polycystic kidney
Bleeding	Urinary obstruction – Calculus
Heart attack	Tumours
Pancreatitis	Analgesic drugs
Calculus	
Bladder tumour	
Enlarged prostate	
Glomerulonephritis	

When the causes of renal failure are acute, normal function may return if the cause can be removed or eliminated. Chronic failure may progress over months or years and become life-threatening. There is a reduction in the volume of urine produced and in acute cases there may be severe symptoms of vomiting, drowsiness, etc.

Urinary tract infections occur when germs enter the urinary tract and cause symptoms such as pain, burning during urination and more frequent need to urinate. These infections often affect the bladder and can spread to the kidneys, where they cause fever and back pain.

Kidney stones are very common, and when they pass, they may cause severe back and side pain. Causes of kidney stones include:

- an inherited disorder that causes too much calcium to be absorbed from foods
- urinary tract infections
- obstructions.

Factors that contribute to stone formation

- Too little fluid
- Chronic infection
- Certain medications
- Urinary tract blockage
- Inactivity for weeks
- Genetic and metabolic diseases

The most common symptom of a stone in the kidney is renal colic, and the most common symptom of a stone in the bladder is difficulty in passing urine.

Prostate enlargement can have dramatic effects on the male urinary system. Because the urethra runs through the middle of the prostate any prostatic enlargement will cause urine flow to be affected.

An enlarged prostate can give rise to:

- difficulty in passing urine
- total obstruction
- dribbling of urine
- frequency of the flow.

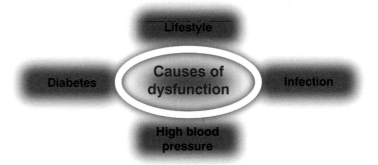

With **diabetes**, the small blood vessels in the body are injured. When the blood vessels in the kidneys are injured they cannot clean the blood efficiently. The body will retain more water and salt than it should, which can result in hypertension. Weight gain and ankle swelling, protein in the urine and blood waste build up are some of the problems.

Diabetes may also cause damage to nerves which can cause difficulty in emptying the bladder. The pressure resulting from a full bladder can back up and injure the kidneys. Also, if urine remains in the bladder for a long time, due to incomplete emptying **infections develop**.

Uncontrolled high blood pressure can damage many organs, including the kidneys. The filtration system is made up of many tiny structures supplied by blood vessels. If the blood pressure increases, the vessels can burst, causing loss of function. This can then lead to renal failure.

Not unexpectedly, **lifestyle** can have an effect on the renal system. Exposure to certain drugs and chemicals can give rise to renal failure. Undiagnosed urinary tract infections, viruses and bacteria can severely affect renal function. High levels of salt in food can often lead to hypertension. Caffeine in tea and coffee can act as a diuretic and raise blood pressure, thus causing mild hypertension.

Dysfunction of the renal system — Activity 5

Describe the main causes of renal stones and list where they may be found.

Diagnostic techniques and treatments

X-rays can usually identify the presence of stones or lack of function. Specialised x-ray techniques using contrast injections (urography) or ultrasound may be used to identify the size and location of the stones and test kidney function.

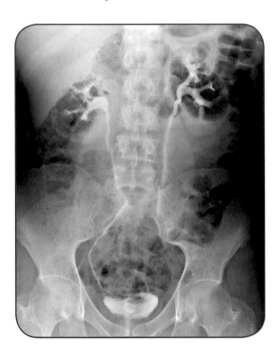

Visualisation of the urinary system using x-rays

Blood and urine tests may help a doctor to find out what is causing a stone, infection or failure and plan the best treatment. **Dipsticks** may indicate the presence of sugar in diabetes or blood in cases of infections. The presence of protein can also be detected which is a sign of kidney damage. They change colour to indicate the level of the problem.

Urethroscopy is a technique where a fibre-optic instrument is passed through the urethra and maybe into the bladder, to examine or to treat certain

conditions affecting the urinary tract. Alternatively, a fibre-optic instrument may be inserted directly into the kidney through the skin to remove a stone whole, or break it into small fragments. This can also be achieved using lithotripsy.

A kidney transplant is an operation in which a person whose own kidneys have failed receives a new kidney from a donor. There are two types of kidney transplants:

- from living donors, usually relatives
- from non-living donors.

A living donor may be someone in the immediate or extended family who wishes to donate a kidney to the person in need of a transplant. There are advantages and disadvantages to both types of kidney transplants.

Dialysis is required when the final stages of kidney failure develop and 85–90% of kidney function is lost. Dialysis keeps the body in balance and does the following:

- removes waste
- removes excess salt
- prevents excess water building up in the body
- keeps a safe level of potassium, sodium and bicarbonate in the blood
- helps to control blood pressure.

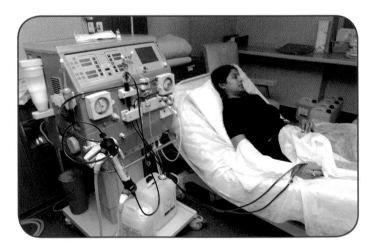

The person is connected to this three times a week

There are two types of dialysis, haemodialysis and peritoneal dialysis.

In haemodialysis, an artificial kidney (haemodialyser) is used to remove waste, extra chemicals and fluid from the blood. To get the blood into the artificial kidney, the doctor installs two tubes into the blood vessels in the arm or leg. A pump passes blood into the machine. The blood is kept at body temperature and has an anti-coagulant added to it to prevent it clotting in the machine. Inside the machine the blood flows between sheets of membrane. On the other side of these membranes flows a fluid called dialysate. This has the same composition as normal 'clean' blood and so the urea and other wastes pass from the blood through the membranes into the dialysate.

In peritoneal dialysis, the blood is cleaned inside the body using the body's natural filtering membrane (the peritoneum). The doctor surgically places a plastic tube called a catheter into the peritoneum. During the treatment, the abdominal cavity (called the peritoneal cavity), is slowly filled with **dialysate** through the catheter. The blood stays in the arteries and veins that line the peritoneal cavity. Extra fluid and waste products are drawn out of the blood and into the dialysate by diffusion.

Assessment activity 12.2.5

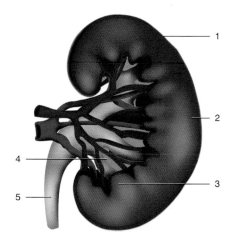

Janet   CASE STUDY

1 Identify each of the structures labelled 1–5 in the diagram and describe their function.

2 Describe how urine is produced.

3 Janet has been diagnosed with a severe renal dysfunction. Explain to Janet how her daily routines and lifestyle could be affected by the dysfunction.

4 Janet's dysfunction has not got any better and she is now suffering from renal failure. She will need dialysis while she waits for a transplant. Explain what will happen during both these events.

12.2.6 Musculo-skeletal system

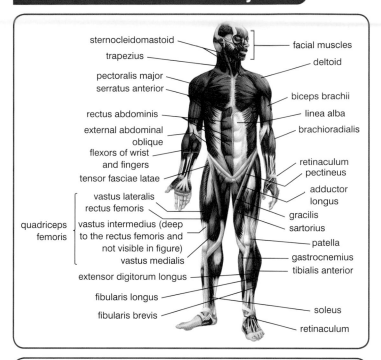

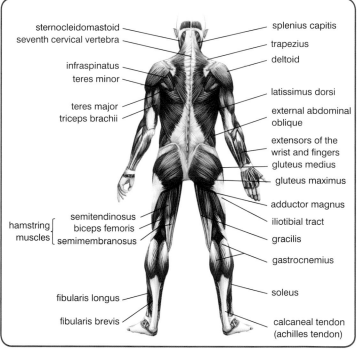

Anterior and posterior views of muscles

The musculo-skeletal system is composed of muscles, bones, cartilages, ligaments and tendons. Altogether they fulfil many functions, including:

• movement
• maintenance of posture
• support
• protection of internal organs
• heat production.

Muscle

Depending on its structure and function, muscle is classified into three types:

- **cardiac** or heart muscle
- **smooth** muscles found in the internal organs
- **skeletal** muscles, also known as striped or voluntary muscles.

Skeletal muscles are attached to bones of the skeleton. Each muscle is able to contract and relax in order to bring about movement. There are over 600 voluntary muscles in the human body.

- **extensors** open a joint and **flexors** close it
- **adductors** move the body part inwards and
- **abductors** move it outwards
- **levators** raise a part and **depressors** lower it
- **constrictor** or sphincter muscles surround and close an opening.

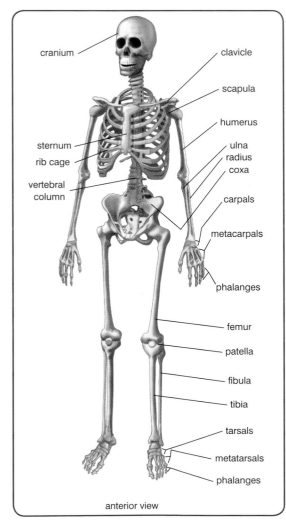

The human skeleton

Bone is a complex matrix of protein fibre, collagen and minerals. Bone has high levels of calcium and to a lesser extent magnesium. The matrix or web-like structure of normal healthy bone gives it strength and makes it light and flexible. The spaces inside some of the bones contain bone marrow, which generates blood cells.

There are approximately 213 bones in the human skeleton, joined together by tendons and ligaments to protect and support muscles and underlying tissues.

Cartilage is part of a joint where two bones meet and allows movement to occur. Where bones join together, they can also form structures that provide protection for the body's organs. The skull is not one bone, but many and provides protection for the brain. The ribs, **sternum** and the spine form the rib cage, which protects the heart and lungs.

Together bones and muscles give humans their unique shape which distinguishes them from other life forms.

Dysfunctions of the musculo-skeletal system

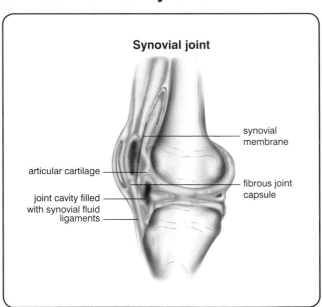

Arthritis is an inflammation of the joints, which develops in various ways, gradually wearing away cartilage. Cartilage lines and cushions the joints, allowing bones to move smoothly during activity. When this cartilage deteriorates, the bones rub together causing pain and swelling.

Osteoarthritis can cause permanent damage, stiffness, and deformity. Although osteoarthritis can result from direct injury, it also commonly occurs in adults over age 55 for no apparent reason.

Rheumatoid arthritis can attack individuals of any age. It affects all the connective tissues in the joints as well as the organs of the body. The precise cause of rheumatoid arthritis is unknown, but it is believed that a virus triggers the disease, causing an auto-immune response in which the body attacks its own tissues.

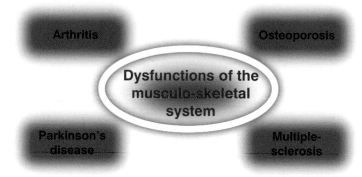

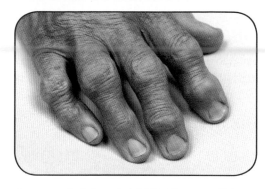

A very painful and debilitating condition

In rheumatoid arthritis, the synovial membrane that lines and lubricates the joint becomes inflamed. The inflammation gradually destroys the cartilage and as scar tissue replaces the damaged cartilage, the joint becomes misshapen and rigid.

Complications of rheumatoid arthritis may also cause damage to the:

- heart
- lungs
- nerves
- eyes.

To **diagnose** arthritis, a physician observes the patient's symptoms and administers a standard physical examination. X-ray studies and laboratory tests may be recommended to confirm joint swelling and to determine the extent of damage the arthritis has caused.

The most **effective treatment** programme for arthritis consists of drug therapy, exercise, and rest. Non-steroidal anti-inflammatory drugs such as ibuprofen and naproxen may also be used to treat the symptoms. In osteoarthritis the joints may be injected with **corticosteroids**. The injections relieve inflammation and pain and are quite effective.

Severe cases of rheumatoid arthritis may require surgery to remove inflamed synovial tissue. With either form of arthritis, **artificial joints** may be implanted to replace those damaged beyond repair.

Osteoporosis is a disorder where the bones become weakened by loss of protein matrix from the bone. This can lead to an increased risk of broken bones from the slightest accident. When the bones are significantly thinned, a cough or a sneeze is likely

to cause a fracture of a rib, or the partial collapse of the spine (vertebra). All bones are at risk with osteoporosis. Bones naturally become thinner with age and bone is constantly being replaced with new bone. Women are more at risk when the menopause occurs, as they lose bone mass at a faster rate. This is because the hormone oestrogen, which promotes bone formation, declines after the menopause and so bone destruction outstrips bone formation. Other contributing factors are:

- removal of ovaries
- poor diet
- lack of exercise
- corticosteroid drugs.

Osteoporosis affects people in a number of ways:

- Broken bones (fractures), can lead to severe pain, lasting for a number of weeks.
- Sufferers, especially the elderly, become more dependent on others to look after them.
- There is a 20% increase in mortality in the first year after a broken hip.
- Collapsing **vertebrae** lead to increased curvature of the spine and loss of height.

Diagnosis of osteoporosis is made from the symptoms, from bone x-rays and by measurement of bone density by photon absorption.

Treatments available for osteoporosis include:

- hormone replacement therapy (HRT)
- **biphosphonates**, a type of medication used to arrest the progress of osteoporosis
- **calcitonin**, a hormone now used to reduce the effects
- calcium supplements
- vitamin D and calcium preparations
- strong pain killers (analgesics).

Parkinson's disease and multiple sclerosis are not diseases of the musculo-skeletal system but their symptoms affect the functioning of muscles and so they have been included in this section. They are in fact dysfunctions of the nervous system.

Parkinson's disease is a progressive disorder, characterised primarily by uncontrollable **tremors** in the limbs, a shuffling gait, and generalised muscular **rigidity**. It most often strikes people over the age of 60.

It is usually not fatal, but it leads to changes in the entire body, making the patient more susceptible to other diseases. It can be present in a mild form for 20 or 30 years, but a severe form can lead to serious disability within 5 to 10 years.

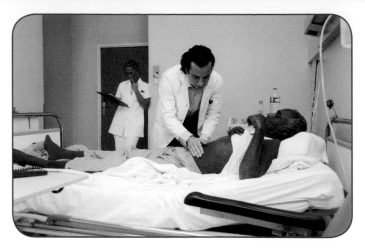

Clinical examination can provide valuable information

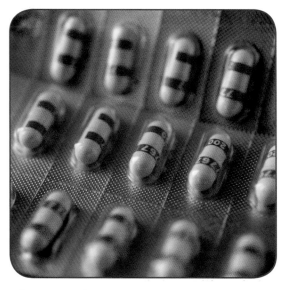

Often the only treatment available

The cause of Parkinson's disease is unknown. No inherited, physiological or environmental factors have been identified, but it is known that Parkinson's disease results from a chemical imbalance in the brain. Sufferers have been shown to have low levels of a **neurotransmitter** called **dopamine**.

Tremors can worsen during rest periods and at times of increased anxiety, but may decrease when conscious efforts are made. As the disease progresses, the speech may slur and sentences trail off. Small muscle movements become increasingly difficult, reducing the ability to write, eat, chew, and swallow; all movements become stiff and slow. Excitement and tension can cause these symptoms to worsen, as can depression, which is common.

Diagnosis of Parkinson's involves a medical history, physical examination, and observation of the symptoms. If tremors are the only symptom displayed, tests may be done to rule out the possibility of other disorders.

Treatment of Parkinson's disease consists of correcting the dopamine deficiency. A drug called Levodopa is prescribed to help the brain manufacture more of its own dopamine. Levodopa and anti-cholinergic drugs decrease nerve-to-muscle transmission, reducing drooling, tremor and rigidity.

Multiple sclerosis (MS) is a chronic disease of the central nervous system. Degeneration of the protective myelin sheath, the insulating covering of the nerve fibres, causes the body's functions to become impaired. In some cases the patient becomes wheelchair-bound, or even dies. In other cases, the disease may flare up once in a lifetime and leave the individual with minimal disabilities.

The exact cause of multiple sclerosis is not known. Some studies indicate that the disease follows exposure to a virus that may lie dormant. MS may then be triggered by a second exposure, or by stress.

Another theory suggests that multiple sclerosis affects people who have some defect in their immune system. It is thought that after viral exposure, the immune system mistakenly identifies the myelin covering of the nerves as foreign tissue and tries to destroy it. After the first attack, there is usually a period of remission for as long as two to three years. Subsequent attacks may occur at irregular intervals and cause gradually increasing disability.

Diagnosis of MS is made by examination of MRI scans and by eye tests to determine the speed of responses in the optic nerve. A lumbar puncture may also be carried out whereby a sample of the fluid that is found in the centre of the spinal cord is removed. The presence of high numbers of white blood cells in this fluid also points to a diagnosis of multiple sclerosis.

Since there is no cure for multiple sclerosis, **treatment** concentrates on relieving the symptoms. Possibilities include:

- muscle relaxants to ease muscle spasms
- corticosteroid drugs to shorten attacks by reducing nerve tissue inflammation
- **B-interferon** to help reduce symptoms
- surgery to halt tremors has been helpful in select groups of patients.

Physiotherapy needs and **assessment** are an important part of treatment programmes for many dysfunctions of the musculo-skeletal system. A range of techniques is used to relieve pain and stiffness and to improve mobility, co-ordination and posture. Manipulation and tailored exercises help to ease pain, build stamina and mobilise joints, while **hydrotherapy** is used to strengthen and relax muscles.

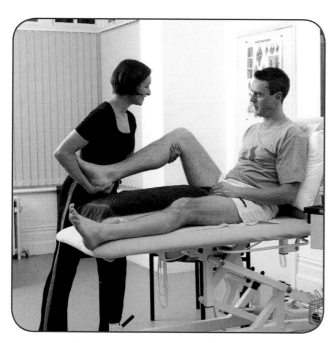

Treatment in action

If surgery is needed to replace the hip or knee, the physiotherapist will help the individual to regain muscle strength and movement. Treatment programmes for patients with Parkinson's disease often include physical therapy and exercise regimes.

Dysfunctions of the musculo-skeletal system — Activity 6

1. Describe **two** dysfunctions of the musculo-skeletal system.
2. How do the symptoms differ in each dysfunction?

Assessment activity 12.2.6

CASE STUDY

You have been asked to give a presentation to a sports club on musculo-skeletal dysfunction; use the questions below to help you.

1. Name one dysfunction of the musculo-skeletal system. Identify the possible causes of the dysfunction.
2. Explain the methods available that would help to diagnose the dysfunction.
3. Describe how the functions of the musculo-skeletal system can be affected by the dysfunction.
4. Explain **two** methods of treatment available and how they can help the individual.

Contents

About this unit

Within this unit you will investigate:

- patterns of development
- factors that influence development and norms of development
- theories of play and how play can affect development
- you will also need to plan and make a learning aid for a child in the 0–8 age range.

Children develop very quickly

Children at play

Introducing this unit

How many times have you heard people say that a child is 'advanced or slow for their age'? A great many people have some idea of what children can do at certain ages but a thorough awareness of child development is essential for anyone interested in the care and education of young children. This will include the **milestones** in all areas of development in the first eight years of life. However, there are a number of factors that can influence and affect the development of the child and these must be considered in some detail. Individual development can be affected by a variety of external factors and early years workers need to be able to take this into consideration when planning targets for the child. The areas covered in child development are physical development, intellectual development (including language and communication), emotional and social development. These are known as P.I.E.S.

As play is **integral** to the development of the child, it is important to consider how play influences development, and the benefits of play activities for each area of development. There are a number of categories of play, and children move through different stages of play as they mature and grow. The early years worker will need to be aware of these and use them in the day-to-day planning for the individual child.

Children love to see and touch items and activities, and will achieve great enjoyment from using various learning aids. Many homemade learning aids have proved to be invaluable for meeting individual and specific needs. It is beneficial for anyone involved with young children to be able to plan and make a **learning aid** for the child, which will provide a useful resource and aid in a range of areas of development.

13.2.1 Patterns of development

Children at different stages of development

Over the years there has been much research carried out to determine what most children can do or achieve at a given age. This has enabled people to devise charts, which **itemise** what is now known as the **norms of development**, e.g. if the majority of children can walk by the age of 15 months then that will eventually become the norm by which all children are measured. It is acknowledged that some children will walk well before this age and some will not walk until much later but the average or norm is fixed because the majority of children have developed that skill by that age. Gradually, charts were drawn up to publish the norms of development across all areas such as:

• physical growth
• physical development
• intellectual development (including language development)
• social and emotional development.

This enables **professionals** to map an individual child's **progression** or development against the norms. If a child is deemed to have **delayed development** then it is possible that a programme can be devised and designed to **minimise** that delay and enable the child to make progress. If a child is ahead of the norms, then again the short-, medium- and long-term goals need to be set with this in mind.

It must be kept in mind that these norms of development are taken from the moment of birth

at what is assumed a nine-month **gestation period**. Babies who are born prematurely will appear to have delayed progress against these charts and this must be taken into account.

> ### Discussion point
>
> In pairs discuss the advantages and disadvantages of using developmental charts when considering the development of an individual child.

Children will follow the same pattern of development as they mature and grow. You will notice, if you have any involvement with very young children, that they will gain control physically, initially with their head. They will be able to hold their head and will develop the ability to move their head purposefully in response to sound or movement. They will gradually develop the ability to sit for short periods until they can sit unaided, and then move to gain greater control for crawling and eventually walking. The child will also be able to have greater control over arms and hands before they master the techniques for walking.

Throughout children's growth and development there are things that mark important points in the child's life, e.g. the first word, the first tooth, the first step. Growth and development usually follow a pattern and they are **sequential**, e.g. a child does not run before they can walk. It must always be remembered that each child is an individual and does not always develop or grow at the same rate as another child. However, there are average ages when certain milestones are met and these will be listed later, but it does not mean that there is no variation from this. The norms of development are discussed in more detail later.

Physical growth

After the baby is born, it is important that checks are kept on physical growth and size. Measurements will be taken on a regular basis and mapped on a **centile chart**. There are separate charts for girls and boys and they have been worked out using data for normal, healthy children. If a child is on the 50th **centile** then they are in line with the average for that age. If they are on the 86th centile for height then they are tall for their age. These charts are used as a reference for average growth patterns. The measurements that are used are the child's weight and height.

The baby's head circumference is also measured until it is established that normal growth patterns are being recorded. Once the measurements are plotted, if the curve runs parallel to one already printed on the chart, then it is linked to healthy growth. Using centile charts is a relatively straightforward method of detecting growth and weight problems early on in a child's life.

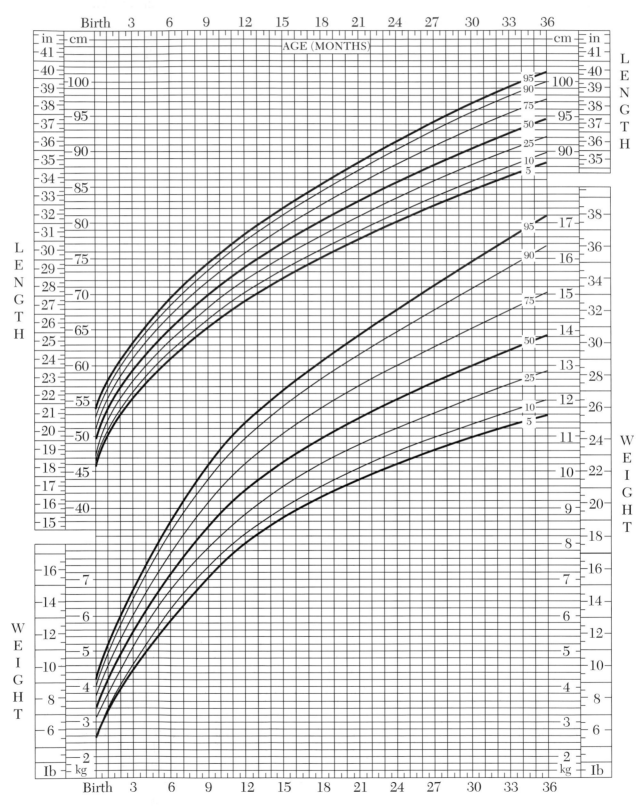

Centile chart

Physical development

Physical development includes the large and small muscle groups, which are often referred to as **gross** motor development and **fine** motor development. It includes the growth of the child and regular checks are made by **health professionals** that this is progressing at the right rate. If it is not, then it may be possible to put measures in place to aid development or prevent further setbacks.

Fine motor skills

Fine motor skills refer to the small muscles that are used in **precise** and **deliberate** movements. They develop fully over a considerable time and may not be totally **refined** until the individual is fully **mature**.

Age	Fine motor skills
Infant 0–1 year	Can hold and shake toys and rattles
	Can place small items in larger container
	Can pick up some items using finger and thumb
Toddler 1–3 years	Skills develop at a steady pace as the child becomes more adept with self help, mark making and drawing skills
	Can turn pages of a book one at a time
	Can put on coat
	Draws 'big head' person
	Enjoys rolling clay/playdough and attempting to make objects
	Enjoys simple jigsaw puzzles
Pre-school child 3–5 years	Can fasten coat (sometimes with help)
	Starting to use scissors effectively
	Can make items with clay/playdough
	Recognises own name when written and may attempt to copy it
	Can write own name
	Can draw detailed figures
	Can form numbers and letters
	Can complete jigsaw puzzles of 20+ pieces
School age Limited to 5–8	Fine motor skills continue to be refined
	Writing becomes more detailed
	Can write stories
	Pictures become more detailed and figures are smaller
	Self help skills are well developed
	Can complete complex puzzles

Gross motor skills

Gross motor skills refer to the use and development of the large muscle groups and development is measured by an individual's ability to use those muscles effectively, e.g. crawl, walk, run, climb, etc.

Age	Gross motor skills
Infant 0–1 year	Sitting unaided
	Rolling
	Crawling
	Walking (some children)
Toddler 1–3 years	Will further develop walking and associated skills and will use push- and pull-along toys to aid this development
	Able to balance when squatting (many people lose this skill through lack of use)
	Able to climb
	Can kick a ball
	Walks up and down stairs (one foot in front of other)
	Runs with confidence
	Confidently steers wheeled toys
	Jumps from steps or blocks
Pre-school child 3–5 years	Balance is improving
	Can sometimes catch ball when thrown
	Can hop
	Can kick a moving ball
	Confident in use of large equipment, e.g. climbing frame
	Can run quickly and change direction to avoid objects
	Gaining in confidence with all large equipment, e.g. swings, climbing frames
School age Limited to 5–8	Confidence improves in all areas
	Can develop new skills quickly, e.g. roller blades
	Can ride bicycle
	Adept at ball skills

Sensory skills

These skills are linked to the senses, i.e. sight, hearing, touch, taste and smell, and are integral to survival. The senses develop as the child matures and grow until they become finely tuned. Sensory skills are closely linked to the development of other skills, as **co-ordination** is usually linked to the inter-dependence of the visual and physical. If the senses are **impaired**, e.g. **visually**, then it is often necessary for the individual to develop other sensory skills to a higher level than they might otherwise need. The sense of touch may become more important especially in the ability to read **Braille**.

Children at play   Activity 1

Arrange to visit an early years care and education setting.

1   Observe children playing outside.

2   How are they using their large muscles?

3   What skills have they developed, e.g. can they run, jump, ride a tricycle?

4   Observe children playing within the unit.

5   List the fine motor skills you observe, e.g. picking up small items, drawing.

6   Link your observations to the use of sensory skills.

Intellectual development

Intellectual development covers language development, including verbal and non-verbal communication and cognitive development.

Language development

Talking is good

When considering the development of language skills it is necessary to give some thought as to what language is and what the purpose of language is.

Language is one of the means by which human beings **communicate** with each other. Individuals communicate in many different and complex ways and all use **symbolic representation** to convey messages.

Chinese whispers   Activity 2

Have you ever played the game commonly known as 'Chinese whispers'? One person whispers a message to the next and it is repeated around a group of people. The last person then says the message aloud. It invariably is totally different from the initial message, as people's listening skills are not finely honed.

1   Play this game in a group of four.

2   Was the message distorted?

3   Note how the message was distorted, e.g. totally incorrect or just the end.

4   Try to work backwards as a discussion group to find out where the distortions occurred.

5   Now play the game with more people.

6   Was the result the same?

Feeling special

Language has definite purposes, some of which are itemised below:

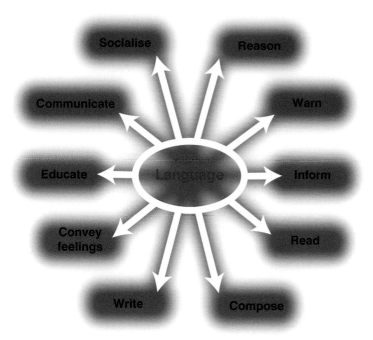

There is much debate as to whether the ability to use language effectively is determined **genetically** or if we learn language because of our **environment** and encouragement by those around us. Two theorists linked with this area of development are Noam Chomsky and B.F. Skinner. Chomsky takes the view that the ability to develop language skills is innate and that nature is the determining factor, whilst Skinner believes that the environment and nurture are primarily responsible.

Noam Chomsky	As other animals do not develop spoken language, Chomsky believed that human beings have an innate capability, both physically and intellectually, to acquire and use language. The physical features of the mouth, tongue, lips and **palette** provide us with the physical means of controlling the variety of sounds required for meaningful language. He believed that parts of the brain were **pre-programmed** to understand language and that human beings have the ability to comprehend complex sentence structures and grammar. He referred to this as a Language Acquisition Device (LAD).
B.F. Skinner	Skinner believed that language was learned after birth as a result of making sounds and imitating those around us. As individuals hear words, they will attempt to repeat them, and with positive **reinforcement** the infant will eventually develop the correct pronunciation, which will again receive positive reinforcement. Sounds and words that are not part of the accepted language will not be reinforced and will be lost. This is part of the process he referred to as Operant Conditioning.

Theory into practice

Reflect on one hour during the day.

Make a list of the different ways you used language.

Language acquisition and development

Pre-language includes the babbling and noises that infants make following birth until the time that speech is able to be understood, and usually is regarded as the first 18 months or until the child's vocabulary starts to develop. Infants start to develop the processes involved in interactions and conversations from the very early stages of life.

Theory into practice

Follow this sequence of events.

A very young child might be cradled in the arms of an adult who will talk to the child in short sentences and maintain eye contact. The adult will stop talking and the child will vocalise and gurgle. The child will stop and the adult will respond. This sequence of events may continue for a while. The infant is developing the skills that will later be used in conversation, e.g. taking turns, maintaining eye contact and remaining quiet while the other person vocalises.

Anyone with contact with very young infants will realise that this takes place very early on in a child's life.

Starting a conversation

Activity 3

Try to arrange to observe a young baby and carer. This may be a friend or relative or from a video or television programme.

Make notes on the following:

- the noises the baby makes
- the language the carer uses
- the tone of voice
- eye contact between baby and carer
- facial expressions of both baby and carer
- comment on how language is being developed/promoted in this situation.

Language development

Age	Language development
Infant 0–1 year	Crying initially and then signs of eye contact. 4–6 weeks. Cries for a purpose, e.g. alone, wet, etc. Infant may follow speaker's voice with eye movement and may stop crying when spoken to. 6–8 weeks. Develops a smile. Gurgling in response to sounds. 3–4 months. Infant will move or raise head in response to sound. 4–5 months. Makes sounds to attract attention. 6–8 months. Start of babbling and use of repeated sounds, e.g. dadadada. Responds to tone of carer's voice. Starts to enjoy music and action rhymes. Begins to anticipate actions in rhymes, e.g. will chuckle at appropriate point. 9 months. May show understanding of simple words. 9–12 months. Imitation of simple words. Pointing and vocalising – often indicating that they want the object. Vocabulary starts to develop. First proper words.
Toddler 1–3 years	Vocabulary continues to increase rapidly. Will indicate things by using one word often accompanied by pointing. Increase in vocabulary, particularly nouns. Starts to use simple phrases. Will repeat new words and sentences.
Pre-school child 3–5 years	Children will develop a greater understanding of grammar, including the use of positional vocabulary, adjectives and pronouns. Vocabulary will increase greatly at this time and children will indulge in meaningful conversations with peers and adults.
School age child Limited to 5–8 years	Gradually children will develop a more sophisticated use of language and will be able to give structure to their sentences and use grammar in a fairly complex way. They will begin to enjoy the complexity of language and sound and gain pleasure from poetry. They will experiment with language structure and develop prose and poetry. They will enjoy a 'play on words' and gain pleasure from verbal jokes. Can follow complex directions.

Verbal and non-verbal communication

Language skills also include the non-verbal aspects of communication: tone of voice, body language, gesture and eye contact being some of the most important points. Written words are marks that have **representational meaning** to others who have learned to interpret the symbols. Individuals without speech may communicate using sign language but, as with other languages, there are many variations.

Children's activities   Activity 4

Arrange to visit an early years and education setting. Observe and make notes about the range of activities the children are engaged in.

1 List the activities where children are alone.

2 List the activities involving more than one child.

3 Note what kind of language is involved.

4 Listen to how the early years care and education workers encourage the children in conversation and their use of language.

5 If possible, join in and talk with the children.

Once children have developed the ability to communicate effectively, they never seem to tire of it. Early years care and education workers will soon be aware of the variety of sounds that children will play with. They take great joy in singing and many games will involve rhymes and verses. However, there are many children who have speech and language difficulties and it may be necessary to involve other professionals such as speech therapists.

Cognitive development

Cognitive or **intellectual** development includes the development of thinking skills and thought processes and also includes the development of language and the skills associated with it.

It is important that children are provided with a stimulating environment, which will help motivate them and increase their eagerness to discover new **concepts**. Many of the sequences of cognitive development are linked to other areas of development, e.g. being able to complete a simple jigsaw puzzle is linked to physical development as well as cognitive or intellectual development. It is difficult to establish milestones in this area as it is largely dependent on a child's experiences and adult **intervention**, e.g. whether or not a child knows the **primary colours** will depend very much on whether anyone has told them the names or encouraged them to identify them. The list on the next page is only a guide and depends on the experiences of the individual child.

Will it fit?

Age	Intellectual development
Infant 0–1 year	Will search for a toy even if it has been removed
	Can place smaller objects inside other containers
	Will 'post' objects
Toddler 1–3 years	Enjoys counting rhymes
	Points to pictures and tries to name them
	Makes marks on paper with pencil or crayon
	Knows main parts of body and will point to them
	Copies simple shapes
	Can play matching games
	Can complete simple (e.g. 3–4 piece) puzzles
	Understands some mathematical concepts, e.g. big/little
Pre-school child 3–5 years	Can re-tell familiar stories
	Knows primary colours
	Can count by rote up to ten
	Has developed further mathematical concepts, e.g. long/short, heavy/light
	Able to put sets together, e.g. one cup, saucer, plate, knife, fork, spoon
	Understands the structure of a day
	Recognises name when written
	Starting to copy letters and numbers
	Understands positional vocabulary, e.g. behind, beside
School age child Limited to 5–8 years	Enjoys and understands games with rules
	Understands concepts of past, present and future
	Problem-solving skills are being refined
	Can work out simple mathematics in head
	Writing is more developed
	Can relate story in writing
	Concentration level increases

How do children learn? — Activity 5

Arrange to visit an early years care and education setting. Observe the children at play.

1. List the activities promoting intellectual development.
2. Were the children talking to each other?
3. Were they trying to solve problems?
4. Did the staff try to extend the learning in any way?
5. If so, how?

Social and emotional development

Emotional and social development are often linked together as it is sometimes hard to separate feelings from relationships. Emotional development is also strongly linked with the development of **self concept** and **self esteem**.

Emotional development

Age	Emotional development
Infant 0–1 year	Children at this age are very loving and affectionate
	They may also be afraid of strangers
	They often become concerned if people around them are sad or upset
	They are generally content and happy
Toddler 1–3 years	They begin to develop a sense of independence
	They develop a sense of identity
	They respond to praise
	They enjoy developing new skills
	They can understand feelings
	They enjoy play
Pre-school child 3–5 years	They become more imaginative in play
	They can develop fears at this time
	Starting to develop a sense of fairness
	They respond to explanations
	They enjoy responsibility
School age child Limited to 5–8 years	More able to control emotions
	Develop strong friendships
	Developing moral awareness
	Understand right from wrong
	Play in complex groups

Child Development
13.2.1 Patterns of development /
13.2.2 Factors that influence development and norms of development

Social development

Age	Social development
Infant 0–1 year	They copy actions – waving, clapping hands, etc. They like to play simple games, e.g. peek-a-boo They will respond to simple instructions They recognise familiar people They like adults to be around them
Toddler 1–3 years	They need support from others They enjoy playing where other children are They like to be appreciated and will 'perform' in front of an audience They enjoying playing with other children They enjoy copying adults and enjoy adult company
Pre-school child 3–5 years	They will copy other children They can share toys They are developing self help skills They will care for others They will talk openly in a group Able to follow rules Developing socially acceptable behaviour Have developed a strong sense of fairness They enjoy conversations with adults and other children
School age child Limited to 5–8 years	Play in groups Friendship groups are well established Will work together to solve problems Self help skills are well developed

Can we solve this problem?

It is important for anyone working with children in the early years sector to have some understanding of the milestones of development in young children. You will need to study **one** child, of at least eight years of age (which could be yourself) and consider the *different areas* of development.

1 Produce a Guide, which might be used by early years workers, in which you identify **three** patterns or milestones for each area of development. You should include the following areas of development:

- Physical
- Language
- Intellectual
- Social and emotional

Your work should be detailed and accurate.

You might like to illustrate the Guide.

13.2.2 Factors that influence development and norms of development

At home

As the infant grows and develops there will inevitably be a number of factors that will affect the process. Some of these will have a positive effect but some will not. The balance of factors which help with the holistic development of the child is easily disturbed. Examples of the main factors that influence development are:

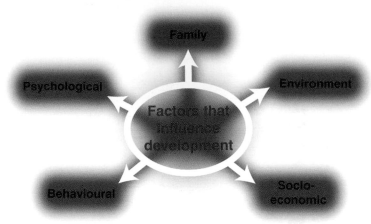

The family

The family situation that a child finds itself in can have a great influence on the development of the child. The position in the family can also affect development. The first child may receive more attention initially and may be given additional responsibility as they grow older. Younger children may receive help from older siblings. This can have positive effects but can also have some negative ones, e.g. if older children answer questions on behalf of a younger child, speech can be delayed.

Family life

Discussion point

In pairs discuss your own position in the family, e.g. only child, eldest.

List what you perceive to be the advantages and disadvantages of that position.

Family structure

The structure of the family can have a profound effect on the development of the child but not necessarily a negative one. Family structure varies considerably and is often formed by individual circumstances.

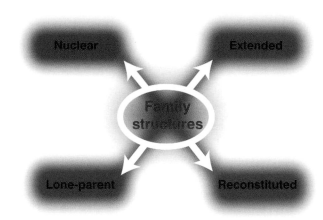

Family type	Advantages and disadvantages
Nuclear	The nuclear family consists of the immediate family and is made up of parents and siblings (including adopted children) living together.
	It is often a very close, tight-knit community and was thought to be the stable unit in society.
	The family unit provides for itself and cares for the individual members but there may be added strains during times of need or illness where help and assistance is required from outside the family unit and the extended family may be able to help.
Extended	The extended family consists of the other relatives, e.g. grandparents, aunts, uncles and cousins.
	The extended family often lives in the same locality and occasionally in the same house.
	It can provide care and stability especially in times of need.
	It can often ease the strain of parental responsibilities as children can be cared for by others in the family.
	In some cultures the extended family is governed by the grandfather figure, especially when the extended family lives in the same residence.

Family type	Advantages and disadvantages
Lone-parent	May be of either sex and may be supported by an extended family. Relationship with partner may have ended through bereavement or the relationship may have broken down for a variety of reasons. Strains of parenting can be problematic. Difficulties can occur if parent is ill and additional childcare is required.
Reconstituted	Usually formed when a male and female, each with their own children, come together to form one family group. Often a very supportive relationship. Extended families can also be supportive to the newly formed family. Sometimes there are some initial difficulties until the family members settle into their new roles.

Mealtime

Theory into practice

Consider the advantages and disadvantages of each family grouping.

Roles and responsibilities of parents/carers

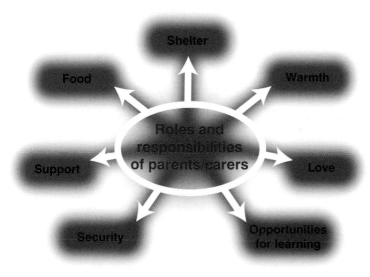

Provision	
Food	It is the parents'/carers' responsibility to provide food and nutrition for their children. If this is not provided then growth and development can be considerably impaired. The food provided should have variety and contain the **elements** of a balanced diet. Children who receive a good diet will have energy to play, and will be able to concentrate and apply themselves to tasks in hand.
Shelter	Adequate shelter/housing must be provided for the safety and well being of the child. **Inadequate** and poor housing will inevitably have a detrimental effect on the health and the development of the child.
Warmth	Warmth is one of the basic needs of life, for without it no one can function to the best of their ability. In the very young the cold can lead to **hypothermia** very quickly and in the older child concentration is affected.
Love	Human beings are, in the main, very sociable creatures and like the company of other people. The need to be wanted and loved by others is very strong, and one of the purposes of family structure and the role and responsibility of carers is to love, nurture and protect the young and **vulnerable**.

Provision	
Support	Support is very closely linked to love. Individuals need support in order to increase and raise self confidence and self esteem. This helps the young develop into contented individuals who are nurtured and prepared to take their place in society as they grow.
Security	Parents/carers have a responsibility to ensure safety and security for their family members especially the young and vulnerable. As children are very curious about their environment, it is essential that the parents/carers are ever vigilant for **hazards** and dangers.
Opportunities for learning	Parents/carers should always be a good **role model** for the children in their care. They should provide resources and activities, which will stimulate the imagination and provide opportunity for learning and development. Language development is particularly important for children, and adults should converse with them regularly and often, introducing new vocabulary as appropriate.

such as making puzzles, listening to stories, talking games, competitive games, etc., enables children to develop intellectual skills and they additionally develop problem-solving skills, depending on the stimulation of the activities. The television programmes children watch have a strong influence and parents should monitor their suitability and limit the amount of viewing time.

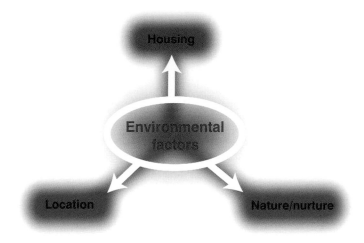

Location

Enjoying learning

Environmental factors

Environmental factors include life at home, the condition of the housing as well as the location and surrounding community. Children who have opportunities to play with and interact with other children in their neighbourhood develop social constructs with greater ease than those who are more solitary in nature. Participation in activities

Location can affect development

The location of a child's residence can have far-reaching effects on that child's life. In the majority of cities and towns there are desirable areas to live in as well as more run down areas. In some areas there are more parent and toddler groups, pre-schools and play parks for children. In other areas there may be very few facilities for a family to access on a regular basis. Lack of amenities and facilities can isolate young families and this will have an effect on the overall development of the child.

Housing

Poor housing can have a **detrimental** effect on the development of the child as it may mean that there is not enough space for the child to indulge in adequate play activities. Overcrowding will affect the development of children and, as each person needs their own space, it will adversely affect the possibility of concentration.

Additionally, there are other aspects of poor housing that will inevitably affect the whole family but have greater impact on a young and developing child. Poor housing usually indicates that the house will be in a less popular area and that the premises may be damp and cold. This may well have an effect on the health and well being of the child and on the attitude of the whole family. If the economy within the family is low then there may not be much opportunity to address these issues and that will affect the morale and general outlook of the family.

Environmental influences — Activity 6

John attends an early years care and education setting near to where he lives. He does not mix a great deal with the other children. When the early years care and education worker talks to John's mother, she finds that he spends much time watching the television and videos and they rarely go out as they live in a 'rough' area.

1. How might John's physical development be affected?
2. How might John's language development be affected?
3. How might John's intellectual development be affected?
4. How might John's emotional development be affected?
5. How might John's social development be affected?

Ellie — Activity 7

Ellie is six years old. She has three younger sisters and a younger brother. They live in a two-bedroom house and at the moment the baby boy shares the bedroom with his parents and all the girls share the small second bedroom. The family income is only just adequate for them to eat healthily but there is little left for toys and books. Her parents care a great deal about their children and want to do the best they can for them.

1. How might Ellie's development be affected by the family situation?
2. List any measures her parents could take to compensate for the lack of resources at home.
3. How might lack of space affect her?

Nature/nurture issue

The nature/nurture debate has been going on for a long time and people have differing views about it. Most people consider that both have a part to play in the development of the individual.

The '**nature**' side of the debate focuses on the premise that the child is programmed naturally to develop in a certain way. We have already considered Noam Chomsky's point of view about the acquisition of language. Many people believe

Do you have enough space?

that intelligence is pre-determined and that the capabilities of a child's mind are pre-ordained.

The '**nurture**' side of the debate focuses on the environment and upbringing of the child. Development and intelligence can be positively affected by external factors such as education, housing, social learning and stimulation of the mind.

Discussion point

In pairs discuss the nature/nurture debate.

List the factors you think might be affected by nature.

List the factors you think can be affected by nurture.

Social and economic factors

Child development can be adversely affected by living conditions and by the disposable income available. Poverty and disadvantage can harm early child development even from before birth. If the mother is malnourished then this will also affect the development of the unborn child. As the infant grows, the socio-economic factors will continue to play a significant role in the child's life. If parents have enough money to buy books and toys for children, this will be beneficial in the use of language and the increase of vocabulary. Parents' own reading ability also has a profound effect on the development of the child and it is one of the government targets that all adults are functionally literate and numerate.

Factor	Effect
Social class	Social class has a major bearing on child development. Research has established that the higher class has a better diet, better housing, more space per person per household. In general there is a greater interest in education, especially at pre-school level.
Financial status	The disposable income within a family has a direct effect on the development of the child. If the income is low then the family may live in poor accommodation and be unable to afford the correct types of nutritional food required for health and well being. There may be a lack of educational resources such as books and toys or there may be over-crowding, which does not encourage learning. Conversely, some children will live in families with a high income and have many advantages. However, it is important to remember that disposable income is not always spent on what is required by the family unit and that children from low income families can be well looked after and cared for. It is the attitude of responsibility that is vital for the well being of all members of the family.
Gender	Children learn about gender roles from their families and those in authority in their lives. Although most people try not to discriminate on the grounds of gender, there are some cultures where discrimination, particularly against the female, is prevalent. In cases where the female is discriminated against, this could have a detrimental effect on education and thus on their overall development.
Culture	Culture has a direct effect on learning and development. As already mentioned, some cultures value males in preference to females. Many cultures value education and place great emphasis on it.
Discipline	Discipline is important for a child but too much or too little will have a profound effect later in life. Parenting styles can affect the development of the child. They are divided generally into three types: authoritarian, permissive and authoritative. Authoritarian: parents expect children to do everything they are told. Permissive: parents allow children to have a great deal of freedom. Authoritative: parents allow children to choose and be involved in family decisions. Children are allowed to be individuals and are respected as such. They are listened to and decisions are explained to them.

Psychological factors

Everyone experiences different stresses in their lives and children will react to stress in a similar way to adults. Stress in a child's life can be caused by family problems and arguments, bereavements in a family, and other negative issues. This can have a detrimental effect on the development of a child and can lead to delays in certain areas. The child's behaviour may change and this change can manifest itself in many ways. The child may become withdrawn, lack conversation, lose their appetite or they may be short tempered and easily moved to tears or they may become aggressive and argumentative.

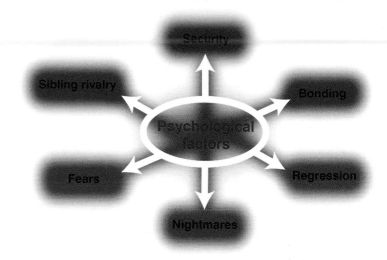

Factor	Effect
Security	Children need to feel secure. It is one of the basic needs in a young child's life. If the child does not feel secure then all other areas of development will be affected. You have already looked at Maslow's Hierarchy of Needs and will be aware that unless the basic needs for the child are met, progress in other areas will be hindered.
Bonding	This is an important process that all children should experience in order to aid balanced emotional development throughout life. It is the process whereby the infant develops strong emotional attachment to their main carers. If this process is interrupted or stopped then the effects might be long lasting. John Bowlby (1907–1990) carried out much research into this area. Bowlby's Attachment Theory became one of the most important areas of research and affected how people viewed the role of the main carers in the life of the young child and how it affected overall development. Children are capable of forming multiple bonds and can develop well if their emotional well being is catered for.
Sibling rivalry	Sibling rivalry or jealousy is very common, especially with the arrival of a new baby. The normal pattern of the household is disrupted and there will need to be a time of adjustment to the new arrangements. It is important that each child feels valued and that quality time is spent with each. It is best if adults refrain from comparing children as it may make one feel undervalued or inadequate. It is usually beneficial to involve the child in the routine for the new baby. It is worth noting that some regression is normal and that this often disappears very quickly.
Fears	Fears are very real and may result from lack of understanding or from not being involved in the communication cycle. Occasionally older children may relate stories that might frighten a child. As with other factors that affect the development of the child, it is important to try to find the root cause and tackle it at source.
Nightmares	Children usually have nightmares because they have a lack of understanding or a fear of something unusual. Parents, carers and early years workers should be mindful of television programmes that children watch and they should ensure that they are suitable. Children must be reassured and comforted until they have settled down and as their feelings are very real, the adult should acknowledge this and approach the situation with **sensitivity**.
Regression	Regression may be caused by a number of factors and it is important to try to ascertain the origin. It may be that the family has a new baby or that parents are going through a difficult patch or that there is a serious illness at home. Whatever the cause, the child must be managed with care and consideration and will need more attention at this time. This may only last for a short while, but adding more pressure and stress will never help the situation.

Sibling rivalry?

Behavioural problems

Factor	Effect
Aggression	**Aggression** is a difficult factor to deal with in young children. Often the child does not realise that it is undesirable to behave in this way. If it can be managed in a calm and patient way then this can have a more positive effect. Encouraging the child to realise the effect their aggression has on others can also help the situation. Help them to develop **empathy** in as many situations as possible. Explain how they might gain attention in a more gentle way and by behaving in a positive way. Aggression in school-age children is often more complex and may require specialist help with its management.
Attention seeking	All children like attention. They will seek attention numerous times every day, and if adults do not give that attention appropriately, the child will find other ways of getting it. Early years workers should provide attention when the child is behaving in a desirable way, and praise and smiles are very powerful reinforcement tools. If positive behaviour is ignored then the child will seek and gain attention in more dramatic ways, e.g. being aggressive, destructive or having a **temper tantrum**. Often the child will gain a great deal of attention for this type of behaviour, and if that is the only way to gain attention then the negative behaviour will continue as it is being reinforced. Providing attention when the child is being kind and working well will help reinforce that type of behaviour for the future.
Temper tantrums	Temper tantrums can be triggered by a variety of issues. The child may be seeking attention or may be frustrated. It is often the two year old who is associated with tantrums and this may be caused because the child is coming to terms with who they really are and their language is not developed or mature enough to cope with what they wish to do. This frustration is best dealt with by the adult remaining calm and relaxed, for the child can quickly detect anxiety in others. There are a number of strategies that can be used, such as distraction or considering the child's request calmly. Provide activities that encourage success and give appropriate praise and support. It is important to try to ascertain the underlying cause of the tantrum and then ensure that the child's safety is not **compromised** in any way.
Lying	There are numerous reasons why children lie. It may be that they wish to keep their parents happy, or that they wish to impress friends or even that they are afraid of telling the truth. Occasionally fact and fiction become muddled in the child's mind. Sometimes encouraging children to keep to the truth is difficult but it is often better to remain very 'matter of fact' about it. Remember, if a child hears adults telling lies, no matter how small, they are encouraging dishonesty in the child, for the adult is often a role model and the child will copy actions and words.

Child Development
13.2.2 Factors that influence development and norms of development /
13.2.3 Theories of play and how play can affect development

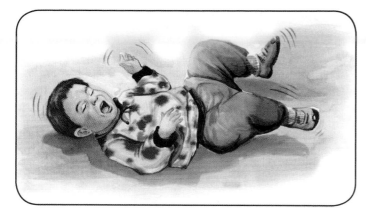

Attention seeking?

Assessment activity (AO2)

Factors that influence development
CASE STUDY

You will need to consider the factors influencing the development of the child chosen.

1. Produce a section within the Guide, in which you give an in-depth description of the factors which have influenced the development of the child chosen, explaining their effect on the child's development.

2. Compare the child's development and the norm for each area of development. Explain any variations from the norm.

Remember that confidentiality is important.

You should use vocational vocabulary as appropriate.

13.2.3 Theories of play and how play can affect development

The areas of development in young children are often remembered using the word PIES or SPICE.

P   physical development
I   intellectual or cognitive development (including language development)
E   emotional development
S   social development

or sometimes

S   social development
P   physical development
I   intellectual or cognitive development
C   communication skills
E   emotional development

When considering the overall development of the child, these are the areas that are included.

How play influences physical development

Play is vital to the overall development of the child but many aspects and types of play can influence physical development. The most obvious type of play is that which will help with the development of the large muscle groups. This is known as gross motor development and children will develop skills as they run, climb, balance and use other large equipment **effectively**. The fine motor skills are

Developing gross motor skills

developed through other aspects of play including creative and manipulative. The children will gain greater control over the small muscle groups as they use modelling materials such as clay and playdough. Creative activities will encourage pencil and brush control, which will later develop into writing skills.

Theory into practice

Devise an activity for a four-year-old child that will help promote physical development. List the resources you will require.

How play influences cognitive development

The influence of play on cognitive development is far-reaching and there has been much research into this field. Three people who have provided much insight into the way children think and learn are:

- **Jean Piaget**
- **Lev Vygotsky**
- **Jerome Bruner**

Early learning

The theorists given below developed their own specific theories relating to the development of children. The list is not exhaustive but provides examples of theorists and the theories in which they believed.

Theorist	Details of their work
Jean Piaget	Piaget noticed that very young children have skills, which are linked to the senses and muscles, i.e. sensory-motor. He called these skills schemas. A child quickly learns how to grasp a rattle and put it in its mouth. The child can then transfer this action to a different but similar-shaped object. This is known as **assimilation**. When the object is totally different then the schema must be adapted – this is known as **accommodation**. Assimilation and accommodation are the two parts of **adaptation**, which is a major part of the learning process. Piaget divided the process into different stages: • sensory-motor: birth–2 years • pre-operational: 2–7 years • formal operational: 7–11 years • concrete operational 11+ years. He felt that children learn by discovery or by first-hand experiences. His **typology** of play is discussed later in this section.
Lev Vygotsky	Social Learning Theory. He believed that social interaction has a great influence on our learning. He challenged Piaget's work, as he felt that learning did not go through specific stages but was a continual process from birth to death. He maintained that there was a difference between what a child's actual development level was, and the stage of development that could be attained through adult help and support. This difference he called the 'Zone of Proximal Development' and he claimed that true learning takes place in this zone. He placed great emphasis on social interaction, with learning being mainly dependent on interaction and collaboration with adults and peers.
Jerome Bruner	Constructivist theory. Jerome Bruner developed a theory of cognitive growth. He believed that intellectual growth developed in stages, each one building upon the other. This structured approach led to the idea of a 'spiral curriculum' with basic ideas repeated until grasped and then they are built upon and an upward direction taken. This process is known as 'scaffolding', with the adult providing the structure and the means for learning and progression. He felt that intellectual development moves through three stages: • enactive – learning through action • iconic – knowledge stored in visual images • symbolic – intellectual concepts and abstract thought.

The benefits of play

Play is the fundamental activity of childhood. It provides many benefits and without play children's well being and overall development will suffer greatly.

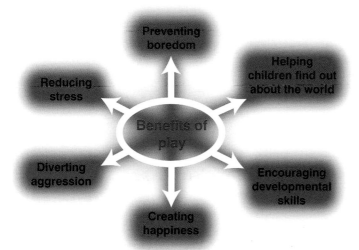

Early science

Benefit	Information
Preventing boredom	Young children are rarely bored. They initiate some form of play and quickly become absorbed in it. Play might be with other children but may also involve other toys. They usually have a great deal of energy but even if they are recuperating from illness they are still able to be involved in detailed play activities.
Reducing stress	Many people do not recognise that children become stressed just as adults do. The triggers may be different but the result is just as real. Through play children can deal with their problems and anxieties in a safe and secure environment.
Diverting aggression	Children may deal with their aggressive feelings by using play as a means of alleviating tensions. Clay and playdough are ideal as the child can pound and manipulate the clay to their hearts' content and they may feel much better after a while. Activities where the child can hammer, e.g. workbench or wooden pegs, are also beneficial in helping the child who is feeling aggressive.
Creating happiness	Children gain happiness from play of all kinds. A feeling of well being is created from vigorous physical activity or from creating a picture. Developing skills creates a feeling of achievement and pleasure.
Helping children find out about the world	Through play, children can gain knowledge and skills. It is good if they can have experiences of the natural world as they explore and experiment. Science and curiosity go hand in hand and children should be given opportunities to discover things first hand wherever possible. Knowledge of different cultures and customs can be experienced through creative activities, stories, drama and role play.
Encouraging developmental skills	Play helps children develop new skills and embed existing ones. It is often through play that the child comes to realise that the written word is symbolic and has meaning. They should be given opportunity to write at all times, e.g. note pad beside the telephone, 'prescription' pad in the hospital. Physical skills will be developed through everyday play activities, e.g. using large equipment for gross motor development and modelling media for fine motor development. Every activity that young children engage in will help develop skills in some way.

Happiness is catching

How play can be used as a therapeutic process

Occasionally things go wrong in a child's life and 'play as therapy' is widely accepted by **psychologists** and medical practitioners. It is believed that children will express their deepest feelings and underlying problems during play and that they might keep them hidden under other circumstances. Anna Freud (daughter of Sigmund Freud) first developed the concept of play therapy and used it to **diagnose** and to **treat** problems in a child's life. The therapist is specially trained so that they do not direct the play but encourage the child to express their feelings throughout in a safe environment. This is often used when children have been through painful experiences, such as abuse, and it is too distressing for the child to cope with. Negative feelings can be transferred to the toys or acted out and it is normal for children to use play to deal with unpleasant events or situations they do not understand.

Types of play

Piaget's typology of play

Samir	Activity 8
Samir is three years old and attends her local nursery school. She is just starting to copy some of the letters of her name but is not very good at it. She likes to pretend that she is writing stories and letters.	

1 How might the early years workers in the nursery extend her learning and provide other activities to support her?

Learning the rules

Type of play	Characteristics
Practice play	Children will continue to practise skills until they have a good level of understanding, i.e. they have developed a new schema. You may notice a child painting vertical lines and if you watch other aspects of play, they may be building towers and stacking blocks. They are developing a 'vertical' schema.
Symbolic play	Linked to logical thinking and the acquisition of language. The child is able to represent their world through images and symbols. One thing can represent another, e.g. a cardboard box can be a car. They will gradually realise that the marks made on paper have meaning and in fact symbolise words. This is the start of writing and reading skills. This is the stage when the child is curious about the world and will always be asking questions. They will believe that objects have life 'animism', e.g. may refer to the 'naughty table' if they bump into it. Piaget felt that the child at this stage was 'egocentric' and could only see things from their own perspective.
Games with rules	As children mature they will be able to play games with rules and take turns. Once the rules are established they are very important and the child will be upset if the rules are broken. It is only later that there can be changes and that rules can be negotiated, e.g. stepping on lines on the pavement – if it becomes boring they can be changed to include other parameters.

Hughes typology of play

(As used on the National Occupational Standards of Playwork level 3.) These types of play were devised by Bob Hughes and form the variety of play practice in children.

Type of play	Characteristics
Symbolic play	Play which diminishes risk but allows potentially 'dangerous' situations to be explored.
Rough and tumble play	Mock fighting, tickling and developing strength of muscles.
Socio-dramatic play	Acting out real or potential situations.
Social play	Play with the rules for the characters and social interaction being changed or amended at will.
Creative play	Play which allows new ideas to be developed as on-going.
Communication play	Play using words, manners or gestures, e.g. rhymes, singing, role play.
Dramatic play	Play in which events that the child is not directly involved with are being dramatised.
Deep play	Play which allows the child to develop survival skills and deal with fear.
Exploratory play	Play in which the immediate environment is explored, e.g. throwing, handling objects.
Fantasy play	Play in which the child can change things so that they have their own way even if against all the rules of reality.
Imaginative play	Play where the imagination rules and anything can happen.
Loco-motor play	Movement for its own sake.
Mastery play	Developing skills.
Object play	Hand-eye co-ordination in manipulation.
Role play	Exploring ways of being in another social context.

Rough and tumble play

Categories of play

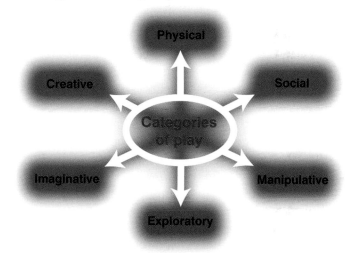

Theory into practice

Arrange to visit an early years setting and watch the children as they engage in activities.

List the different activities you see and place them in the six categories mentioned above.

Creative play

Categories of play	Characteristics
Physical	Development of muscles (large and small) through play. Running, jumping, climbing, skipping, swimming and use of large equipment, e.g. tricycles, see-saws, climbing frames. Safety of the child is important and there should be use of impact-absorbent surfaces at all times.
Creative	Can include a variety of activities ranging from painting, drawing and collage to drama, construction and music. Children develop many skills when indulging in this type of play and gain great satisfaction from the end result as well as the process.
Imaginative	Pretend play, make believe, role play or fantasy play are other ways of describing the use of the imagination in play. It enables the child to act out fears and anxieties as well as the challenges and fun of taking over other characteristics in play.
Exploratory	Children seem to have an innate curiosity and should have opportunity to explore in a safe and secure environment. Discovering things first hand is exciting and challenging. It is important that children have the chance to find out about the real world and the natural world for themselves.
Manipulative	Skills involved in developing the fine muscles particularly in the hand. The child will refine control of grasping, holding and placing as well as precision in mark making and eventually writing.
Social	Enjoys the company of other children. Co-operates with others. Strong relationship between language/communication development and social play.

Stages of play

Solitary play

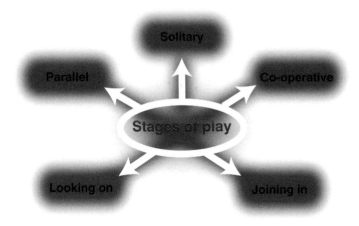

Discussion point

In pairs discuss activities that might encourage children to indulge in co-operative play.

Child Development
13.2.3 Theories of play and how play can affect development /
13.2.4 How to plan and make a learning aid for a child (0–8)

Stages of play	Characteristics
Solitary	Children of all ages enjoy solitary play but it is the first stage of play and is mainly seen in the very young child. Children under 2 will play alone quite happily and even when with other children they will be absorbed in their own activity.
Parallel	At this stage it may appear that the child is joining in with others but in fact they are playing alongside but still each is involved in their own activity. At this stage the child will appear to be more confident and enjoys the company of others.
Looking on	Often the child will indulge in this type of spectator play whereby they watch what is happening and learn from the experience before trying it for themselves. The child will be using this as an opportunity to gain confidence.
Joining in	This is often referred to as partnership or associative play and is the first step toward full co-operation during play activities. Often children will have friends and they are all involved in the same activity, e.g. painting, but not carrying it out as a total collaborative exercise.
Co-operative	This is the type of play that is very beneficial for all who are involved. Children develop the ability to share and work as a group. They can look at a problem and start trying to solve it by listening to each other's ideas. The child is moving away from being totally egocentric and language development is increasing.

Assessment activity (AO3)

Research theories relating to play   CASE STUDY

1 Carry out research using **three** relevant sources of information, e.g. existing toys/catalogues, books or the Internet. You will then need to make reasoned judgements, in order to analyse how **two** theories of play can be reflected in the development of the child chosen for the study.

2 Provide two examples to support your views.

Your information must be accurate and you should use vocational language effectively.

Make sure your evidence is applied to the child chosen.

Let's get on

13.2.4 How to plan and make a learning aid for a child (0–8)

Planning activities is a task that the early years worker will be involved with on a daily basis and this should be carried out in a **logical** and **structured** way. Within the role of planning activities the worker will also be involved in making learning aids for young children. This could range from designing and making a game that the young child might play, making a puppet or story aid to encourage concentration and language development, to making a chart to encourage involvement in a topic or activity, e.g. height or weather chart. The range is only limited by your imagination. The worker should focus on how the learning aid will contribute to the overall development of the child. Good planning and careful thought will ensure successful outcomes.

Careful planning should ensure that the activity will meet the required needs in the chosen area(s) of development. In this way it is necessary to consider the **aims, objectives,** and **outcomes** to be achieved by the child who will be using the learning aid.

It is then important to list the **resources** needed and work out or estimate the cost. During this planning stage it is essential that the early years worker decides what the learning aid is designed to achieve. What do you want the child to get out of this exercise? Do you want them to know more about science, colour, sorting or creative aspects of their development?

Aim

The aim of the activity is what the early years worker intends to introduce the child to. It is an 'umbrella' statement that **encompasses** what is to be carried out during the activity. For example, to introduce the child to a simple science activity involving melting snow.

The detail of what it is to be achieved is given in the objectives. The aim sets the scene and limits the activity to a specific type of activity. However, the activity should be flexible enough to incorporate some change of direction if necessary. The learning aid assists in the aim of the activity being met.

Objectives

The objectives are what the child will be able to achieve. In order to plan the objectives it is quite useful to start with the words: 'By the end of the activity the child will. . . .' For example:

- understand that heat causes snow to melt
- be aware that snow is cold
- demonstrate that snow reduces in volume as it melts.

The objectives break the activity down into small units, each of which is measurable.

All my own work

The learning aid linked to the activity should be safe and well thought out. The early years care and education worker will need to consider what it is designed to achieve and which areas of development is it focusing on. When considering any learning aid there are a number of issues to be thought about:

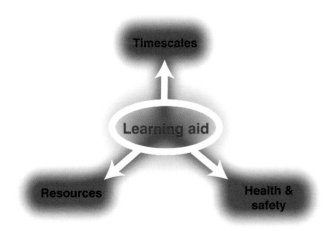

Outcomes

The outcomes are the overall achievements by the child and whether the activity has accomplished what it was intended to. When looking back at the activity and learning aid and deciding what could be changed in order to improve the event, it will be necessary to consider whether the outcomes have been achieved and what could have improved the overall experience for the child.

> ### Discussion point
>
> Neesha works in an early years care and education setting. She is planning to make cress sandwiches with the 4-year-old children in her care.
>
> In pairs discuss what learning aid she might make to help the children and what the separate tasks the children might be doing involve, e.g. counting one slice of bread per person, buttering bread.
>
> Write down at least four objectives linked to the activity.

Resources

When planning to make a learning aid it is necessary to decide what resources will be required. It is good practice to gather all the resources together before you start so that everything is at hand. It is useful to itemise all materials required and any other equipment such as drills, glue, etc. Remember, your learning aid might be used for outdoor activities and so might need to be weather-proofed or painted appropriately. Cost will be a further factor to take into consideration when designing your aid.

Resources

Health and safety issues

It is necessary that all health and safety issues are considered when organising and preparing activities. This will include carrying out a risk assessment and noting if any elements of the task constitute a risk. It will then be necessary to put in place ways of minimising that risk, and if that is not possible then the early years care and education worker must decide whether or not the activity should be abandoned. Your learning aid must be safe and appropriate for the age group that are going to use it. Remember, very young children have a tendency to put things in their mouths. There should be no sharp edges (consider rounding off sharp corners even on laminated card) and paint must be child-safe. The policies of the early years setting must be followed.

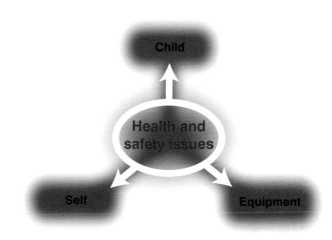

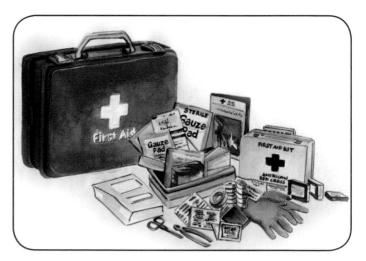

Safety is important

Theory into practice

Jane is going to bake small cakes with a group of four children.

1. Provide an aim for the activity.
2. Explain what your learning aid is.
3. List the resources she will need for the activity, e.g. ingredients for the cakes.
4. Work out a realistic timescale for the activity.
5. List the developmental areas that this activity will help promote.

Health and safety issues
CASE STUDY

Jane decided to make small, brightly coloured, wooden blocks for the children in the early years care and education setting to use. Before she made them, she considered all aspects of the activity with a view to health and safety issues.

1. Carry out a risk assessment for this activity.
2. What are the issues of health and safety for the child?
3. What are the issues of health and safety for the early years care and education worker?
4. Does any equipment pose a risk and how might that be minimised?

To think of safety for oneself is important because if the carer is injured then there is the problem of who will look after the children. Do not take any unnecessary risks and always look out for any hazards. When planning and preparing activities, try to consider what could go wrong and then put safeguards in place to prevent that from happening.

Looking after a toddler
CASE STUDY

You are caring for a toddler aged 18 months and you decide to make a learning aid for use with that child. Using P.I.E.S. as a guide make a list of the different aids which you might choose to use for each area of development.
Remember that language development is also included.

Supervision is one of the main factors in preventing harm coming to a child whatever the activity. It is essential in the early years care and education setting that there are enough members of staff to adequately supervise all the children present.

Theory into practice

Remember that children cannot fully enjoy activities and intellectual stimulation if their basic needs are not fully met. When an early years care and education worker is providing for the developmental needs of children it is useful to think of the areas covered by Abraham Maslow. If the basic needs of the child are not met then they will be unable to function at a higher level.

Carry out research to find out about the basic needs that Maslow considered important.

How would these be applied to a young child?

Jenny
CASE STUDY

You have been asked to plan a short intellectual activity for Jenny who is 3 years of age. The purpose is to help her learn about colours.

1. Give the aim of the activity.
2. List at least **three** objectives.
3. Outline a learning aid that you might make to help this area of development.

You might like to use a planning sheet such as the one below:

Planning sheet for learning aid

Date/time	Action	Reason for action
e.g. Monday	e.g. Decide on activity that learning aid will be used with. Consider types of suitable learning aids.	e.g. To link the learning aid to the activity and consider health and safety issues.

Evaluate the learning aid

After an activity has been carried out, it is good practice to evaluate it and look at the benefits and also determine what might need to be altered if it is carried out again. As part of that overall evaluation it will also be necessary to evaluate if the learning aid has been effective in promoting the intended development in the child. There may be feedback from a number of sources about the effectiveness of your aid and these will all help in the overall evaluation. The following headings will provide an outline for effective evaluation.

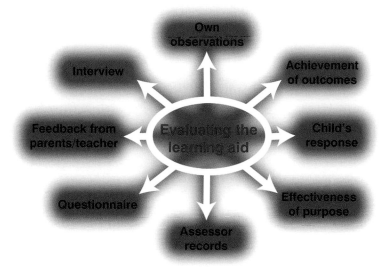

Own observations

If the objectives were correctly stated at the outset then it should be relatively easy to check whether they have been achieved. This might have been observed and you would know that learning has taken place. It is always good practice to go back and consider the objectives that were set initially and check that they have been met. If they have not, then it may be that the activity was more complex than at first anticipated and needs to be revised.

Once the activity has been completed, the worker will need to evaluate what has taken place. It is necessary to think about the activity and learning aid and to consider how effective it has been. When considering this, the early years worker should examine their role in the whole activity. To evaluate successfully, judgements will need to be made.

Achievement of outcomes

It is then possible to look at the whole activity and decide if the main outcomes have been achieved. Did the child produce what they set out to produce

or did they do what they set out to do? If they did, then the outcomes have been achieved. If they did not then there should be a reason and that must be addressed if the activity is to be repeated.

Remember: if the child enjoys the activity they will wish to repeat the activity and experience a second enjoyable session.

Child's response

All activities should benefit those taking part, and in evaluating the activity, it will be necessary to consider what those benefits were. The child should find the activity to be a pleasurable experience and if that is the case then they may well wish to repeat it in the future. Think of the benefits in terms of P.I.E.S., and ascertain which areas of development were addressed and how your learning aid provided for these areas of development.

I'm enjoying this

Carrying out an activity with a child inevitably affects the relationship the early years care and education worker has with that child. It is common for the relationship to be strengthened so that through carrying out an activity the child has developed a deeper relationship with the early years care and education worker.

Effectiveness of purpose

When carrying out any activity with the child, it is important to consider if the learning aid you made was effective in purpose. Prior to making the learning aid, the early years worker would have in mind what its purpose was to be. Now is the time to ask if that was fulfilled or if it fell short of expectations. Children should be involved as much as possible in the activity and it should be their work. It is in this way that they will learn new skills and develop those they already have. Allow children to experiment and ensure that the aid is child centred and child friendly.

Assessor records

In many cases an assessor will have seen the learning aid and may well have witnessed its use in an activity. Assessor records will provide a valuable source of information regarding the effectiveness of the learning aid as they will have been written in an unbiased and objective manner. Someone who understands child development, and will be able to make an informed judgement as to the suitability and safety of the learning aid with regard to age and stage of development for the chosen child will also write these records.

Questionnaire

It will be necessary to check that the learning aid chosen was adequate for the task in hand. The following checklist might prove useful:

Checklist for learning aid	Yes	No
Was it safe?		
Was it correct for the activity?		
Was it used correctly?		
Was the cost of the aid within the budget allocated?		
It the activity was to be repeated would the learning aid remain the same?		

If the answer to any of the questions in the checklist is 'No', it will be necessary to alter the activity plan or learning aid accordingly.

It may also be beneficial to devise a questionnaire that could be given to anyone who saw the activity and use of the learning aid. However, you must remember to word the questions so that they do not present any bias and that a true reflection can be attained.

Feedback from parents/teacher

When you are working with a young child there will inevitably be other adults around and they will observe what is taking place. It is useful to ask for feedback after the activity is completed, and if you have involved others during the planning stages, then often people are only too happy to be asked for opinions later. This feedback will enable you to plan more effectively in the future and any discussion may involve ideas for the designing and making of learning aids in the future.

Interview

Interviews are often a more formal method of gaining feedback but can be very useful in helping with the evaluation of the activity and use of the learning aid. It is helpful to have questions formulated prior to interviewing someone and it is essential that you arrange a mutually beneficial time for this to take place.

Assessment activity (AO4)

CASE STUDY

You are working in an early years setting and have been asked to make a learning aid, which will promote the development of skills, for a child in the 0–8 age range.

- You must explain in detail how you will plan for the physical needs of the child and the impact it will have on the child's development.

- Then you should draw up a plan for the activity, which will include the use of your learning aid.

1 Plan the activity remembering to include:
   - aim
   - objectives
   - suitably challenging outcomes to be achieved by the child using the learning aid
   - accurate timescales.

2 Explain in detail the method of making the learning and the resources used.

3 Describe the health and safety issues associated with the aid, explaining how risks will be reduced.

4 Carry out the activity using the learning aid with the child. Try to be confident in your approach.

5 Evaluate the learning aid in terms of:
   - the child's response
   - achievement of outcomes
   - effectiveness of purpose
   - recommendations for improvement.

Contents

About this unit

Within this unit you will investigate:

- the concepts of mental health
- types of mental illness
- causes of mental illness
- effects of mental illness
- preventative and coping strategies
- support for service users with mental-health needs.

What is considered to be 'normal' behaviour?

Introducing this unit

Whilst it is possible to send people to the Moon and explore the depths of the oceans, there is still much to learn and discover about the workings of the mind. The mind can be defined as those processes that are carried out by the brain, in terms of thoughts and feelings, which may be conscious or subconscious, and may be demonstrated through behaviour.

The person with a normally functioning mind is considered to be mentally healthy. If the mind is not functioning normally then the person is seen as having a mental illness or mental-health problems. Whether a person is considered to be mentally healthy or not is often decided through observation of their behaviour and talking with them.

Although such terms are used as if they are 'facts', they tend to raise more questions than they answer. What is meant by 'normal', 'good mental health' and 'mental illness'? They are words that are in everyday usage but can mean different things to different people. Such differences become important issues when an individual's diagnosis and treatment depends on a common agreement and understanding between the services and professionals involved in providing their treatment and care.

This unit investigates different types of mental illness, suggested causes and the resultant effects and needs they may create. The main preventative and coping strategies together with supportive services are considered along with relevant legislation. The ways in which mental health and illness are defined by society, often through the media, will be examined and the effects of such portrayals on service users considered.

14.2.1 The concepts of mental health

Positive self esteem is a feature of mental health

To understand what is meant by mental ill health or illness, it is important to first define what mental health is. This may not be as straightforward as it might appear.

Theory into practice

Write down the first six words that come into your head when you try to define or explain the term 'mental health'. Now compare your list with other people's and discuss the similarities and differences.

Mental health is?

You are likely to have found some differences. Why do you think this has happened when the term 'mental health' is commonly used as if everyone understands what it means?

M. Jahoda (1958) identified the features of mental health and psychological well being as:

- self acceptance – positive self esteem
- the **potential** for growth and development – not being passive about life
- autonomy – acting independently
- accurate **perception** of reality – being realistic about what is happening in your world
- environmental competence – being able to deal effectively with demands of situations and circumstances
- positive interpersonal relationships – having fulfilling and warm relationships with others.

These are seen as ideal features and depend on cultural factors. Can you relate these features to your chosen words?

Mental health is often defined, in a negative way, in terms of it being present when there is an absence of disease or disability or when you are not ill. How would you write a one sentence, positive definition of 'mental health'?

Theory into practice

Repeat the exercise carried out in the first 'Theory into practice' exercise but now write the first six words you'd use to define or explain 'mental ill health'. Compare with others and discuss the differences.

Mental ill health is?

Rosenhan and Seligman (1989) identified features of mental ill health and maladaptive behaviour as being:

- suffering – experiencing distress or discomfort in everyday life
- maladaptiveness – engaging in behaviour or ways of thinking which makes life more difficult

- **irrationality** – being unable to be understood, or be communicated with, in a reasoned manner
- **unpredictability** – acting in ways which are entirely unexpected to the individual as well as others
- vividness and unconventionality – experiencing sensations which are far more vivid and intense than those experienced by others or experiencing them in a different way from others
- observer discomfort – the individual acts in ways that other people find embarrassing or difficult to watch
- violation of moral and ideal standards – breaking the accepted ethical and moral codes of society.

Discussion point

Consider the features identified by Rosenhan and Seligman. Is mental ill health related just to what the individual experiences, e.g. suffering, or are there other external factors that may have an influence?

As can be seen in the identification of features of mental illness, some of these relate to external factors – factors that are determined by society, its views and judgements. This would indicate that the concept or idea about mental illness is not just about what the individual is feeling but is also about what other people believe is normal behaviour or thinking.

How views of mental health change over time

As people's views change over time, then the concept is also likely to change. This can be seen in terms of homosexuality which was seen, in the past, as an illness, which was treated through the use of **aversion** therapy. Subjects were given mild electric shocks when they showed an interest in photos of people of the same sex and encouraged to become interested in opposite sex photos. In Russia, in the past, people who were seen as political **dissidents**, because they did not believe in the form of state communism being practised, were forcibly 'treated' for mental illness to 'cure' them of such abnormal beliefs.

Discussion point

What views might the majority of people feel are not 'normal' and therefore 'abnormal'? If people hold different views to the majority, does this mean they are 'mentally ill'?

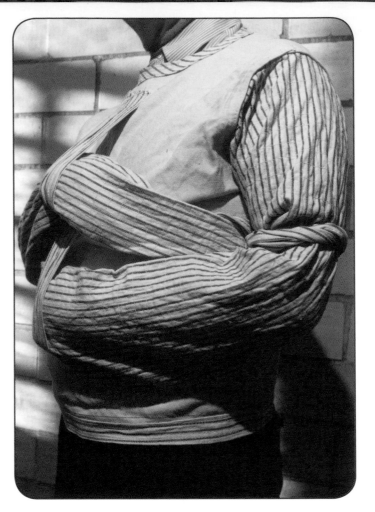

Person in a straitjacket

Historically, there have been differing views taken on what is abnormal behaviour and how it should be dealt with. Some of these views are still current in certain modern-day communities.

An early view of mental illness or abnormal behaviour was that a spirit had possessed the individual. This could be seen in a positive or negative light depending on the 'spirit's message'. If it was interpreted by the priesthood as being a good spirit – usually one that supported their teachings – then it would be seen as a message from the gods and the individual would gain in status and be cared for. If it was seen as a bad spirit or demon, the individual would be beaten, starved and/or exorcised to drive out the spirit. If the person was seen to have a bad spirit at the time of food shortage or a natural disaster, then they could be blamed for their community's misfortune and killed or sacrificed to appease the angry gods.

There is evidence of people having holes drilled in their heads – trepanning – to allow the evil spirit to escape, and relieve the pressure. Exorcisms and trepanning continue to be practised in the UK today by some communities, individuals and religions.

Being cast out by the community

Witchcraft was also seen as being responsible for people's illnesses and behaviour due to the casting of spells and curses, which afflicted the victim. Witches were often old women who were skilled in the use of herbal remedies and were seen as a threat by the local priest or doctor.

The Ancient Greeks believed that abnormal behaviour was the result of disturbance or imbalance of the body's four main fluids or humours. It was seen as an indicator of physical illness and was treated as such. The body was bled or purged to restore the balance between the humours – blood, black bile, yellow bile and phlegm. An excess of one of these was believed to cause behavioural changes, e.g. mania, melancholy, restlessness or **unresponsiveness**.

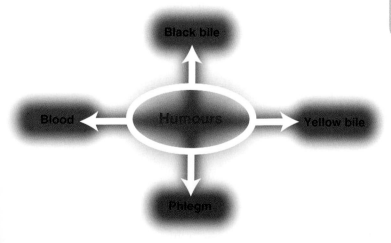

From the 16th century onwards, people who acted abnormally were seen to have 'lost their reason' and some forms of treatment were carried out in institutions known as 'asylums'. This term means a place of refuge and care but they were far from this for many. The word 'bedlam' – a place of uproar! – derives from a shortening of the name of one of the original asylums based in the Priory of St Mary of Bethlehem. Inmates were given icy baths in an attempt to shock them back to normality.

Being shocked back to sanity

Theory into practice

Imagine you are feeling depressed or paranoid and that people are out to get you. What is the likely effect on your mental state of being forced into, and held down in, a bath of icy water, by poorly paid and poorly educated workers who treat you as if you are no better than an animal? Is your condition likely to improve as a result of your 'treatment'?

In the late 18th century, a more 'moral' approach to the response to, and the treatment of, abnormal behaviour started to develop. Philippe Pinel, a French physician, who was in charge of a French asylum, believed people who 'lost their reason' did so because they had experienced environmental stress. This could be caused by relationship or personal problems or as a result of social stress, for example overcrowding.

Philippe Pinel treated such people as individuals, with dignity, compassion and kindness and provided more humane surroundings for their care, in an attempt to help them recover their lost 'equilibrium' or balance. His approach was taken up and used by the Quakers in York.

In the late 19th century, this approach was overtaken – as it was seen as being unscientific – by the development of medical science, the medical profession and the more favoured medical model. As success in curing physical illnesses began to grow, the cure for mental illness was felt to be close at hand. Abnormal behaviour was seen as a symptom, or observable sign, of internal disease that was affecting the workings of the nervous system, brain or body. This could be treated in a number of different ways using medication, therapy or surgery. These approaches, known as the biomedical and psychotherapy approaches, will be investigated later in the unit.

Lack of universal agreement

Historically, the concept of mental health and illness has changed according to **prevailing** beliefs and knowledge. This has led to abnormal behaviour being treated in widely different ways and from different standpoints. This lack of **universal** agreement, as opposed to that which generally exists in the field of physical illness has led to continuing difficulties in defining, treating and prevention of mental illness.

Definitions of mental health/disorders

A number of different approaches have been used in an attempt to define what is considered to be abnormal behaviour and is therefore seen as a mental illness.

- Statistical frequency and infrequency. Behaviour that is typical and therefore frequently observed can be defined as usual or normal. This can be measured statistically using a normal distribution curve. Whatever falls outside the middle ground, and therefore happens infrequently, is considered abnormal. For example, in terms of measuring intelligence, the majority of people have an intelligent quotient (IQ) or measurement of around 100. Those outside the middle ground or the mean (two standard deviations) are considered to have abnormal IQ. It should be noted this applies to both groupings at the extremes – those with very low IQ, as well as those with very high IQ.

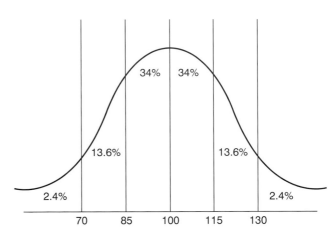

Normal distribution curve showing IQ measurement spread in the population

- Deviation from the social norm. As has been previously identified, behaviour that does not fit in with social expectation can be classified as being abnormal. This has applied to homosexual behaviour in the past. In a religious community, not believing what the majority believe would be seen as abnormal and deviant.
- Personal distress. People who are suffering from distress in terms of being depressed, stressed, aggressive, etc., and possibly showing physical symptoms, such as not eating or sleeping normally, could be suffering from mental illness, as distress is not seen as a normal feature of everyday life.

- Fitting the stereotype. By behaving in a way that people believe mentally ill people behave, the individual meets the stereotype and is socially treated as being mentally ill. This tends to attract negative behaviour from others.
- Models of illness.
  - The medical model suggests abnormal behaviour is a physical indication, resulting from a physical disease, malfunction or illness, of a mental condition.
  - The social model puts forward the view that external pressures, such as losing a job, being bullied, or having a baby can produce a dysfunction within the individual.
  - The existential model suggests that abnormal behaviour is the normal response to an abnormal situation that the person may find themselves in. For example, living in a dysfunctional family could create this response.

Theory into practice

Discuss the different approaches to mental health. Does one approach provide the answer to what is mental illness or is it more likely to involve elements from a number of different approaches?

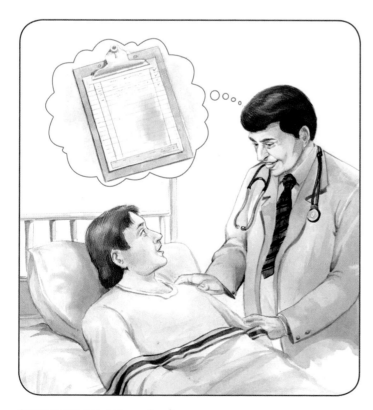

Symptoms are categorised

Methods of diagnosing/measuring mental-health needs

Two classification systems have been developed to help professionals in their diagnosis (identification of an illness by its symptoms). Without some common agreement on what a mental illness, is the type of **prognosis** and treatment could become very varied.

The Diagnostic and Statistical Manual (DSM) was developed in the 1990s to assist medical professionals in identifying a common pattern of symptoms that could then be categorised or labelled as a certain type of illness. This could then lead to a focused treatment using, for example, medication developed to combat a group of symptoms. The DSM-IV system has been revised over time to take into account changes in approach and professional terminology. An example, mentioned earlier, was the removal of 'homosexuality' from the list of disorders. The other system developed is known as the International Classification of Disease (ICD-10) but tends to be less common in its usage.

Mood disorders	Depressive disorders
	Bipolar disorders
	Mood disorders due to a general medical condition
	Substance-induced mood disorders

Taken from DSM-IV Axis 1 Mood Disorders

The DSM-VI system classifies disorders into five general groupings or axes. Within each axis, there are sub-groups of disorders that have some commonality of symptoms, e.g. mood disorders or anxiety disorders. The degree of 'abnormality' can vary from mild to severe within each axis.

Present day images of mental health and how the media influences attitudes to mental health

Socialisation is the process of learning the culture of a society or social group. This takes place through informal primary socialisation whereby learning takes place with the family. Children are taught about their expected behaviour, roles and social position. As a result of this, they start to develop a sense of self, an identity, which also develops its own attitudes and opinions. As the child becomes more exposed to influences outside its own social group, a more formal secondary socialisation process takes place. They learn more about societal expectations through schooling, work and the media as well as from family and friends.

The media provides a framework for thinking about issues and also helps form attitudes and opinions. Older people can believe they are more likely to be mugged that any other group, because of what they read in the papers. However, statistically, younger people are at greater risk of being mugged for their mobile phones and other pieces of modern technology. This is often seen as less newsworthy and therefore features less in media reports than the more emotive attacks on older people. The view of reality loses balance, becomes twisted and subjective.

Headline used in the Sun in 2003

The reporting on mental health and illness issues has often suffered from negative presentation. A study of daily tabloid newspapers during 1996 found that 40% of the reporting on such issues used negative language, e.g. nutters, and this rose to 45% for the Sunday tabloids. This was highlighted in 2003 by the Sun's reporting about Frank Bruno, a famous boxer, television celebrity and charity worker, who was suffering from a mental illness. His condition required a compulsory detention in a psychiatric unit. This was reported as 'Bonkers Bruno locked up'. The public and professional outcry that resulted from this produced an amended headline of 'Sad Bruno in Mental Home'.

Theory into practice

Produce a table showing some of the things you have learned from family, e.g. difference between right and wrong, and importance of good time-keeping, 'don't steal' and 'you'll lose your job if you are not on time'.

The message	An example
Respect others	'Don't speak to your mother like that!'

'He must be one of them!'

Generally, people who have little or no contact with people who are affected by mental illness will develop their attitudes and opinions based on media reporting. When stereotypical images are used, people are likely to take these on board as 'real' images and this can lead to prejudice and discrimination. This has happened, in the past, with stereotypes of the role of women in television commercials. They were the ones who were likely to be seen looking after children and carrying out the traditional domestic roles.

In children's books, foreigners were often portrayed as the villains and girls did 'girly' things!

The positive role that the media has fulfilled in these areas has been to challenge such stereotypes and offer positive counter-stereotypes. It can also encourage 'pro-social' behaviour in that it encourages people to be more understanding. It can also provide the individuals being stereotyped with positive role models.

Theory into practice

How far have things changed? Research current tabloid papers for their reporting of mental illness. Consider the images used on television, especially in 'soaps'. Have you seen such movies as 'A Beautiful Mind' (2002) and others in which people have a mental illness? How are they portrayed? Are there any adverts you are aware of that feature people with mental illness? List your findings under the headings of Positive or Negative and identify why each has been placed there. What is your overall conclusion about present-day images of people with mental illnesses and how the media may influence these attitudes and images?

Positive image	Why?	Negative image	Why?

Legislation and its effects on the care of individuals with mental-health needs

There are two key pieces of legislation currently relating to people with mental-health needs.

The NHS and Community Care Act (1990)

This was aimed at enabling and supporting the continued move from institutional care to community care that had started in the 1960s and 1970s. The intention was that, wherever possible, older people, people with mental-health needs, people with physical disabilities and those with learning disabilities would be cared for in their own community. The philosophy of 'normalisation' was initially proposed in 1972 and moved away from the idea of the protection of people with mental illness through segregation to one of supportive integration into normal life through living in the community. It was hoped this would lead to a breakdown of the stigmatisation and stereotyping process that happens when there is little contact between two groups.

The Act provided individuals with the legal right to have their needs for care assessed. These needs would then be translated into a 'package of care', although such a package depended on the resources being available. There was no legal right attached to this. The care would be organised, monitored and reviewed to ensure it continued to meet the individual's needs.

This was further supported in 1995 by the Carers (Recognition and Services) Act that gave carers the statutory right to have their needs assessed, but again gave no right to have them met.

The Mental Health Act 1983

This was aimed at achieving a balance between an individual's civil liberties, at a time when they are mentally ill, and the need to compulsorily admit them to hospital, for assessment and treatment. This would be done for their own health and/or safety and to protect others.

It provides a clear structure within which safeguards are in place. People can be detained under 'a section' for assessment and/or treatment. The word 'section' relates to the section or part of the Act that authorises a particular form of compulsory detention, e.g. Section 4 covers emergency assessment where an individual can be detained and assessed for up to 72 hours. Section 3 covers admission for treatment for up to six months. There is a right of appeal to the Mental Health Review Tribunal for legal aid and for representation by a lawyer.

Whilst sectioning someone who is severely mentally ill provides them with protection, care and treatment, at a time when they are unlikely to be able to make rational decisions about their own welfare, the Act has had its critics.

Some of the 'sections' under the Mental Health Act by which individuals, who are viewed as being a danger to themselves or others, may be compulsorily detained in hospital are shown below:

Section 2	Admission for assessment for up to 28 days recommended by two doctors at request of approved social worker or nearest relative
Section 3	Admission for treatment for up to 6 months recommended by two doctors at request of approved social worker or nearest relative
Section 4	Admission for an emergency assessment for up to 72 hours recommended by one doctor and at request of approved social worker or nearest relative

The Mental Health Act was put into place at a time when the main focus of care and treatment was hospital based. With the development of community-based psychiatric services, like the Community Psychiatric Nurse Service, more support can be offered in the community. The process of taking someone to hospital when they don't want to go can make their condition worse, if they already believe people are 'out to get them'. They then find they are placed in a 'closed' ward or unit with locked doors.

Theory into practice

Research the two Acts and identify their strengths and weaknesses. Consider how you might feel if you were feeling paranoid and forcibly taken to a closed ward for treatment.

In an attempt to update the 1983 Act and relate it more towards compulsory community-based treatment, as well as bringing it in line with the Human Rights Act 1998, a new Mental Health Bill was drafted in 2002. This has met with stiff opposition from a wide range of people, including service users and professionals, and has been re-drafted. Opposition still remains and further changes are likely before it is presented to Parliament in its final form.

The underpinning knowledge for the unit has not been arranged within the specification in the same order as the Assessment Evidence Grid. The Assessment activity is, therefore, more appropriately placed at the end of Unit 14.

14.2.2 Types of mental illness

Mental ill health can cover a wide range of disorders and illnesses and service users may experience more than one disorder at any time.

Alzheimer's disease

Alzheimer's disease comes under the general heading of Delirium (confusion) and Dementia (deterioration of intellectual ability). Whilst it tends to affect older people, especially those aged over 80, it can be found in middle-aged people. Brain tissue wastes away and is not regenerated. This leads to a shrinking of the brain and an increasing reduction in mental, emotional and physical functioning.

Alzheimer's disease   CASE STUDY

Nadia is 75 years old and lives by herself. Her husband died two years ago and her family moved to another town because of work.

Her neighbours contacted Social Services as they have become concerned for her safety as she is becoming very forgetful. About six months ago, they noticed small changes – she started to lock herself out of the house, on a regular basis, because she kept forgetting to take her keys when she went shopping. In the past, she was always dressed smartly but her clothes have now started to look dirty. She forgot the names of next-door's children even though she had known them for ten years.

Up all night

CASE STUDY

Continued...

She had started to stay up all night and sleep during the day – she often visited a neighbour at 2 am thinking it was in the afternoon. The main worry was she had started to leave the gas unlit on her cooker because she would forget she'd switched it on. Neighbours feared there could be an explosion.

Depressive illnesses

Mood or affective (emotional) disorders are those that involve emotional disturbances that have a severe impact on the individual's life. They include depression, which can involve feelings of great sadness or loss and the withdrawal from contact with others, and loss of appetite, sexual desire, ability to sleep and general detachment from day-to-day life. At the opposite end of the scale is mania, a less common condition, which produces hyperactivity, **euphoria**, excessive talkativeness and impractical, impulsive ideas and behaviour. The third main condition in this grouping is bipolar disorder, which was previously known as manic-depression as it involved mood swing episodes, (periods) of depression and mania.

Bipolar depression CASE STUDY

Charley is buzzing with ideas   Charley is depressed

CASE STUDY

Charley is a middle-aged plumber who works for himself and has been treated for bipolar disorder for a number of years. He can have periods when he is energised by his ideas to make money. He will be up all night developing his ideas to make and sell a new design of tap which can be turned on and off through verbal command. He has drawn his savings out of the bank so he can go to New Zealand to develop his ideas further and visit his sister whom he hasn't seen for 20 years. He's buzzing with ideas and will talk about them to anyone who will listen. He is normally a quiet man who is cautious about spending money and has saved his money for retirement. After a week of little sleep and rushing around, he collapses from exhaustion and is seen by his GP who persuades him to take his medication.

A month later he becomes very depressed, stays in bed all day, eats little and is suicidal, as he believes he is useless and life is not worth living. His neighbour calls his GP.

Generalised anxiety disorder

Anxiety disorders tend to have a commonality of individuals experiencing severe anxiety that interferes with their normal functioning and ability to adjust to and cope with anxiety.

Generalised anxiety disorder CASE STUDY

Nazia woke one morning feeling tense and anxious. She has found the feeling of anxiety has remained with her for the last six months. She worries about everything in general, e.g. crossing the road, getting to work on time, missing the bus, meeting new people, forgetting things when she goes shopping. She is always tense, is unable to relax, fidgets constantly and has difficulty sleeping. She always 'looks worried'. She has been diagnosed as having generalised anxiety disorder.

Personality/perception disorders

Personality disorders are possibly the most complex and difficult group of disorders to describe as they do not necessarily fit into an easily recognisable set of common symptoms. The individual with a personality disorder is likely to behave in a socially immature way and not be able to **empathise fully**, if at all. It represents a failure of the personality to develop and adjust to behaving in a socially and culturally acceptable manner. A number of personality traits are seen to be extreme and are expressed in inflexible and dysfunctional ways. An individual may be seen as having a narcissistic personality disorder as they are totally self-absorbed in themselves and are incapable of caring or loving others. They demand love and attention from others.

Narcissistic behaviour

A person may be diagnosed as having a paranoid personality disorder, as they believe they are being persecuted, spied on and are suspicious of others. Others may develop a borderline personality disorder. They tend to be difficult to live with, as their emotions tend to be unpredictable, impulsive, inappropriate in their actions and unstable in relationships. People with antisocial personality disorders are often referred as being sociopathic or psychopathic. They are seen as having no social conscience or guilty feelings. They act as they wish because they do not take others or the rules of society into account. As with other personality disorders, the individuals tend not to be aware of being ill or behaving in inappropriate ways. Their sense of reality differs from that held by the majority of people.

Schizophrenia is a condition that generally produces a schizophrenic personality disorder. Taken from the Greek (skhizein 'to split' and phren 'mind'), it refers to a split between the mind and reality – the mind retreats into its own private world populated by hallucinations, delusions, emotional disturbance and bizarre behaviour. The hallucinations are false perceptions that are seen or heard. The person usually hears voices that tell them what they should do. Delusions represent false beliefs about reality that often cause paranoia, e.g. they believe they are being spied on.

Paranoid schizophrenia CASE STUDY

Harry had served in the army as a cook for ten years. Two years after being discharged, he started to believe he was a famous retired army general – delusions of grandeur – who was being spied on by the Security Services because he had valuable information they did not want him to pass on to anyone. He knew he was being spied on as a voice from the radio had told him and he'd seen men in white boiler suits and with binoculars on the roof opposite his flat. He had also heard them moving around in the roof space above his flat planting listening devices.

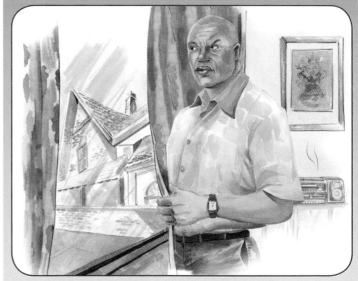

Voice from radio telling him he is being spied on

Autism

Axis 1 of the DSM Classification System includes Disorders of Childhood. These cover attention-deficit/hyperactivity disorders (ADHD), conduct disorders, learning disabilities, mental retardation and autistic disorders.

Autism

Tom's parents have become increasingly concerned about his behaviour and his lack of connection with people. Developmentally, he was considered normal until the age of three. His language development slowed and he became withdrawn. He constantly played repetitive games by himself and any change in routine produced a tantrum. He avoided making eye contact with people, showed little emotion, and did not appear to relate to others, regardless of age. He was diagnosed as having autism.

The main symptom of autism is seen as having a lack of social responsiveness. The child appears to live in their own world and has little need to communicate with others. Behaviour becomes stereotypical and repetitive and any changes in their environment or routine, e.g. cleaning their teeth in the kitchen because the bathroom is in use, will create an adverse reaction in them. Reaction to sensory stimulation, e.g. pain, will produce extreme sensitivity or no reaction. Language is either not used or used differently. Creative ability might be displayed in terms of drawing or music.

Obsessive compulsive disorders (OCD)

Obsessions relate to uncontrollable, repeating and unwanted thoughts that are associated with repetitive, ritualistic behaviour.

Obsessive compulsive disorders

Joseph washes his hands yet again!

Joseph's father died in hospital when he was young and he remembers being told to wash his hands carefully at the end of each hospital visit, so he did not bring any germs home. Thirty years later, following the death of a close friend, he has started to obsessively wash and rewash his hands up to a dozen times each time he has been to the toilet. This is to prevent his hands from becoming contaminated by germs. They are becoming red raw as he scrubs them each time to get rid of any germs. He follows the same procedure or ritual each time. He has been diagnosed as having obsessive compulsive disorder.

Phobias

They are described as being irrational fears that are related to a particular situation or object. The individual is aware that it is irrational and disproportionate to any danger that might be associated with it.

Phobias

Jenny cannot have a shower until her partner first checks the room for spiders. She suffers from arachnophobia – an extreme, irrational fear of spiders that affects her quality of life. She will not shower if her partner is away on business for a couple of nights. She experiences shortness of breath, chest pains, dizziness, pounding of the heart and a feeling that she is about to die. She remembers her mother had a similar fear.

Theory into practice

Can you identify with some of the feelings experienced by the people in the case studies? The difference is that yours are not likely to be as extreme as theirs. You are likely to be able to control them so that they do not prevent your normal functioning. You might have developed strategies to cope with them, e.g. if you are afraid of spiders, you might have bought a 'spider-removing grab'.

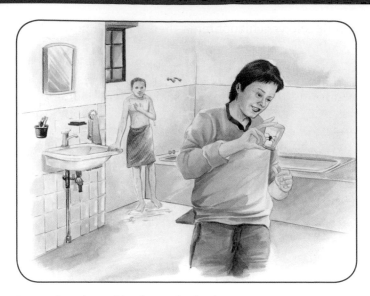

Removing the spider from the bathroom

The underpinning knowledge for the unit has not been arranged within the specification in the same order as the Assessment Evidence Grid. The Assessment activity is, therefore, more appropriately placed at the end of Unit 14.

14.2.3 Causes of mental illness

To look for one cause of an individual's illness is usually too simplistic an approach to take. Cause could be due to a number of factors coming together, at a certain time, to produce an adverse reaction in an individual. Cause can be **multi-faceted** and complex. One set of circumstances may affect an individual in one way whereas it can affect another person differently. It is important to view each person as a unique individual who experiences life in his or her own unique way.

Physical influences

The biological approach to abnormal behaviour sees physical influences playing an important role in an individual's mental health and well being.

- It is suggested that schizophrenia can be caused by excess of dopamine activity or as a result of structural changes in the brain (brains of schizophrenics tend to be lighter) or due to a brain tumour. Possible biological causes for depression have been identified.
- A reduction in the levels of noradrenaline in the brain seems to be linked with depression in some people, whilst a viral infection was present in others who had either unipolar or bipolar

depression. Others have been found to have a relatively inactive frontal cortex whilst hormonal changes, e.g. pre-menstrual or postnatal, can act as a trigger in people who are predisposed to become depressed.
- Alzheimer's involves the wasting away of the cerebral cortex of the brain as a result of disease, brain injury or chemical damage.
- Panic attacks and phobias can be triggered by chemical imbalances that produce the physical symptoms associated with such conditions, e.g. racing heart.
- Injury to the brain as a result of an accident, e.g. falling off a ladder, can also be the cause of mental illness, e.g. antisocial personality disorder.
- Autism, in some children, has been found to be the result of structural or functional brain abnormalities whereas genetic factors have been found in others.

Societal influences

Another cause of mental illness can be societal influences. Depression can result from an individual losing their job. They may feel useless, undervalued and develop a poor self image because they feel no one will want to employ them. They may feel they have let their family down. One of the factors that determines a person's status in society is their job.

Theory into practice

Identify six jobs at random – now put them in order of status or importance. Share your list with another person. Explain why you have made your first and last choices. Where would 'unemployed' go in your list? Why?

If individuals are in a higher status job or career, they are likely to feel good about themselves and their achievements. Feeling good leads to self acceptance, one of the features on M. Jahoda's list (see earlier) of mental health. If they lose their job, then negative feelings can replace the positives and affect their sense of well being and health.

People living in a socially deprived area that has poor housing, services and public image, may find they experience negative reactions of others from outside the area. They may find they are not being offered jobs they are qualified to do and feel it is because they have a 'bad address' – live in an area where people are stereotyped as being criminals and benefit scroungers. They may find that taxis will not drop them off at home because of the area's reputation.

Taxi driving past without stopping

They may find that buses stop running in the evening for the same reason. They may find they have to wait a long time before the landlord carries out repairs. They may find there are few facilities near to where they live compared to other areas. All these things and more can send a subliminal or unspoken message that they are seen as second-class citizens who receive less of a service than others. This in turn can produce stress that, if not dealt with, can trigger such mental illnesses as depression and schizophrenia.

People who use and mis-use drugs, alcohol and substances can receive similar societal messages because of the stereotyping and labelling associated with 'users'.

Theory into practice

What words are used to describe people who are seen as being drug addicts? Mind map the words. Compare them with someone else's mind map. These words are likely to be negative and represent society's view of such people. Being constantly aware that this is how people 'see' you is likely to have a negative effect on your self image and mental well being.

Genetic influences

Genetic influences have been identified as possible causes of some mental illnesses. Studies of twins (Kendler 1983) have shown that where one

twin develops schizophrenia then the likelihood of the other twin doing so is 50% for identical (monozygotic – MZ) twins, whereas it is only 15% in non-identical (dizygotic – DZ) twins. It has also been found that a child of a schizophrenic parent, who has been adopted, is more likely to develop the condition than a child of normal parents, adopted into a family where one parent is schizophrenic (Wender et al 1974).

Monozygotic twins

Studies into twins' anxiety disorders have found a 31% likelihood of one MZ twin developing a panic attack if present in the other but no such likelihood in DZ twins. Studies of close-knit family communities, e.g. the American Amish communities, have indicated that bipolar characteristics can run in families.

Alzheimer's has also been identified as having a genetic basis, again in family and twins studies (Heun et al 2001 and Bergen et al 1997, both cited in Flanagan 1994). It has been found that no one with Down's syndrome (caused by having an extra chromosome – trisomy 21) has survived beyond the age of 67, without developing Alzheimer's.

Socio-environmental influences

There can also be socio-environmental reasons that possibly are at the root of mental illness. This moves away from the societal reasons – the pressures applied by society on the individual – to the more immediate environmental and relationship pressures that affect the individual, on a day-by-day basis. This produces stress, which acts as the trigger for mental illness. Stress, in small doses, can be seen as a positive motivator – the stress that builds up in a sprinter prior to a race is used to explode out of the starting blocks. If stress is experienced over a length of time, the effects become negative as the body and mind become exhausted through having to constantly cope with it.

Sprinter exploding from her blocks

In 1967, two American researchers, Holmes and Rahe, produced a list of life events, taken from 5000 patients' records that had occurred in the months prior to their illness. People were asked to list the events in order of seriousness, in terms of stress. From this, they produced the Social Readjustment Rating Scale (SRRS) that could be used to predict the likelihood of a stress-induced illness. The most stressful life event was death of a spouse followed by divorce, marital separation and jail term. Holidays, Christmas and minor violations of the law were bottom of the list.

Ranking	Life event	Mean value
1	Death of spouse	100
2	Divorce	73
8	Fired from work	47
10	Retirement	45
12	Pregnancy	40
17	Death of best friend	37
27	Beginning or finishing school	26
43	Minor violations of the law	11

Theory into practice

Update the list and put it into a UK context. What would you list as your top ten of most stressful life events? Compare your list with others and identify any cultural, social or religious differences. It is likely that people will have different views on stress – why is this?

Factors of stress (or stressors) also relate to environmental and relationship influences. Living in overcrowded accommodation; constantly not feeling safe or secure; being put down all the time; job demands and feelings of not being in control; excessive noise, temperature extremes; pollution; lack of sleep; anxiety and fear are stressors that can lead to mental illness, in various forms. Not having your own space because of 24-hour caring for a partner, older relative or child with challenging behaviour are also examples of situations that could trigger mental illness through stress.

The range of possible causes of mental illness gives some indication of the complexity involved in diagnosis. It is likely that many mental illnesses have a combination of different related causes. People are individuals and need to be treated as such. This relates to their mental-health needs as much as it does to their physical and emotional needs.

Types of mental illness — Activity 1

1. Select three types of mental illness from the case studies mentioned previously and describe them in detail.

2. Explain, in depth, their possible causes, and discuss how they may be interlinked.

The underpinning knowledge for the unit has not been arranged within the specification in the same order as the Assessment Evidence Grid. The Assessment activity is, therefore, more appropriately placed at the end of Unit 14.

14.2.4 Effects of mental illness

Just as dropping a pebble into a pool causes an ever-widening ripple effect, so can the effects of mental illness on the individual spread outward to affect family, neighbours, the local community and, ultimately, society. There can also be short- and long-terms effects.

The ripple effect

Wayne — CASE STUDY

Wayne, a 20 year old, lives at home with his parents, brother and sister, and developed schizophrenia two years ago. He has been hospitalised for treatment on a couple of occasions and takes medication to manage his symptoms.

The initial effects of schizophrenia on Wayne involved auditory hallucinations and delusions. His family were regular churchgoers and did not feel his 'hearing God speaking to him' was unusual. Nor did his paranoia or fear about the police following him seem too extreme as many young men of his age tended to be stopped and questioned about their activities.

However, when he started to hear God talking to him from the radio, when it wasn't switched on, and his anger about the police following and spying on him turned to violent behaviour at home, they contacted their GP. He arranged for Wayne to be hospitalised until his behaviour could be controlled by medication.

Prior to being admitted into hospital, he lost weight because he ate very little, believing his food was being poisoned. He was in danger of suffering from malnutrition. He stopped taking an interest in his appearance and personal hygiene and accused his family of being agents of the police. He locked himself in his bedroom most of the time, storing his bodily wastes in jars, as he believed they could give people power over him. When he left his room he was verbally aggressive towards his siblings and pushed them out of his way.

Theory into practice

Identify and summarise the short-term physical and psychological effects of the illness on Wayne, prior to going into hospital.

Physical and psychological effects

The short-term physical effects of Wayne's illness are likely to be weight loss, a lowered resistance to infection and headaches as a result of the build-up of toxins in his body due to reduction in the intake of liquids. He is likely to have difficulty sleeping because of his over-active mind. His behaviour – talking to himself, disorganised speech and looking at people in a suspicious way, because he's experiencing paranoia – is likely to draw attention to him, which, in turn, is likely to increase the feelings.

His psychological state of auditory hallucinations and delusion will create feelings of paranoia and persecution, which are manifested in his view of the police and what they and his family are doing against him. This is further demonstrated by his aggression towards siblings. He is likely to quickly make up his mind about things and these conclusions will be based on unusual beliefs created by his illness, e.g. his family are police agents.

Effect on social and emotional health of self and others

He is likely to become socially withdrawn because of his suspicion that people are spying on him. Such withdrawal can make him feel isolated, because he cannot trust anyone, and will worsen his condition.

The social and emotional effects on his family can be devastating, both in the short and long term. Friends of his brother and sister may stop coming around because of his behaviour. They will be uncertain of how he is going to react towards them. They may also hold negative, stereotypical views of 'the mentally ill' and be worried that they may 'catch' something from Wayne! His siblings may be very supportive of their brother or they may feel he is messing up their social lives. His parents may feel torn between supporting him and their other children. They may realise how vulnerable he is but are also aware that their other children have the right to expect to feel safe in their own home and be able to invite friends around.

Labelled

Parents and siblings may find themselves becoming very stressed because of the uncertainty of the situation and not knowing what might happen next. To live in this situation for any length of time could turn stress into depression because of the sense of powerlessness – not being able to do anything about it and feeling no longer in control of their own lives. Prolonged stress can itself lead to heart attacks, strokes, ulcers, raised blood pressure, insomnia and various skin conditions.

This ripple effect could spread to neighbours who are abused by him. Wayne could believe the neighbours are letting the police drill holes in walls and ceilings so they can hear what he is doing and monitor him more closely. They could have difficulty sleeping because of his banging around and shouting in his bedroom, for most of the night, next door.

Ability to cope with daily life

The local community, once they are aware of Wayne's behaviour, could label him as 'mad' or a 'lunatic' or use some other negative term.

Theory into practice

How do you think people in your local community would act towards someone whose behaviour is seen as unusual, abnormal or bizarre? Would they 'label' the individual? If so, what labels or names would be used?

The process of 'sticking labels' on people is known as stigmatising. People are 'marked or branded' by a usually negative term or label and tend to be excluded from mainstream society as a result. This in turn leads to a wider process.

As the diagram illustrates, once a label is 'stuck' on an individual or group of people, they attract a negative image. This develops into a prejudice, a pre-judgement that, if acted upon, will lead to discrimination taking place. This can be followed by harassment.

In the case of Wayne, his behaviour in the local community is likely to attract a label, e.g. 'nutter'. Having been branded as 'one of those' he may also attract other stereotypical labels such as dangerous and head case. People who do not know him will know of him and will make judgements about him based on these labels. Should they meet him on the street, they are likely to act on their prejudices in a variety of ways, most of which will be negative. People might cross over the road so they do not have to pass him. They might talk about him as if he were not there. They might point and say to their friend, 'That's the one I was telling you about – Wayne – you know, Mrs Johnson's boy who isn't quite right in the head.'

'That's the one I was telling you about – Wayne – you know, Mrs Johnson's boy who isn't quite right in the head.'

Theory into practice

If you were Wayne, what effects are these comments likely to have on you and your state of mind? Discuss it in a group or with a partner and mind map it.

Such comments are likely to make the individual feel more alone and isolated. It is likely to push them further into their illness and provide further feeding grounds for their paranoia. Such discrimination could lead to him receiving a poorer service in shops than others. It could lead to him being treated as a second-class citizen because he's seen as being 'different'. It could also lead to harassment by local children calling him names and throwing stones as he walked down the street.

All of these will affect his self image and confidence and will encourage him to withdraw from contact with others.

Ability to relate to others

Not only is Wayne's illness encouraging him to withdraw from contact with others, but also the reaction of others to him and his behaviour is likely to accelerate this process. People with schizophrenia and other personality disorders are not aware of their illnesses and believe their view of the world is the correct one. Those illnesses where people are aware that they are ill, e.g. mood (affective) and anxiety disorders, are not going to be helped by negative labelling and discrimination, which will make them go into themselves more. The more people are treated as 'abnormal', the less able they will be able to connect with others. They are looking for understanding and support, not ridicule.

Effects of labelling on self concept

Argyle (1978) suggested that self-concept or self-image is influenced by four factors:

- the reaction of others provides the individual with an external view of themselves. This is sometimes referred to as the 'looking-glass self' (Cooley 1902) meaning our self image is based, in part, on what others reflect back, or mirror, to us. It is also related to the labelling process or the self-fulfilling prophecy in that the individual, in time, will fit the image that others have created for them. If Wayne is told often enough that he is a 'nutter', he will take that image on board and will start to behave in whatever way a 'nutter' is expected to behave. In other situations, children are praised for producing good work and are told they are clever. As a consequence, they will develop a positive self image.
- People need to compare themselves with others to get some idea of where they stand, and how well they are doing, in the grand scheme of things. A baseline of understanding is needed. Individuals gauge how successful they are by comparing their salaries, size and price of house and car, etc. with others.

'Next door are doing better than us!'

- Self image is also based on the different roles we play in life – mother, son, friend – and their status. This affects the way individuals measure their self worth. Are the roles considered by others to be important, thus giving more status to the self image?
- People use role models, individuals they look up to or like to compare themselves to, and see how they measure up to them. They base their view of themselves on this comparison.

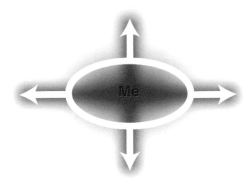

Not only does early prevention, through health checks and education for all, reduce the cost to society of treating serious illness and conditions at a later and more advanced stage. It also indicates the degree of equality that exists within the society. To provide a lesser service to certain groups within society, because of their health conditions, is unfair and morally wrong.

Now consider what have been the influences on your self image, in terms of Argyle's four factors.

What do you think might be the self image of people with mental illness? Identify the factors involved in producing this image.

Cost to society of mental illness

Historically, people with mental illnesses were blamed for any misfortunes that happened to their social grouping. They were used as scapegoats, beaten and cast out into the wilderness, symbolically taking the misfortunes with them.

A study by the Disability Rights Commission 'Equal Treatment: Closing the Gap' (2006 www.drc.org/healthinvestigation) has identified a modern day equivalent in that people with learning disabilities/difficulties and people with mental-health problems face widespread health discrimination. The study found both groups are more likely to suffer major illness, develop serious health conditions at an early age and die of them sooner than other people. This related to cancer, heart disease, high blood pressure and diabetes amongst other conditions. They are less likely to receive adequate treatment or health checks. There appeared to be an assumption amongst many professionals that all health problems were connected to the presenting psychiatric problem or learning disability/difficulty. This is known as 'diagnostic overshadowing'.

The underpinning knowledge for the unit has not been arranged within the specification in the same order as the Assessment Evidence Grid. The Assessment activity is, therefore, more appropriately placed at the end of Unit 14.

14.2.5 Preventative and coping strategies

There is a range of different methods that can help an individual, who has a mental illness, to manage their condition. These can also be used to prevent the illness from occurring in the first place or from returning at a later date.

Access to professional health and informal support

The majority of people, once they are feeling unwell and there is no short-term change in the condition, tend to contact their GP or local pharmacist. Others may go to their local NHS Walk In Service. This applies to physical and mental illnesses although, because of the stigma, individuals may delay going if it is the latter.

In more urgent situations, e.g. if the individual's condition deteriorates, a visit to the local hospital's Accident and Emergency department may be more appropriate.

If partners, family members or neighbours – informal carers – have been struggling to cope with the individual, they may contact Social Services for help and support.

Theory into practice

Identify what help informal carers might be seeking and how it might be met.

Help needed	Help provided
Needs a break from being sole carer providing 24-hour care, seven days a week	Person with illness to go to day care centre twice a week

---

The primary care professionals can help and support individuals and their informal carers by, in the case of GPs and medical staff, prescribing appropriate medication to manage the illness and, in the case of Social Services, providing practical support such as a place at a day care centre or practical help in the home with possible respite care for the family. Referral can be made to secondary tier professionals such as counsellors, occupational therapists, psychologists and psychiatrists.

Positive coping mechanisms

The individual may be introduced to a range of coping mechanisms, all of which are designed to enable them to take control of their lives and overcome their illness. These can also be used to prevent recurrence.

An action plan can be produced with a professional to motivate, provide structure and direction to an individual's life. Such structure provides purpose and direction which many people experiencing depressive conditions lack. An action plan looks forward. It might start with small steps and expectations, e.g. get up by 10 a.m. and clean teeth each morning, and progress to going back to work initially on reduced hours until confidence has been completely restored.

Stress management techniques are actions that can be taken which will reduce stress once it appears, or stop it occurring in the first place. Relaxation exercises, e.g. tensing and relaxing muscles, listening to soothing music, meditation and yoga, are just a few of the techniques that can be used.

Biofeedback is another relaxation technique used to reduce stress levels. The individual is trained to lower their autonomic responses through relaxation techniques. He or she will be linked to a machine, via a sensitive pad, which will give them feedback about their physiological state, e.g. pulse or heart rate, via an electronic signal. By practising relaxation, e.g. deep breathing exercises, the individual can lower the tone of the signal and can reduce their arousal levels.

Monitoring goals and progression

Under the NHS and Community Care Act 1990, people with mental illnesses have the right to have their needs assessed, as part of the care planning process. Once a care plan has been drawn up and implemented, it is essential that it is monitored and reviewed to ensure it is achieving its original goals and remains relevant in meeting the individual's needs.

Monitoring should also relate to such things as medication and other therapies being employed. Is it working and achieving the original goals of restoring the person's health or managing their condition? Improvement in their condition and quality of life would indicate progression towards these goals. If progression is not taking place then alternative strategies should be adopted.

Cognitive techniques

Cognitive psychology suggests disordered cognitions or ways of understanding lead to disordered behaviour. It focuses on encouraging individuals to 'reframe' or see things in a different light. It aims to overcome irrational and illogical beliefs by emphasising the positive rather than the negative aspects of a situation or belief. It encourages cognitive reappraisal or a rethinking to take place.

Is the glass half full or half empty?

Behaviourist techniques

Behaviourists believe bad behaviour is learnt and can therefore be unlearnt. This can be done in a

number of different ways. They differ from other approaches in that they see the cause of mental illness as being immaterial.

In aversion therapy, the individual is injected or given a chemical implant that will produce an adverse reaction if they take the banned substance, e.g. alcohol or drugs.

Systematic desensitisation involves the individual learning to go into a relaxed state before being gradually exposed, over a number of sessions, to whatever they are afraid or phobic of. Each session should see the subject becoming desensitised to the stimulus or fear object.

Flooding is very much a 'sink or swim' treatment where the individual is placed in a situation of maximum exposure to their fear object, e.g. a room with spiders – images and reality – and has to stay until the fear disappears.

All of these approaches involve learning acceptable new behaviours that replace old negative behaviours.

Medication

Medication for mental illness

Drug therapy is also known as chemotherapy. It was the development of drug therapy in the 1950s and 1960s that enabled people to be moved out of 'contained' institutional situations to being cared for in the community. People had been 'stored' or 'warehoused' in institutions for their own, and the community's, good. They were physically cared for but little rehabilitation took place. The new era of drugs – anti-depressive, anti-psychotic and anti-anxiety – meant the symptoms could be managed and controlled in the community.

Drugs enable symptoms to be blocked out or dampened, in the case of schizophrenics, and can lift depression and anxiety. Dosages are individual and it may take some adjustment before the optimum amount is found. There may be side effects that produce worse symptoms – tremors, restlessness, weight gain, dry mouth, lack of emotions, etc. – than those the drug is trying to overcome. Drug therapy can also enable people to lead a normal life.

Counselling and psychotherapy

Talking therapies encourage people with mental illness to gain insight into their behaviour, illness and inner conflict through talking with a counsellor or therapist. Different approaches are used and these are explained under 'Theorist approaches' below.

Electro-convulsive therapy (ECT)

This treatment was widely used prior to the development of drug therapy. It is currently used for depression and involves relaxing the patient, using muscle relaxants and anaesthetics, before applying an electric shock to the temple. This produces memory loss and alleviates depression.

Exercise

The benefits of exercise on a person's sense of well being and self confidence are widely recognised. The subsequent release of endorphins produces a 'feel good' mood. Exercise also produces an enhanced blood supply to the brain, rich in oxygen and nutrients that increase mental alertness. The sense of well being improves self esteem and the exercise can improve self image. In some areas, GPs are prescribing exercise via free membership at a sports centre or a gym. It is also a very powerful preventative technique to use.

Theorist approaches

Psychology can be defined as 'the study of the mind' and 'the science of behaviour and mental processes' (Weber 1991:1). The different views, ideas and hypotheses can be summarised into theories. Most of these theories offer explanations for abnormal behaviour and ways – therapies – of helping restore mental health or balance. A summary of some of these theories and associated therapies is produced in the following table.

Theoretical approach	Theorists	Focus of theory	Therapy
Psychodynamic	Freud, Erickson	Abnormal behaviour is as a result of unresolved, unconscious conflicts	Psychoanalysis – therapist aims to make the unconscious conscious so that the patient can resolve the conflict(s)
Cognitive	Beck, Ellis	Negative internal evaluations of situations or events produce anxiety and exaggerate problems	Therapy aims to restructure negative views to positive views Ellis's approach was known as Rational Emotive Therapy
Humanistic	Rogers, Maslow	Each individual is unique and has the ability to achieve to their full potential – sometimes this gets blocked and help is needed to re-focus	Person-centred counselling enables client to find own solutions, through use of empathy, congruence and unconditional positive regard
Behaviourist	Pavlov, Skinner	Abnormal behaviour is learnt so can be unlearnt	Aversion therapy – people are conditioned to behave in different way Desensitisation involves relaxed, gradual exposure to fear; flooding involves maximum sudden exposure

These theorists offer different explanations for abnormal behaviour and ways of managing it.

> ### Theory into practice
>
> Research into two of these approaches and compare the different therapies. Which approach would you prefer to experience? Why?

> The underpinning knowledge for the unit has not been arranged within the specification in the same order as the Assessment Evidence Grid. The Assessment activity is, therefore, more appropriately placed at the end of Unit 14.

14.2.6 Support for service users with mental-health needs

Support is provided by a wide variety of service and support organisations based in institutions and in the community. Professionals in these organisations, whilst working to similar care values and standards of care, come from different disciplines. They will adopt a way of working that will relate to the medical or social model of care or somewhere on the **continuum** between the two. Their training will develop different skills and approaches to working with mentally ill people.

Hospital-based services are likely to include admission services, such as the Accident and Emergency Department for emergency assessment and possible admission to either an acute psychiatric ward or unit or a closed ward for involuntary admissions. Outpatient clinics and day hospitals/units also offer non-residential help. Some hospitals may have halfway houses in their grounds that are used to prepare patients for a return to living, and coping, in the community.

The staff involved in providing assessment, care and treatment include:

- psychiatrists
- clinical psychologists
- psychiatric nurses
- ward staff
- day care staff
- hospital-based social workers
- residential support staff
- occupational therapists
- general medical staff would also be involved in general medical matters, e.g. a broken leg.

Community-based services can involve those services that support people living in their own homes or in supported houses and hostels.

The professionals may come from a medical background, e.g. community psychiatric nurses, GPs and occupational therapists or from a social work/care background, e.g. approved mental-health social workers, counsellors, therapists, support and care workers, day centre officers and domiciliary workers.

Professionals are increasingly working in multi-disciplinary teams, both in the community and in hospitals. This approach helps produce a more focused and informed approach together with better co-ordination and less duplication of services.

Job roles

The job roles for those working with service users who have mental illness vary but are still governed by the common care values and nationally set care standards. Within the same type of job, e.g. hospital-based psychiatric nurse and community psychiatric nurse, the emphasis and therefore skills, knowledge and care provided, differ. Working on a locked ward with patients who have **acute** conditions and are living in a group situation with people, not of their own choosing, who have differing illnesses and needs requires a different approach to working on a one-to-one basis with someone, living alone in a bed-sit, refusing to take their medication.

Joseph

Joseph is living in a bed-sit and is being supported by Amy, a community psychiatric nurse. He spent a month in a closed psychiatric ward after being diagnosed as having paranoid schizophrenia. He was cared for by various nursing staff, as there were three shifts a day, but had a key worker, John, whose role it was to oversee his care.

Both staff work in different ways with Joseph, although they are both psychiatric nurses.

Both nurses have undergone similar training but are applying their skills in different ways, based on the environment in which they work and the emphasis on approach. Both are working for the benefit of the individual. It is the needs of the individual that change and require different responses.

John working with Joseph in hospital	Amy working with Joseph in the community
John sees him five days a week	Amy visits Joseph in his bed-sit once a week
He, along with other nurses, gives him his medication each day – Joseph has to take it	She checks he's been taking his medication – she needs to persuade him to take it
Although he is Joseph's key worker, he also works with others on the ward – if there is a crisis, he may not be able to spend time with Joseph	She is the only nurse working with him – her role is one of monitoring and support – she has set times to see him – she can respond to him on an individual basis
John is involved in the management of a group of people – the patients on the ward – and tends to use group work skills	She works with him on a one-to-one basis – helping with practical issues such as benefits and basic social and living skills, e.g. healthy eating, on a more personal basis than is possible in hospital
He does one-to-one work with Joseph, assessing his needs, managing his medication and preparing him for discharge – the emphasis of the approach is based on the medical model	She uses person-centred counselling skills to help him find his own solutions for day-to-day problems – her aim is to enable him to live an independent life in the community – this approach focuses more on the social model

Theory into practice

Research, using primary evidence, e.g. talking with a professional who works with people with mental-health needs, where possible, the job roles of two hospital-based professionals and two community-based professionals. How does the emphasis of their roles differ? Do they work to similar standards? What are their views on mentally ill people?

An important support role is fulfilled by advocates. These are people who speak on behalf of individuals who are unable, for whatever reason, to express their own views and needs. They ensure the individual's rights are not ignored. Organisations such as MIND speak out in general on behalf of people with mental illness. Individual representation at appeals and tribunals is carried out by solicitors, welfare rights advisors, and support workers. Informal advocacy may involve a family member, speaking on behalf of their relative, asking a GP to refer the individual for a day care place. Professionals have a responsibility to advocate on behalf of their patient or client to ensure they receive the best service possible to meet their needs.

Speaking on behalf of others

Charities supporting people with mental-health needs

Charities and voluntary bodies are another source of help and support for people with mental illness and their carers. They act as national and local advocates for service users and people who have mental-health problems. They challenge society's negative views and the poor service many experience when dealing with service providers. They support individuals in appeals and negotiations. They take on test cases to clarify the law and individuals' rights to be treated fairly and as individuals.

Locally, self help groups exist so that individuals and their carers can share common experiences and work together to bring about change. Some charities provide services, e.g. advice services and befriending/visiting schemes to fill gaps they believe exist in current service provision. Others provide services that have been **commissioned** by Primary Care Trusts and Social Services, e.g. day centres.

Theory into practice

MIND, SANE, Samaritans and Turning Point are national mental-health charities. Working in groups, choose one charity and research their background and the services they provide. Present your findings to the whole group.

Another group could investigate if there are any local self help groups and report back on their findings.

Empowerment of service users

Since the White Papers of the 1980s that led on to the 1990 NHS and Community Care Act, legislation and policy has focused on putting the patient or client at the centre of the caring process. This has been a very empowering process that has given the individual and their carers control over their own lives and the choices they can make. This process was emphasised in the 1990s through the Care Values Base that was intended to underpin care workers' approach to their work. As well as confidentiality, the other two focuses were to promote equality and diversity as well as rights and responsibilities.

This approach was developed further by the establishment of National Minimum Standards that were identified under the Care Standards Act of 2000; The NHS Plan 2000 and National Service Frameworks, all of which focused on providing a service that was organised around the needs, preferences and choices of informed patients and their carers. The involvement of service users in focus groups, user groups and forums so that the service providers and planners can find out their views, needs and feedback on current services has issued in a new era of partnership working between service users, carers and professionals.

This has been added to by the establishment of complaints procedures and the clear spelling out of people's rights. Without knowing what an individual's rights are, it is difficult to know if they are receiving what they are entitled to. This applies not only to services and equipment but also to attitudes and interactions. Departments have been created to objectively investigate complaints, and advocates support service users and their families through this process.

Theory into practice

Research which department would investigate complaints by patients in a hospital. This could be done via the Internet or by visiting a hospital to pick up a pamphlet on their complaints procedure.

Implications of voluntary and involuntary admission to hospital

People who are ill would usually choose to go into hospital if it would make them better or at least improve their health. Patients would tend to work positively with professionals so they could get better. The relationship would be based on trust and a sense of placing themselves into the hands of professionals in whom they had faith. This trusting relationship would be part of the healing process because the patient would expect to be cared for. The same could not be said for someone who has been forced to become a patient.

Theory into practice

Refer back to the case study regarding Harry, who had paranoid schizophrenia. Imagine how he would feel if he was forcibly taken to a hospital believing people were out to get him. What sort of relationship is likely to develop between him and the staff? How might this affect his recovery?

Staff are faced with ethical issues on a daily basis relating to involuntary admission. Is it right to force treatment on someone who doesn't want it? Is it right to detain someone against their will because it is 'thought' they might harm someone else? Is it right to detain someone for longer than a criminal who had been found guilty of a similar offence, e.g. assault, because of their illness? These are issues that society generally leaves for professionals to resolve, within the confines of the law.

Assessment of appropriate services for service users

The 1990 NHS and Community Care Act gave individuals the right to have their needs assessed as part of the care planning process. The meeting of such needs, unless there is a statutory requirement to meet them, depends on locally set criteria and available resources. Governments are unhappy about passing laws that give people the right to have their needs met because of the cost implications. Government would be handing over financial control to front line professionals. There are never enough resources to meet everyone's needs and the politicians see their role as deciding on financial priorities.

The assessment process should include all the key people involved, e.g. the potential service user, family, neighbours (who might be informal carers) and others. The aim is to identify clearly what the individual's needs are and who is meeting them, if at all, at present. From that basis, planning how the needs can be met becomes the next step.

Mental Health Act 1983

Whilst the NHS and Community Care Act aims to support the individual by meeting their caring needs, the Mental Health Act offers a different type of support. It aims to maintain a balance between the individual's civil liberties and the need to make decisions about their welfare and treatment, when they are unable to do so for themselves, because of their mental state. Compulsion is seen as the last resort and voluntary or informal admission is the preferred outcome.

If compulsion is used, then the Act protects the individual by clearly laying down the periods of time such action can last and the appeals process to be followed. The Mental Health Act Commission was set up to act as watchdog over patients' rights and interests. Such protection is essential. It was not unknown in the 1800s, and before, for wealthy older family members to be certified as 'mad' and locked away in private asylums so that other family members could gain access to their money and property, as they were no longer deemed capable of managing their own affairs!

Theory into practice

Explain how the two Acts support each other and the individual. In what ways could they be improved?

Assessment activities (AO1 – AO4)

Service user X   CASE STUDY

1. Produce a guide for new members of staff about mental illness. As the introduction to the Guide, explain, in depth, the concept and definition of mental illness. This should be followed by a comprehensive overview of **three** of the following types of mental illness, explaining their possible causes and relating these to mental-health needs. You can choose from:
   - Alzheimer's
   - depressive illnesses
   - generalised anxiety disorder
   - personality/perception disorders
   - autism
   - obsessive compulsive disorder
   - phobias. (AO1)

2. For the Guide, produce a case study for service user X who has one of the mental illnesses you have written about. (AO2)

3. Using the case study, describe and fully explain **three** likely effects of your chosen illness on the service user, relating your work, and examples, to day-to-day situations, in general and specific terms. (AO2)

4. Complete the Guide by considering and making reasoned judgements about the main preventative and coping strategies and analyse how two health or social care services could support your service user. (AO3)

5. The Guide should clearly explain how causes can be interrelated and the difficulties involved in separating them out. (AO1)

6. Produce a presentation, with speaker notes, which describes one of the following pieces of legislation – NHS and Community Care Act 1990 or Mental Health Act 1983 – and discuss the possible impact of such legislation on people with mental illness. (AO3)

7. Conclude the presentation by evaluating, giving **two** examples of how mental illness is or has been defined. (AO4)

8. Research into, and produce evidence of, how the media portray people with mental illness. Consider **one** positive and **one** negative effect of this, and make reasonable recommendations for how this can be improved upon. (AO4)

Unit 15 Social Trends

Contents

About this unit

Within this unit you will investigate:

- social trends and patterns of family life – the ways in which our lives today have changed in recent years (the last 50 years)

- reasons for changes in the structure of the family and the roles of individuals within families and households. This will include analysing changes in people's attitudes and changes in the structure of society. This involves a **macro** and **micro** approach

- changes to service provision available to the family and individuals – you will need to be aware of statutory, private, voluntary and informal providers and how these have adapted to major structural changes in society, for example the **ageing population**

- how to use data to explore and draw conclusions about the trends and patterns of family life by studying primary and secondary research of both a quantitative and qualitative nature.

This unit is assessed through one exam paper consisting of five questions, which will test your ability to interpret data and analyse the reasons for the patterns shown.

Family life has changed from 50 years ago

Which is the typical family today?

Introducing this unit

If you were to do a quick survey of the other members of your class and asked them about their family, it is likely that you will find that they belong to a wide range of family types. Equally, if you were to ask your grandparents about changes they have experienced during their lifetime, they would provide you with a fascinating image of how society has changed in recent years. One of the main differences between life today and in the past is the much greater diversity of relationships we are likely to experience. It is becoming increasingly difficult to define a typical family and all of the groups shown in the photographs could be regarded as typical in our society. Your great grandparents' lives would have been fairly predictable. They would have married at a young age and would have had a large number of children, several of whom might not have survived beyond their first birthday. The couple would have remained married throughout their lifetime. Your great grandmother would almost certainly have outlived her husband and they would have remained in the same community throughout their lifetime. Unless they were rich they would have left school by the age of 14 and the husband would have worked in the same job until he retired. There was a high level of predictability about their lives. They would probably have lived in an extended family very close to their other relatives.

Your life is likely to be very different, particularly if you are female. The certainties of the past have disappeared. Social scientists use the term modernity to describe the period up until the late 20th century. This was characterised by life being very predictable and the pattern of life was unchanging. We are now living in a more post-modernist world, one characterised by the phrase 'the pick and mix society'. You are able to select your lifestyle and relationships much as one used to select the pick and mix bag of sweets from Woolworths. You could choose the varieties you liked and the next time you went into the shop you could make different selections. Life is becoming a little like that – we can now move from one relationship to another without feeling guilty or being **stigmatised** by our society.

In this unit it is necessary to look at the trends of family life and consider explanations for such trends by looking at economic and societal changes. When studying trends it is important to look for patterns in the information. Does the data suggest an increase or decrease? If so, has the change been rapid or gradual? Have there been fluctuations in the data? Perhaps there was a sudden increase for a short period of time. Why might this have occurred? You do not need to include statistics in your explanation – just look for an overall picture. You will have a lot of opportunity to practise this skill throughout this unit.

15.2.1 Social trends and patterns of family life

Nuclear	Extended	Reconstituted	One parent
Dual worker	Childless	Same sex	Single person

Some of the family and household relationships available to individuals in society today

The nuclear family

> **Nuclear family:** the group that most people today recognise as the typical family. It is the family which politicians and the media tend to promote. Other family types are compared with the nuclear family which is still seen as the norm by most people.

Despite the changes that have occurred in the last 50 years, the most common relationship is the one-family household, which often has a maximum of two children. This is known as the nuclear family, sometimes referred to as the cereal packet family. It consists of two parents and a number of children who live in relative isolation from other family members, remaining in contact by telephone, text, email and the occasional visit. It would be a mistake to suggest, as some observers do, that the nuclear family has been replaced by alternative relationships, as it remains the type of family that most young people aspire to live in. The majority of people do spend at least part of their life in a two-parent family.

The advantages of living in this type of family are:

* It provides a stable environment for the primary socialisation of children. This is where children learn the norms, values and culture of society. They understand through rewards and sanctions what is regarded as acceptable and unacceptable behaviour.
* It provides for the physical needs of its members – food, clothing and shelter. It is regarded as an economic unit and parents have the financial responsibility for their children.

* It functions to provide stability for the adult members, both sexually and emotionally.
* Most health care is provided within the family before specialists become involved.

Some of the disadvantages that individuals see in this type of relationship are:

* The family can be too intense and suffocate individuality. Women in the past often tended to suffer as a result of the roles they were expected to play – domestic work and childcare.
* The dark side of the family – child abuse and domestic violence can often be difficult to detect in a small family environment.

Of all households in 2005, 57% were couple families compared with 70% in 1971. The biggest fall has been in couple families with three or more dependent children (Social Trends 2006).

The number of children

Mother born 1930s average 2.46 children

Mother born 1980s average 1.74 children

Trends in birth rates

165

A significant trend in the last 50 years has been the continued decline in the birth rate and fertility rate.

> **Birth rate:** the number of babies born per thousand of the population per year.
>
> **Fertility rate:** the number of babies born per thousand women of child-bearing age per year.

The fertility rate has fallen from 91 in 1961 to 55 in the year 2000. This clearly results in a decline in completed family size. The peak of 2.46 children was reached for women born in 1934. This corresponds with the 1960's baby boom. Family size has declined for subsequent generations and is projected to decline to around 1.74 children for women born in the mid 1980s. Women born in 1958 and now at the end of their child-bearing years have an average of 1.99 children. This decline in average family size has major health and social care implications which will be discussed later in the unit.

Extended families

> **Extended family:** a family consisting of more than two generations living together or in close proximity. The family can be extended vertically through grandparents or horizontally through, for example, two or more brothers living together with their wives and children.

Until recently this family structure had been in decline but because of significant changes within society a revival may be taking place. The growth of the multi-cultural society has led to the extended family becoming a part of many Asian communities. The ageing population, combined with the cost of care has meant an increase in sons, and particularly daughters, having to take responsibility for their parents in the later years of their lives. A survey in 2005 by 'Propertyfinder', an estate agency website, found that almost 16% of those questioned were considering moving a parent into their home in that year. This finding supports other research which suggests that '3-g families' (those with three generations under one roof) are on the increase. An interesting recent development has been the growth in the number of children in their 20s continuing to live with their parents, largely because of spiralling housing costs and student debts. Some of this

generation may have children of their own thus creating a type of extended family.

Some of the advantages of the extended family are:

- More adults to share the responsibility of bringing up children such as helping with childcare and babysitting.
- The emotional burden can be reduced because more people can contribute towards any family problems or crises that may arise.
- Younger members of the family may benefit from the wisdom and experience of their grandparents.

Some of the potential disadvantages are:

- Lack of space for individuals to develop their personality and freedom.
- There is less opportunity for the family to move geographically because of the relatively large numbers.

Reconstituted families

The reconstituted family

Reconstituted family: sometimes called a step family, this is formed when one or both partners have been married before and following divorce or death remarry and may bring their children with them into the new relationship.

This family type is on the increase largely because of the rise in divorce and the increase in remarriage and cohabitation. Reconstituted families are unique because children are likely to also have close ties with their natural parent. Children may find themselves pulled in two directions and they may have tense relationships with their step-parents. On the other hand, the children may benefit by belonging to a closer happier family away from one of their natural parents who was experiencing relationship difficulties. The General Household Survey showed that 10% of all families with dependent children in Great Britain were stepfamilies in 2004/05. Over 80% consisted of a stepfather and natural mother. This is clearly because children tend to stay with their natural mother rather than their father when a separation takes place. The 2001 census showed that 38% of cohabiting couples with dependent children were stepfamilies compared with 8% of married couple families.

One parent families (lone parent families)

Lone parent/one parent family. This can be formed through either the death of a partner, divorce, unmarried mother/father, or through choice.

The most common lone parent is formed through divorce. Despite the media often giving the impression that the number of teenage pregnancies is out of control, the figure is relatively low, although England and Wales does have one of the highest teenage conception rates in Europe. In 2003 there were 8,024 conceptions for under-16 girls of which 57% led to an abortion (Social Trends 2006).

The percentage of households that are lone parent with dependent children has risen from 3% in 1971 to 7% in 2005 (Social Trends 2006). There are now approximately 1.7 million lone parent families in Britain, making up about 25% of all families. It is estimated that about one-third of all children will spend some time in a lone parent family.

Lone parents continue to be criticised by many social observers for some of the problems in society, for example anti-social behaviour and under-achievement at school by some students. This attitude is usually based upon prejudice and ignorance and a misconception that such problems did not exist in the past before lone parenthood existed to the extent it does today.

Different families   Activity 1

1 What is meant by the term 'lone parent families'? Explain the advantages and disadvantages of this type of family.

2 Why is the 'extended family' no longer a viable situation? Explain the advantages of having an extended family.

3 Explain the advantages and disadvantages of the 'nuclear family'.

4 What is meant by the 'reconstituted family'? Explain the advantages and disadvantages associated with this type of family.

Dual worker families and conjugal roles

Dual worker family: this is where both partners contribute to the family income by having paid employment.

Conjugal roles: the roles played by adult males and females within a family. They may be *segregated* (separate roles for the male and female) or they may be *joint* (shared equal roles between the adult male and female).

The dual worker family has become an essential feature of many relationships for a number of reasons. The increased cost of bringing up children and the child-centred nature of family life ensure that two incomes are required. Women have achieved increasing equality and independence both within the home and in the workplace despite the continuing existence of discrimination and sexism.

One effect of these changes is the move away from segregated roles towards joint conjugal roles within the family. The latter suggests that household and childcare tasks are shared much more equally within a relationship and that the '**new man**' is a feature particularly found in young couples.

Not everyone is convinced that men have reduced the triple shift placed upon women (paid work, housework and caring for relatives when they are sick). Many **feminists** continue to believe that women are disadvantaged in a relationship and that men continue to exploit their partners.

Childless couples

Another interesting trend is the growth in childless couples. There has been a rise in childlessness for women at age 35 from 15% of those born in 1949 to 27% of those born in 1969. The proportions of women reaching the end of the child-bearing years (age 45) who remained childless rose from 13% in 1949 to 18% of those born in 1959. A survey of 2,428 adults conducted in 2006 by the Skipton Building Society found that one-fifth was choosing to remain childless. The possible explanations for this trend are: rising consumer debt, pension worries and rising house prices. In addition there is some evidence that many people are choosing to enjoy their lifestyle instead of adding more pressure with the cost of bringing up children. This is often referred to as the growth of **individualism** in society.

Homosexual couples

Elton John and partner

Same sex couples have been given greater recognition through the Civil Partnership Act, 2004. This allows civil ceremonies to take place in front of a registrar and two witnesses at registry offices throughout the UK. This gives civil partnerships the same legal weight as marriages, apart from the fact that the ceremony cannot be carried out in a church or religious building. A lot of publicity was recently given when Elton John entered into a civil partnership with his long-time partner. Same sex couples remain a controversial issue within society and people are often divided on religious and cultural grounds in their attitude towards such relationships. This is particularly true when issues of adoption arise for couples of the same sex.

> ### Theory into practice   Family size
>
> Look up the 2006 census data on www.statistics.gov.uk and study the trends in completed family size, fertility rates by age of mother and the average age of mothers when giving birth to their first child (Tables 2.15, 2.16 and 2.17).
>
> What do these statistics suggest about changes in family size and women's attitudes towards childbirth? Discuss your findings as a whole group.

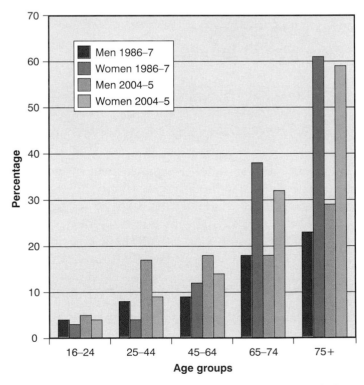

Table A: People living alone: by sex and age, Great Britain 1986–87 and 2004–05
Source: Social Trends 2006, p 23

Single person households

There has been a rise in single person households from 18% of households in 1971 to 29% of all households in 2005. The largest increase has been with people under pension age. The term 'singledom' has been applied to this phenomenon and it is sometimes found amongst established couples choosing to have a close relationship whilst living in separate homes.

One of the key implications for health and social care is the large number of men and women aged 75 and over who live alone and the impact this has upon care provision. This will be discussed at a later stage.

Homelessness

Samia Smith supporting a Shelter appeal

Valid and accurate figures on the number of people who are homeless are notoriously difficult to find. The actress Samia Smith promoted a Shelter Appeal highlighting the growing number of children living in poor housing conditions and the impact this has on their health and future life chances. Shelter, the main pressure group working with the homeless, hopes to get a pledge from the government to end bad housing for the next generation of children and to commit to building more council and housing association homes.

The statistics for the homeless are likely to underestimate the real number because many people are not recorded as homeless because they are staying with friends and relatives and sleeping

on their floors. From a health and social care perspective the issue of homelessness presents a particular difficulty. Many of them suffer from physical and mental health problems and they are part of a shifting population. The statutory authorities have an obligation to ensure that suitable accommodation is available for applicants who are eligible for assistance, have become homeless through no fault of their own, and who fall within a priority need group. Such groups include families with children, and households that include someone who is vulnerable, for example because of pregnancy, domestic violence, old age, or physical or mental disability. The main problem is that there are simply not enough places to accommodate everyone in need.

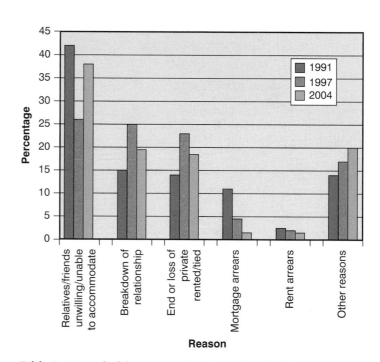

Table B: Households accepted as homeless by local authorities: by main reason for loss of last settled home
Source: Social Trends 2006, p 153

Unemployment

Unemployment statistics are another good example where those reading the data need to be suspicious as to what extent they present an accurate picture of the number of people out of work. The figures tend to show those who are seeking employment and may exclude many women who are not registered as unemployed because of childcare commitments and people who are temporarily unemployed. In addition, of course, some people may be on the unemployment list but working in the black economy.

Unemployment rates are linked to sex and ethnic group as is shown by Table C.

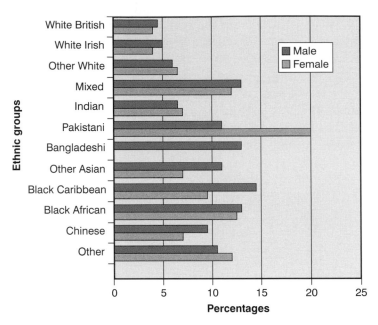

Table C: Unemployment rates: by ethnic group and sex 2004
Source: Social Trends 2006, p 61

Migration and immigration

Immigration: people moving into a country to live.

Emigration: people leaving a country to settle elsewhere.

The movement of people in and out of the UK increasingly creates a **multi-cultural society** which has implications for health and social care services. The pattern of people entering and leaving the UK changed during the 20th century. During the first four decades there was a net loss of people due to migration, but since 1983 there has generally been a net gain. In 2004 nearly 222,600 more people migrated to the UK than left it.

The issue of migration has always been politically controversial and continues to be so, with the media concentrating upon asylum seekers and refugees and some politicians exploiting people's fears of changes taking place in their communities.

Births outside marriage

Although most children are born to married couples, there has been a large increase in the proportion of births occurring outside marriage. In 1980 12% of births in the UK were outside marriage. By 2004 this figure was 42%. This figure is amongst the highest in all European countries. However, it must be placed alongside the fact that most of the increase in the number of births outside marriage has been a result of an increase in jointly registered births rather than those registered to only one parent. This suggests a stable cohabiting couple and does not support the view that children are being born to couples not in a relationship.

Cohabitation

One clear trend in recent years is the increase in cohabitation whereby a couple live together in a permanent relationship without having gone through a legal marriage. According to the General Household Survey for 2002, amongst those aged 16–59, 25% of non-married men and 28% of non-married women were cohabiting. The significance of this data for marriage has led to two opposing interpretations. Some see it as an alternative to marriage and a rejection of marriage as an institution. Others view it as a trial marriage which in most cases will eventually lead to a formal marriage. Most cohabiting couples intend to and do get married if they have children.

The conclusion to draw from these trends is that the pattern of family life is much more diverse and complex than at any time in the past. As an individual one is likely to experience several of the relationships outlined above throughout one's lifetime.

Assessment activity 15.2.1

	1971	1981	1991	2001	2005
One person					
Under state pension age	6	8	11	14	15
Over state pension age	12	14	16	15	14
One-family households					
Couple					
No children	27	26	28	29	29
1–2 dependent children	26	25	20	19	18
3 or more dependent children	9	6	5	4	4
Non-dependent children only	8	8	8	6	6
Lone-parent					
Dependent children	3	5	6	7	7
Non-dependent children	4	4	4	3	3
Two or more unrelated adults	4	5	3	3	3
Multi-family households	1	1	1	1	1
All household (millions)	18.6	20.2	22.4	23.8	24.2

Table D: Great Britain households by type of household and family (percentages)
Source: Social Trends 2006, p 22

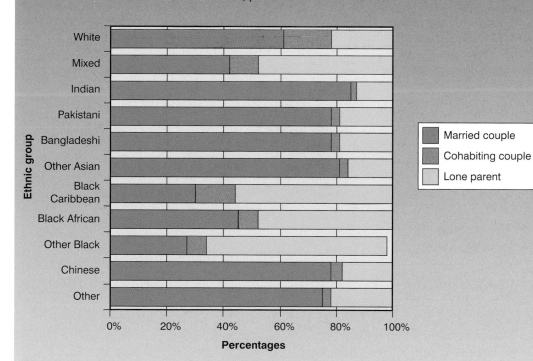

Table E: Families with dependent children: by ethnic group and family type 2001
Source: Social Trends 2006, p 25

Using the tables answer the following questions:

1 Identify and explain two trends in the data on one-family households and lone parents in Table D.

2 Identify two reasons why the data in the tables might not give an accurate picture of family structure in society.

3 Identify and explain two trends in the data in Table E.

4 To what extent is the married couple family the typical family in Britain today?

15.2.2 Reasons for change in the structure of the family and roles of individuals

It is important to explain the reasons for the trends identified in the previous section. A number of key changes have taken place in society influencing every life stage from birth to death. Some of the changes have been brought about by changes in legislation, others through a shift in attitudes and values.

Divorce

Marriage breakdown, often leading to divorce, is a familiar feature of family life in the 21st century. The drawing up of pre-nuptial agreements by the rich and famous is a reflection of the reality of a likely breakdown in the relationship. The diagram below shows some reasons for the change in divorce:

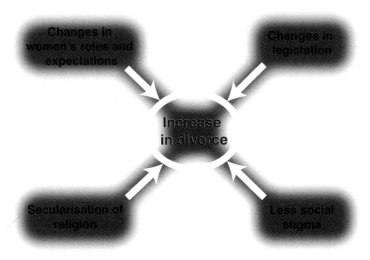

Many observers of society would suggest that the increase in divorce has been a key reason for wider changes within the family and the increase in diversity identified in the previous section. The most significant change took place in 1971 when the Divorce Reform Act came into force. This act removed the need for 'guilty parties' to be identified, replacing this with 'irretrievable breakdown' as the sole grounds for divorce. Such changes made divorce considerably easier and are the main reason for the dramatic rise in the divorce rate after 1971, from 74,000 divorces in 1971 to 126,000 divorces in 1976. New legislation came into force in 1984 reducing the period a couple needed to be married before they could petition for divorce, this changed from three years to one year.

More recently, in 1996 partners simply had to assert that the marriage had broken down and they had undergone a 'period of reflection' to consider whether a reconciliation was possible. Greater use of mediation was encouraged. This change reflected a growing concern amongst observers and politicians that divorce was too easy and individuals were not taking marriage seriously and that they should consider ways of overcoming any difficulties they may have. The **New Right** and **New Labour** were influential in this change of approach and they reflected a growing concern about instability within the family. Despite the attempt to reduce the number of divorces, in 2004 there were 167,100, the fourth successive annual rise. The average age of divorce has increased over time from 39 in 1991 to 43 in 2004 for husbands and from 36 to 40 for wives for the same period. This can partly be explained by the growth in **empty nest families** and **empty shell marriages**.

Changes in legislation alone would not explain the rise in divorce. With regard to divorce, it is important to look at the way women's roles have changed in the last thirty years. The growing independence of women and their increased status in society has led to them no longer having to tolerate an unhappy marriage. Since the 1990s most divorce petitions have been initiated by women. Attitudes have changed from the time when only men could divorce women. It took until 1923 for some equality to be established. Women no longer need marriage as a means of economic support; other means are available through work or the welfare benefit system. Abusive relationships may have been tolerated in the past because women had fewer options; today they know they do not have to stay in situations that they find unbearable. However, it is important to note that some women are still dependent upon their partner's income and many domestic abuse situations fail to reach the courts.

Secularisation: the decline in religious beliefs, religious behaviour and the role of the church.

Fewer people feel bound by traditional religious teaching and consequently church vows such as 'until death do us part' play less significance in a relationship. However, church white weddings remain popular but they are one option from a long list of wedding procedures.

Today there is much less social stigma attached to divorce as most of us know people who have separated and the media constantly reminds us of celebrities who have relationship problems and others who have undergone multiple marriages.

Remarriage

In order to understand the impact of divorce upon the family and relationships it is important to look at patterns and trends in remarriage.

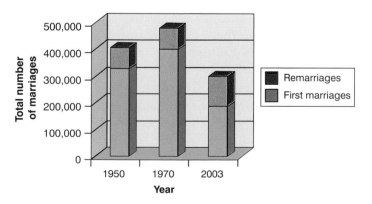

Table F: Marriage and remarriage trends through the 20th century

Serial monogamy: the pattern of marriage in which an individual can have several marriage partners over the course of his or her lifetime. It is becoming increasingly common in British society.

Increasingly it is likely to witness a wedding, which involves at least the bride, and/or groom stepping down the aisle for at least the second time. This suggests that marriage is still regarded with status – what has changed is that people are unwilling to stay in an unhappy relationship but are willing to try again. This is an important fact to remember when considering the family and its stability or instability in society.

Weddings — Activity 2

The Church of England has launched a campaign to promote the advantages of church weddings over civil ceremonies by marketing its 16,000 parish churches at a series of national wedding shows. Since 1994, the number of civil ceremonies in 'approved premises' has risen to more than 50,000 a year, while the number of Church of England marriages has dropped by 40% to around 60,000, one in four of all weddings.

1. Do you think that a decline in church weddings indicates a growing rejection of marriage and a decline in its importance?

2. Describe the pattern shown in the table on marriage trends.

3. Give examples of the growth in secularisation in society.

4. In what ways has the increase in divorce benefited family members and what problems does it possibly create?

Contraception

When attempting to explain the changing role of women, reference must be made to the change in sexual behaviour and the freedom brought about by the development of contraception. Women in the UK from the 1960s onwards were the first to be able to control their fertility with any degree of reliability with the introduction of effective and safe contraception. This has freed men and women to have sex without necessarily intending marriage or even a relationship. It is also, of course, an important means of avoiding sexually transmitted diseases.

Other significant advances that have increased women's control over their own fertility include:

IVF treatment	Hormone treatments
Surrogate motherhood	Fertility drugs

Such advances have been paramount in providing women with choices about their lives which were not available 50 years ago.

Abortion

The legalisation of abortion in 1967, its amendment in 1996 and the Human Fertilisation and Embryology Act 1990 provide further evidence of the increase in options available to women today. The 1967 Act was a means whereby 'back street abortions' were greatly reduced and women were given the chance to seek proper medical attention.

Abortion is allowed up to 24 weeks on condition that continuing with the pregnancy involves a greater risk than having a termination to:

- the physical or mental health of the woman, or
- the physical or mental health of the woman's existing children.

Abortion is allowed after 24 weeks if there is:

- risk to the life of the woman
- evidence of severe foetal abnormality, or
- risk of grave physical and mental injury to the woman.

An abortion must be:

- agreed by two doctors
- carried out by a doctor, and
- carried out in a government-approved hospital or clinic.

About 87% of abortions take place within the first 12 weeks of pregnancy. In some parts of the country it is difficult to access abortion after 12 weeks.

Cultural and racial diversity

Culture: the way of life of a particular society or social group. It normally includes: customs, shared values and social norms.

Race: the belief that it is possible to divide the human population into groups having distinct inherited physical characteristics.

Ethnic group: people who share common history, customs, identity, language and religion.

It is more appropriate to look at diversity (differences) between people on cultural rather than racial grounds. Most towns and cities in the UK contain people from many different ethnic and religious backgrounds. This creates the multi-cultural society that now exists in this country. This is clearly shown in Table H on page 175.

Such diversity requires health, social care and childcare workers to be sensitive towards the particular needs and requirements of people from different cultures and backgrounds. Society also needs to show tolerance towards norms and values which may be different to those of the majority of people. Research carried out at Essex University in 2000 indicates that only 39% of British-born Afro-Caribbean adults under the age of 60 are in a formal marriage, compared with 60% of white adults. Moreover, this group is more likely than any other group to intermarry. Relationships between Asian parents and their children are also very different from those that characterise white families. Children tend to respect religious and cultural traditions, and they feel a strong sense of duty to their families, and especially to their elders. However, there is growing evidence that third

Theory into practice

Table G: Abortion rates: by age
Source: Social Trends 2006, p 31

What are the main trends in abortion shown by the above data?

	White British	White Irish	Mixed	Indian	Pakistani	Bangladeshi	Black Caribbean	Black African	Chinese
Christian	75.7	85.7	52.3	5.0	1.1	0.5	73.7	68.8	21.1
Buddhist	0.1	0.2	0.7	0.2	-	0.1	0.2	0.1	15.1
Hindu	-	-	0.9	44.8	0.1	0.6	0.3	0.2	0.1
Jewish	0.5	0.2	0.5	0.1	0.1	-	0.1	0.1	0.1
Muslim	0.1	0.1	9.7	12.6	91.9	92.4	0.8	20.0	0.3
Sikh	-	-	0.4	29.2	0.1	-	-	0.1	-
Any other religion	0.2	0.3	0.6	1.7	0.1	-	0.6	0.2	0.5
No religion	15.7	6.2	23.3	1.8	0.6	0.5	11.3	2.4	53.0
Not stated	7.7	7.4	11.6	4.7	6.2	5.8	13.0	8.2	9.8
Total (1000s)	50,366	691	674	1,052	747	283	566	485	243

Table H: Main ethnic groups by religion 2001 (percentages)
Source: Social Trends 2006, p 14

generation Asian children are rebelling against these traditions, as witnessed by the recent disturbances in cities such as Oldham and Bradford.

Increasing older population

Queen celebrates 'grey power' with a party at the palace

Sixty year olds have been renamed **GOTYS** – Getting older, thinking younger – by social and economic analysts who say that many 60 year olds feel in the prime of life and are 'ageing positive'.

This 'ageing population' is a key factor in explaining many of the recent social trends in society.

Year	Under 16	Over 65
1971	14.3 million	7.4 million
2004	11.6 million	9.6 million

A comparison of under 16 and over 65 age groups
Source: Social Trends 2006

By 2021 it is projected that 17.6% of the population will be under 16 and 19.7% will be aged 65 and over. This can be explained by the continuing fall in the birth rate combined with longer life expectancy because of improving medical advances, healthier lifestyle and better working practices and environmental conditions. The huge impact of this on the health and care services will be examined in the next section.

Decreasing birth rates

Year	1961	1971	1981	1991	2000
Fertility rate	91	84	62	64	55

Decreasing birth rate/fertility rate
Source: Social Trends 2006

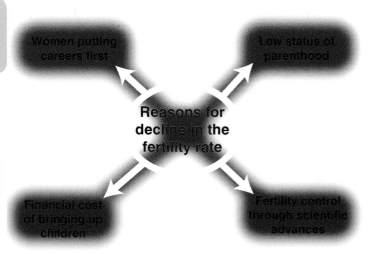

Women putting careers first

Low status of parenthood

Reasons for decline in the fertility rate

Financial cost of bringing up children

Fertility control through scientific advances

The fertility rate has decreased by almost 50% in the last 40 years. This hugely significant trend is clearly the result of women having greater independence and control over their lives. The growing importance of women in the workplace, combined with their changing priorities, means that it is very unlikely that society will return to the high fertility levels experienced at the end of the 19th and early 20th century.

Having a baby   Activity 3

Year	1971	2004
Age of mother	23.7	27.1

Age of mother at birth of first child
Source: Adapted from Social Trends 2006

Big rise in pregnancy among the over 40s as women delay first baby.

After spending her 20s building her career in management, Marion Frostrick tried to get pregnant in her early 30s. She found she could not conceive. She spent the next 10 years trying and finally resorted to IVF. She got pregnant aged 41 and now, aged 47, she works as a management trainer and lives with her husband and two children in Oxford.

(Adapted from an article in the *Independent* 24.02.06)

1. What are the main reasons women are delaying having their first baby and having smaller families?

2. Discuss the main advantages and disadvantages of the big rise in pregnancy among the over 40s.

3. To what extent has the ability of women to control their fertility played a significant part in the growing equality of women in society?

Smaller workforce and economic factors

One consequence of an ageing population has been to add pressure to a workforce which is growing at a much slower rate than the over 65 population. The working population (16–65) produces the income and wealth to support the dependent population (0–16 and 65+). As the following table shows, the problem is not so much with children, where a decline in the birth rate has reduced the pressure on this age group, but with the rapidly expanding number of people living to 75+. Not only does this group put extra pressure upon the health and social

care services but they are part of the 'pension time bomb' that the government constantly reminds us of.

Age group	1971	2021	% change
Under 16	14,256,000	11,399,000	−25%
25–34	6,991,000	8,834,000	+26%
35–44	6,512,000	8,279,000	+27%
65–74	4,764,000	6,610,000	+38%
75+	2,644,000	6,129,000	+131%

Extracted age groups 1971–2021
Source: Adapted from Social Trends 2006

As a consequence of the increased burden of care for older adults on the working population, John Hutton, the Work and Pensions Secretary, announced in February 2006 that a rise in the state pension age is inevitable for people aged 50 or younger. A later retirement age would be introduced by 2020 and the proposal to equalise retirement for men and women at 65 may have to be put back to as late as 69 by 2050.

Another consequence of a smaller increase in the working population is the problem of recruiting staff in shortage areas of work, particularly the lower paid sections of the health and social care services. This problem is likely to increase as the smaller under-16 age group reach the age of employment.

The problem of a smaller increase in the working population was highlighted in an article in the *Observer* (10.08.03) which interviewed Cheryl Baptiste, who arrived in East London from Grenada in 2000 to work in the NHS. Across Britain many thousands of NHS staff have travelled from around the world to work in Britain's health service and continue to arrive in increasing numbers. If they were to leave, the healthcare system would collapse. Cheryl works at Homerton Hospital which serves part of Hackney, East London, and she works alongside staff from Finland, South Africa, the Philippines, Turkey and China. This situation does not just apply to nurses; almost two out of five consultants at the hospital are not British.

Migration and immigration

The difficulty of recruiting workers is increased by the fact that migration out of Britain for both men and women is highest in the 25 to 44 age group, whilst those over retirement age and children under 15 had the lowest numbers emigrating.

According to a report by the World Bank, in October 2005, Britain has lost more skilled workers to the global 'brain drain' than any other industrialised country. More than 1.44 million graduates have left the UK to work in countries such as the United States, Canada and Australia. That far outweighs 1.26 million immigrant graduates in the UK, leaving a net 'brain loss' of some 200,000 people.

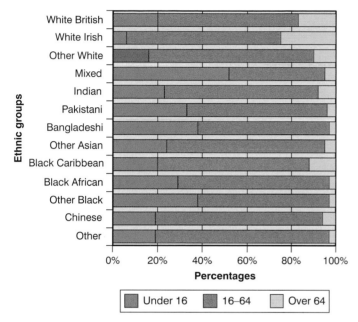

Table I: Population by ethnic group and age 2001
Source: Social Trends 2006, p 13

This table divides the population into the two 'dependent' groups and the working population. It is important to realise that these are very general categories. Increasingly it is more realistic to extend the 0–16 age group to 0–18/21 as 40% of young people are now entering higher education and not the workforce. Secondly the 16–65 age group includes those unable to work through unemployment, disability, etc. and are therefore not economically active. Increasingly, either through choice or economic circumstances, a growing number of the 65+ age group is employed in some form of economic activity. Many employers are keen to recruit this age group as they see them as reliable and experienced.

Theory into practice

What are the major trends in age and ethnicity shown in Table I?

Changing role of women

The most significant social change in the last 50 years has been in the status of women in society.

This is highlighted in a piece of sociological research undertaken by Sue Sharpe. In a 1976 survey she discovered that girls' priorities were 'love, marriage, husbands, children, jobs and careers, more or less in that order'. When the research was repeated in 1994, she found that the priorities had changed to 'jobs, career and being able to support themselves'. The Spice Girls and 'girl power' in the 1990s is one illustration of this change of role.

The increased status and importance of women in the workforce is clearly shown in the table below:

Gender	1971	2005
Male	92	79
Female	56	70

The percentage of UK working age population in employment, by gender
Males aged 16–64, Females aged 16–59
Source: Social Trends 2006

It is important to point out, however, that women still earn on average less than men and are often found in the lower paid sectors of the economy, particularly sections of the health and social care services. The **'glass ceiling'** continues to remain a barrier for many women.

Changing concept of childhood

Until the introduction of state education and child labour laws at the end of the 19th century children were seen as an economic asset – an extra pair of hands to bring some money into the household. Today children are an economic liability to their parents, particularly with the advent of mass higher education. The family has become a child-centred institution in which children's interests tend to be put at the forefront.

In addition, children are now seen as vulnerable and in need of protection. This has given rise to a huge increase in services targeted at children, for example social services register of 'at risk children' and the role of paediatric services in health care. The Children Act 1989 established the importance of children placing their interests as **paramount** and this was reinforced by the Children Act 2004 which put into legislation the Green Paper *Every Child Matters*. Children are now consulted upon the break-up of their parents' marriage and the Child Support Act 1991 protects children's welfare in the event of parental separation. Such changes have had a significant impact upon both the structure of the family and relationships within it.

The definition of childhood has changed dramatically

Changes in educational provision

The length of time young people spend in education has increased both at the lower and upper ends. The proportion of three and four year olds enrolled in all schools in the UK has risen from 21% in 1970/71 to 65% in 2004/05. In addition 35% of three and four year olds were enrolled in other non-school settings offering early education, such as playgroups in the private and voluntary sectors, either instead of, or in addition to their school place.

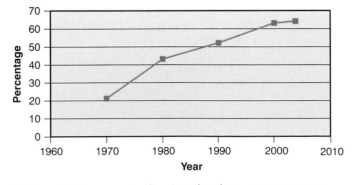

Table J: Children under five in schools as a percentage of all three and four year olds

Source: Social Trends 2006, p 34

Year:	1970/71	1980/81	1990/91	2003/04
Total: (000s)	621	827	1175	2446

Number of students in higher education 1970–2004
Source: Social Trends 2006

The impact of this unprecedented increase upon the family and other carers cannot be underestimated, as students and parents are increasingly responsible for their financial costs whilst at university. Free higher education is no longer financially viable for any government.

Educational attainment

The trend in educational attainment at all levels tends to be linked to:

- ethnicity
- social class
- gender.

Table K on page 179 is based on data from the Department for Education and Skills and shows a pattern of an overall increase for all ethnic groups in the benchmark 5 A*–Cs at GCSE Level. However, there is a clear correlation of achievement with ethnicity.

> **Theory into practice**
>
> Look back to Section 15.2.1. Can you think of any possible reasons to explain the pattern in the data?

Social class is a very complex concept but it is usually measured using occupation because this impacts upon many other features of a person's life including income, health, life expectancy and status. Despite governments' attempts to reduce the impact of social class on achievement, significant inequalities remain as is shown by the following:

Percentage of students with at least A or AS levels at age 21 in 2003:

- professional and intermediate: (middle class): 69%
- skilled non-manual: (middle class): 65%
- skilled manual: (working class): 46%
- partly skilled: (working class): 39%
- unskilled: (working class): 33%.

(continued on page 180)

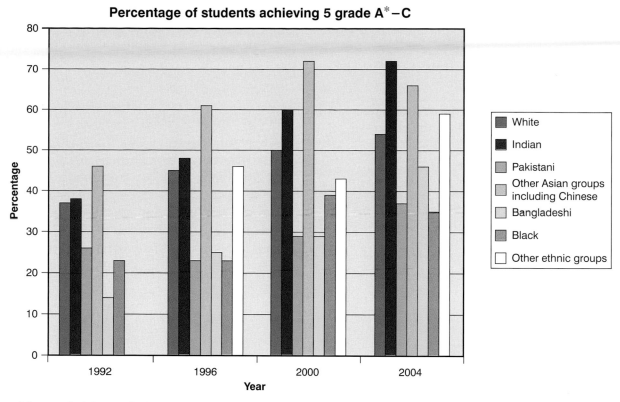

Percentage of students achieving 5 grade A*–C

Table K: Ethnicity and educational achievement as measured by numbers achieving 5 A*–C grades at GCSE (figures are for England and Wales)

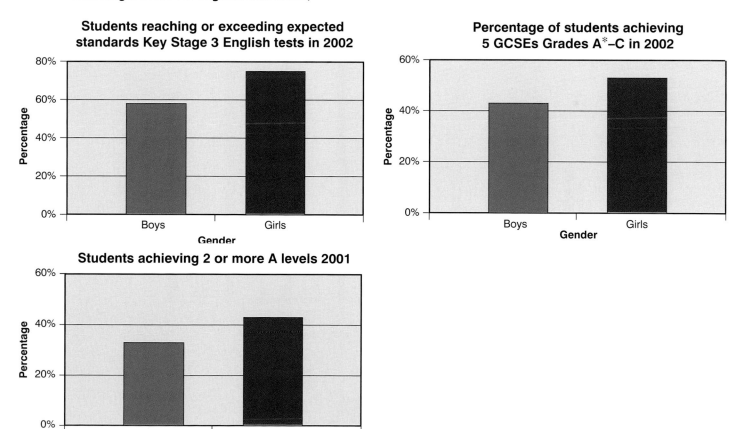

Table L1–3: Educational achievements (figures for England and Wales)

There are many possible explanations for this correlation including family background, language development, economic and financial issues, environmental factors and the type of school the student attends.

The most dramatic change in recent years has been the growing gap between achievements of boys and girls.

The possible explanations for this dramatic improvement in the performance by girls can be found by referring to the changes in occupational structure and in women's roles in the home. In addition, schools in the last 30 years have concentrated upon improving girls' achievements to compensate for their relatively poor performance in the 1950s

and 1960s by encouraging girls to study non-traditional subjects such as science and technology, and to continue their education beyond the school-leaving age.

Theory into practice

Work in three groups: one to investigate the relationship between educational achievement and social class; one the link between ethnicity and class; and the third the relationship between gender and achievement. Look for the evidence and the possible explanations. Report back to the whole group. Access to Sociology textbooks in your library would be very useful. Also interview your Sociology teacher if available.

Assessment activity 15.2.2

CASE STUDY

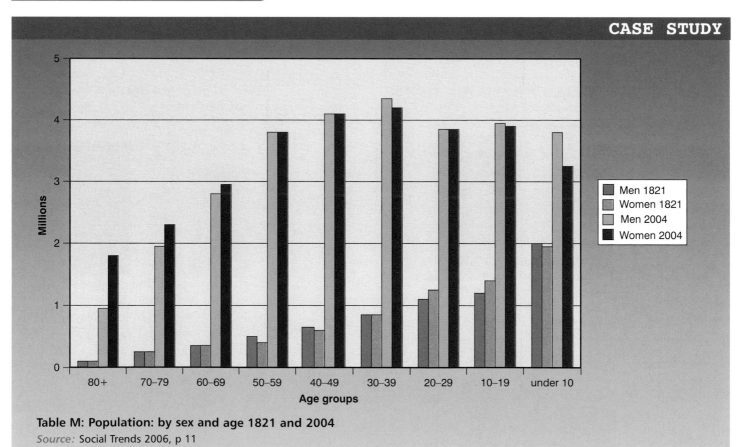

Table M: Population: by sex and age 1821 and 2004
Source: Social Trends 2006, p 11

1 Define the term 'ageing population' (2 marks).

2 Identify two ways the table shows that our society is ageing (2 marks).

3 Identify and explain two differences between the data for males and females (4 marks).

4 Discuss the impact of an ageing population upon other family members (12 marks).

15.2.3 Changes to service provision available to the family and individuals

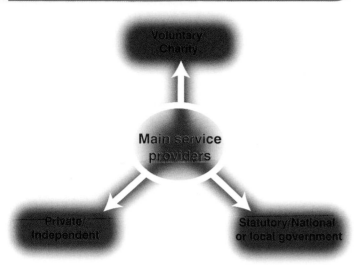

The groups shown above have to provide a service that meets the current needs of service users and so have to closely follow the significant changes that have taken place in the family and wider relationships. Two key groups that demand attention are: children as a result of changes in family structure and the potential for greater breakdown in relationships, and the impact of the ageing population upon older adults.

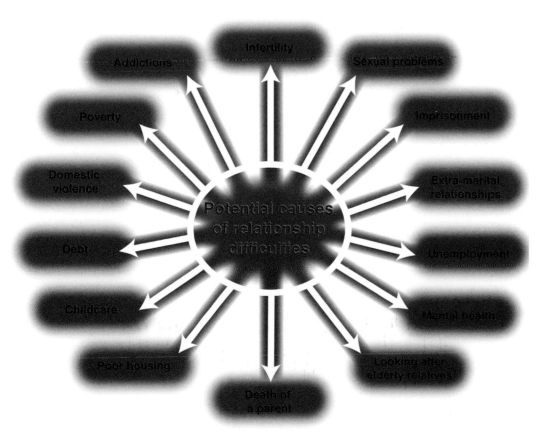

Services to reduce family breakdown and assist individuals during family breakdown

Family breakdown and divorce impose a huge cost on the taxpayer estimated at about £5 billion a year. This is currently made up of social security benefits (£3 billion), social services (£266 million), health (£190 million) and other costs. This may well be an underestimation of the true cost to society. Added to costs are the potential adverse effects of the social and emotional impact on couples and children and it is easy to recognise why the government is concerned about the trend towards relationship instability.

The reaction to such changes can be illustrated by the DfES proposal *'Moving forward together: A Proposed Strategy for Marriage and Relationship Support for 2002 and beyond'*. The proposal set out the government's desire to help and support couples undergoing relationship difficulties. Such problems can result from a wide range of interlinking factors.

Assistance during family breakdown

One of the many attempts by governments to support families, particularly in disadvantaged areas, was the establishment of SureStart. One of its many objectives was 'Strengthening Families'. This aimed to:

- Promote effective and appropriate support to families (couples and parents at key life stages) and in particular at times of change, challenge or crisis.
- Encourage and support innovation among family support organisations.
- Address social exclusion through the provision of support.
- Contribute to the five outcomes listed in *Every Child Matters* (for the purposes of supporting families): be healthy, stay safe, enjoy and achieve, make a positive contribution and achieve economic well being.

One of many independent charities working to reduce family breakdown is the National Families and Parenting Institute, which was set up in 1999 as part of the government's programme 'Supporting Families'. This organisation raises money through fund raising alongside a government grant, and they also run promotion campaigns such as the annual National Parents' Week.

Perhaps the most well known registered charity addressing family breakdown is Relate (www.relate.org.uk). This is the UK's largest provider of relationship counselling and in 2005 they saw 150,000 clients. Their vision is: 'A future in which good couple and family relationships form the heart of a thriving society'.

Their success is largely based upon their many volunteers who in 2005 gave 94,000 voluntary hours valued at £2 million. Their funding comes from:

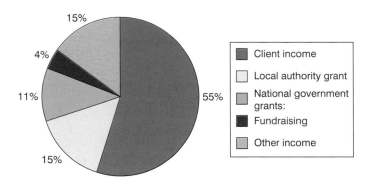

15%
4%
11%
55%
15%

- Client income
- Local authority grant
- National government grants:
- Fundraising
- Other income

Table N: Income sources for Relate

Evidence of the growth in counselling services to families is the huge expansion in private counselling services available throughout the country. One can also access services online, and the media has become preoccupied with addressing relationship issues even down to the 'Jeremy Kyle Show' which in its own way tries to help people in some of the most challenging situations.

Child protection services

Child protection continues to be a controversial and emotive issue. It is difficult to find valid data on the number of children needing protection. Why is this? Most people assume that the figures for the abuse of children are on the increase, if only because we are more aware of the problem today than at any time in the past. The little detailed evidence we have of 19th-century family life suggests that children were far more at risk then through child labour, neglect and prostitution than they are today. Society is much more child centred and concerned with child welfare in the 21st century.

The official statistics of the number of children on child protection registers can be seen in Table O:

What trends are there in the data? Whether or not there has been an increased need for child protection, the fact is that as a society more resources are allocated to children than almost

	Under 1	1–4	5–9	10–15	16 and over	All ages
Males						
Neglect	49	45	39	36	30	41
Emotional abuse	8	16	22	22	19	19
Physical abuse	24	18	15	16	15	17
Sexual abuse	6	6	9	11	17	8
Multiple/other	13	15	15	16	19	15
All males (actual numbers)	1,400	4,000	4,000	3,900	200	13,600
Females						
Neglect	49	44	37	32	26	38
Emotional abuse	8	17	23	21	15	19
Physical abuse	22	18	12	13	16	15
Sexual abuse	6	8	12	18	28	12
Multiple/other	14	13	16	17	15	15
All females (actual numbers)	1,400	3,600	3,700	3,700	310	12,700
Both (actual numbers)	2,800	7,600	7,700	7,600	510	26,300

England (percentages)

Table O: Children on child protection registers by sex, age and catagory of abuse 2003
Source: Social Trends 2005, p 120

any other group. It is interesting that a breakdown of charitable expenditure by the top 500 charities in 2003/04 reads as follows:

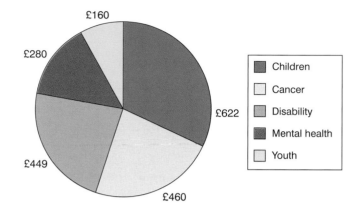

£160	
£280	
£622	Children
£449	Cancer
£460	Disability
	Mental health
	Youth

Table P: Largest charities by expenditure (£millions)
Source: Charities Aid Foundation

Statutory involvement in child protection can be traced back over 100 years to 1889 when the 'children's charter' was passed. This enabled the state to intervene for the first time in relations between parents and children. Even then the police could arrest anyone found ill-treating a child, and enter a home if a child was thought to be in danger. This clearly shows that child abuse is not something that emerged in the second half of the 20th century. A series of acts followed strengthening the legislation. One of the most significant was the 1970 Local Authority Social Services Act which created Social Services departments.

As far back as 1974 weaknesses were exposed in child protection with the death of Maria Colwell at the hands of her stepfather and this led to an attempt to co-ordinate efforts to safeguard children at risk. The Children Act 1989 and the Child Protection Act 1999 further strengthened the legislation protecting children.

Further weaknesses were exposed in the child protection services by the death of Victoria Climbie

However, mistakes were still made and in 2003 the tragic death of Victoria Climbie led to the biggest shake-up in 30 years in the child protection services – the appointment of the first children's minister, Margaret Hodge, and the government Green Paper, *Every Child Matters*. In 2005 Professor Al Aynsley Green was appointed as England's first children's commissioner and Estelle Morris was appointed to oversee the government's reform of the children's services workforce.

This clearly shows the concern the statutory authorities have with child protection issues and also the difficulty of balancing care with interference into private family matters – something which the police and government are very sensitive about.

Our growing awareness of child protection issues has led to an increased workload for the **voluntary** sector working with children. Childline, set up in 1986 by Esther Rantzen, joined the NSPCC in 2006 to make its work more effective and to co-ordinate resources.

The NSPCC, established in 1984, is perhaps the best-known charity/voluntary group working for children.

Theory into practice

Find out about the work of the NSPCC, and how it is funded, by visiting the website: www.nspcc.org.uk

Discuss as a whole group how and in which ways the organisation contributes to child protection.

Assistance with care for family members

With the ageing population, more pressure is being placed upon formal and informal carers. The support older family members need can be provided formally by health and social services, voluntary organisations and community projects or informally by spouses, extended family, neighbours and friends. The older adult often wants to retain their independence and it is more economical for them to remain in their own homes rather than add to the burden placed upon care homes and nursing homes. If they do not require 24-hour care, services are available in the community to enable older people to retain their independence. Social Services can provide, with a voluntary agency, a meals on wheels service to ensure a healthy diet is achieved. Occupational therapists can make adaptations to homes to enable mobility to be maintained. Home

Care Services are available to help with dressing, getting in and out of bed and taking medication. Community alarm services provide some security and ensure immediate help is available, if required, in an emergency.

The number of 'home help' hours purchased or provided by councils in England has increased over the past decade to meet the growing demand.

	1994	2004
Number of hours of care provided directly by local authorities or purchased by them	2.2 million	3.4 million
Percentage provided directly by local authorities	81%	31%

Care provision 1994–2004
Source: Social Trends 2006

The number of hours purchased by the local authority from the independent sector has increased from 0.43 million in 1994 to 2.34 million in 2004 and this has now become the main type of provision.

The proportion of households receiving high-intensity care, more than five hours of 'home help' or home care contact and six or more visits per week has increased from:

- 16% in 1994 to
- 45% in 2004.

Low-intensity care (two hours or less of home help or home care and one visit per week) has fallen from:

- 34% in 1994 to
- 13% in 2004.

It is important not to underestimate the level of informal care provided for people over 60.

Despite the decline in the extended family, Table Q clearly suggests that family members, particularly spouses and partners, provide most care. For those aged 75 and over caring is mostly provided by the younger generations such as children, children-in-law or grandchildren.

Carers UK (www.carersuk.org), a leading pressure group campaigning on behalf of informal carers, identifies 10 facts about caring:

- One in eight adults are carers – around six million people.
- Carers save the economy £57 billion per year – an average of £10,000 per person per year.

	60–74	75 and over	All respondents
No help	64	46	56
Spouse or partner	23	16	20
Son	6	11	8
Daughter	9	17	12
Son-in-law/ Daughter-in-law	3	7	4
Sibling	1	2	2
Grandchild	2	5	3
Friend or neighbour	4	8	6
Other unpaid	2	4	3
Privately paid employee	2	10	6
Social or health service worker	1	8	4
All respondents (actual numbers)	**2,760**	**1,942**	**4,702**

Table Q: Reported sources of help for people aged 60 and over who have difficulty with daily activities or mobility by age (England, 2003) (percentages)
Source: Social Trends 2006, p 121

- Over 3 million people juggle care with work.
- The main carer's benefit is £46.95 for a minimum of 35 hours.
- 1.25 million people provide over 50 hours of care per week.
- People providing high levels of care are twice as likely to be permanently sick or disabled.
- Over one million people care for more than one person.
- 58% of carers are women.
- By 2037 the number of carers could have increased to 9 million.
- Every year over 2 million people become carers.

The involvement of privately paid employees, social, or health service workers increases dramatically for those adults who are over 75. This is likely to be because of widowhood, which increases dramatically at this age, so that the chances of living alone increase, particularly for women.

Respite care is an important service which enables the informal carer to have a short break in order to provide some relief from caring. Such care can be provided through a number of private, statutory or voluntary organisations, for example hospitals or residential homes.

For older adults requiring 24-hour supervision a potential 'care crisis' is causing great concern.

Pensioner attacks care home crisis

67-year-old Joan Mortimer is set to move to her fourth nursing home in three years. Her current home will close in two weeks, with the owners blaming new rules and low fees for the decision.

Source: Adapted from BBC News 17.07.02.

Hundreds of residential homes throughout the UK have closed in recent years largely because of poor rates of return and increasing bureaucracy. This is putting added pressure on hospital services and informal carers.

Brian   CASE STUDY

Brian's father died recently and Jane, his mother, is now living on her own. Jane is aged 82 and she relied upon her husband for some help in terms of mobility and basic care needs. Jane is keen to retain her independence and Brian is concerned about how she is going to cope. Brian lives over 120 miles away from his mother.

1 What statutory, private and voluntary services could Brian contact in order to help his mother retain her independence?

2 Describe the roles of three key workers who are likely to be useful to Jane.

Financial support for children and families

A survey by Woolworths in 2004 estimated that on average it will cost parents/carers £164,000 to bring a child up to the age of 18 – all those holidays, designer clothes, electronic gadgets, etc.!

The government has played a supportive role in this cost since the establishment of the **Welfare State** following the **Beveridge Report** at the end of the Second World War. This financial help started with the introduction of Family Allowance in 1946 and was extended in 1979 with the full implementation of Child Benefit. This **universal benefit** is currently paid each week (2006/07) at the rate of £17.45 for the first child and £11.70 for all subsequent

children. The vast majority of support for families and children today is, however, based upon a **means test** (related to income) and is targeted towards those most in need.

In 2004 the government spent £22 billion on state financial support for families and children. This is more than double the sum spent in the mid-1970s. Since the number of children has been falling, spending per child has risen from £13.41 per week in 1975 to £32.57 in 2003.

In 2003/04, 56% of lone parents with children, and 10% of couples with children were receiving income-related benefits (source: Social Trends 2006). The range of benefits available can be noted in the table below:

	Single person with dependent children	Couple with dependent children
Income related		
Council tax benefit	48	8
Housing benefit	45	7
Working tax credit or income support	46	5
Job seekers allowance	1	2
Any income-related benefit	56	10
Non-income related		
Child benefit	97	97
Incapacity or disablement benefits	8	9
Any non-income-related benefit	97	97
Any benefit or tax credit	98	98

Table R: Receipt of selected social security benefits among families below pension age (percentages by type of benefit, 2003/04)
Source: Social Trends 2006, p 125

Theory into practice

Carry out research to find out more about the benefits available to families and children.

Give a brief presentation to others in the group.

Despite the falling birth rate there has been a substantial increase in the demand for pre-school places for the under-fives. The government has made it clear that they want more young parents to be able to return to work and since 2004 it has guaranteed a free school place for all three year olds from the term following their third birthday. Children in this category are entitled to five 2.5-hour sessions for 33 weeks a year. The projected annual cost of providing these places is £2.4 billion.

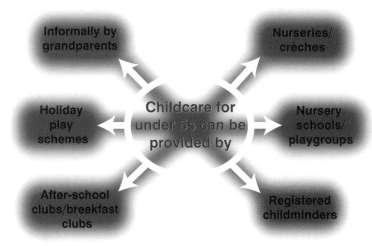

It is clear that governments have to make critical decisions regarding the quantity of services they are able to provide and the political consequences have to be considered. The ageing population and the growing demand for pre-school education have to be placed alongside the demand for more resources towards health care in general, as well as other key areas of expenditure, for example defence. One likely outcome is that individuals will have to take a growing level of responsibility for themselves and their families unless the taxpayer is willing to provide a substantial increase in income.

Theory into practice

Using the website: www.gingerbread.org.uk find out about the work of Gingerbread. Find out how it is funded and the services it offers to lone parent families.

Assessment activity 15.2.3

CASE STUDY

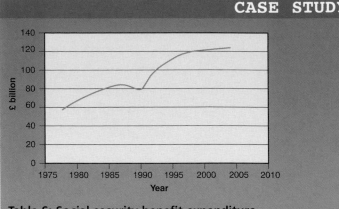

Table S: Social security benefit expenditure in real terms (£billion at 2004/05 prices)
Source: Social Trends 2006, p 116

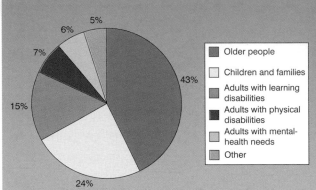

Table T: Local authority personal social services expenditure by recipient group (percentages, England, 2003/04)
Source: Social Trends 2006, p 116

1 What was the total amount of expenditure in 1997/98 (1)

2 Identify one possible reason why expenditure fell slightly between 1986/87 and 1989/90 (1)

3 Describe the trend shown in the data on benefit expenditure (2)

4 Identify and explain two possible reasons why the largest portion of expenditure by local authorities is on older adults (4)

5 Discuss the role of social services and their work with children and families (12)

15.2.4 Using data to explore and draw conclusions about the trends and patterns of family life

When using data to explore issues, important aspects of social research must be considered such as:

- the differences between primary and secondary, and quantitative and qualitative research
- the different research methods that can be used to collect data
- the main processes involved in all research methods, for example sampling
- how to evaluate research findings using key concepts such as reliability and validity
- the problems involved when researching people's lives over a period of time and how these can be overcome
- the ethical issues involved when researching aspects of family life.

What do you mean you want me to investigate the hypothesis that divorce has increased mainly because of changes in women's status, using quantitative and qualitative primary and secondary research methods avoiding ethical issues?

Quantitative data, qualitative data and methods of collecting primary data

Quantitative data: data which can be put into numerical form, for example numbers, percentages, tables, graphs and charts.

Most of the data used in this unit has been obtained from secondary sources, and is quantitative in that it originated from official, mainly government sources, for example the ten-yearly census.

Secondary data: information that a researcher can use but has been collected by someone else.

In health, social care and childcare there are a number of secondary sources that are useful to the researcher. Some examples are:

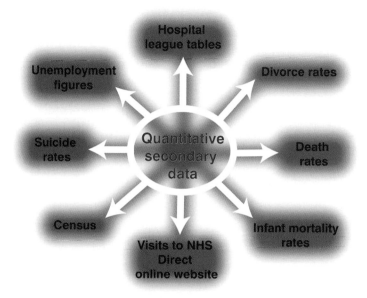

The strengths of official statistics are:

- they are easily available
- they can be used to show trends over time
- they tend to be reliable
- they allow hypotheses to be tested
- they can be used as a comparison with other primary research.

The main weaknesses of collecting secondary data are:

- the data can tend to be superficial and lack depth
- the data has been collected for a specific purpose and may not be easy to adapt for other research
- some statistics collected by the government may have a political motive, for example unemployment statistics might be 'manipulated' to present a better picture.

Quantitative primary research is usually undertaken using a survey with a **questionnaire** containing closed questions or a **structured interview**. The questions will be **pre-coded** with a choice of alternative responses, often of a 'yes/no' nature. The survey can either be posted for completion, or left for the respondent to complete in their own time, or they can be read out and completed by the researcher. Such methods are likely to produce a mass of statistical data that can be easily presented and analysed. Questionnaires are useful for collecting factual data or people's attitudes on a topic, for example euthanasia.

Closed questions could be used to determine family roles, for example to what extent roles are shared equally in a relationship. For example: Is childcare (a) shared (b) largely the responsibility of the mother or (c) largely the responsibility of the father in your relationship? An open question might ask: 'Do you think childcare should be equally shared in a relationship – please give your reasons?' or, 'How would you describe who takes responsibility for the children in your relationship?' If the respondent is confused, it is useful to have 'follow-up' or 'prompt questions', such as: 'Can you explain on a day-to-day basis who takes overall responsibility for the children – is it shared or mainly the responsibility of one person?'

Questionnaires   Activity 4

1. Design a questionnaire containing at least ten questions to investigate people's attitudes towards the service they receive from the NHS. Include both closed and open questions.

2. Show others in the group the questionnaire produced and ask them for their opinions.

A third type of quantitative primary research is the use of an **experiment** whereby one carries out research similar to that in the natural sciences such as Chemistry. This method is rarely used in social research because of ethical concerns about experimenting with people and the possible consequences that might follow.

Primary research: information collected by the researcher at first hand using an appropriate method.

Qualitative data: data, which instead of numbers relies upon words to express feelings, values and attitudes.

Examples of secondary qualitative research could be personal documents such as letters and diaries that a person may have written, for example about family life during the war. A fascinating insight into life during the Second World War can be gathered through studying letters that servicemen sent home to their relatives. They offer a very personal view of life and are rich in quality and depth which quantitative data usually lacks. Many historians have found out about life in London during the 17th century using the diaries written by Samuel Pepys. The 'fly on the wall' reality programmes on television such as Big Brother use qualitative approaches to observe human behaviour and can be a valuable secondary resource.

Primary qualitative research includes:

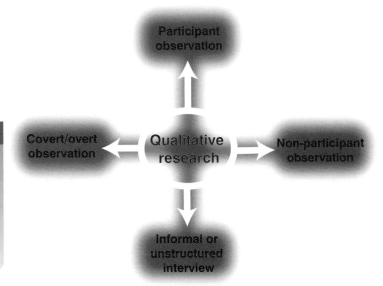

An excellent example of qualitative research linked to health and social care is the work of Erving Goffman (*Asylums* 1961). He was interested in how mental illness is defined and how the mentally ill were treated in the middle of the 20th century. As a consequence he decided to undertake some research in a psychiatric hospital playing the role of a Physical Education Assistant. He thought that asking questions would not produce an accurate picture of the way hospitals worked; he needed to see life himself from the inside. His study was **participant observation** using a **covert** undercover method. Researchers in the media who want to expose corruption often adopt this approach. There are, however, serious ethical concerns with such investigations.

Observation as a method of research

It's good being able to study the lives of real people and seeing them as they really are – this is reality TV – better than doing that questionnaire on relationships my Health and Social Care teacher wants me to do

Observation needs to go through the following stages:

Choice of group to study

⬇

Participant or non-participant study

⬇

Joining the group

⬇

Watching the group or taking part

⬇

Leaving or exiting from the group

⬇

Writing up the report and drawing conclusions

Observation has a number of strengths for studying issues in health and social care, for example:

- seeing people behaving normally in a natural environment should enable an accurate picture of reality to take place
- the study is based upon the participants – the researcher should have less impact and therefore less bias
- this method can 'dig deep' into the activities taking place
- the researcher may discover things which they could not have anticipated and would not have been revealed through quantitative research.

However, there are some difficulties involved in using observation. These could include:

- not being able to study large numbers of groups and so the research has to be small scale, therefore making generalisations less likely
- the method is often very time consuming
- occasionally the presence of the observer may change the behaviour of the group – this is known as the 'Hawthorne effect' (based upon the study of an observer at a factory whose workers thought their productivity was being assessed and consequently worked harder in the observer's presence)

- serious ethical issues are raised with some observation – should one ever observe people without their consent?
- occasionally the researcher may put themselves at physical and/or psychological risk if they are investigating a controversial or sensitive topic.

Carrying out research **Activity 5**

1. In small groups identify three topics/issues relevant to health, social care or early years that could be usefully studied using observation.

2. What problems might one have undertaking such research into the chosen groups?

Data sampling methods

When undertaking a piece of research it is usually impossible to interview, talk to or observe everyone in your chosen population.

Population: the total number of people you are planning to study, for example everyone between the ages of 13 and 19 if you were investigating teenage attitudes towards drug use.

To overcome this problem a sample of the population is surveyed. There are a number of different types of sample available including:

- random sample
- stratified sample
- quota sample.

A *random sample* is the simplest and least sophisticated. It works like the National Lottery where a number of balls are selected with each ball having the same opportunity of being selected. In the example above one could select a sample size of 100 teenagers from a school by putting all the teenagers' names in a hat and picking out names until a total of 100 are obtained. The problem with this method is one could end up with, say, 70 boys and 30 girls and gender might be linked to attitudes towards drugs. In others words the sample is unlikely to be an accurate cross-section of the population.

Stratified random sampling should be more accurate. The intention is to get a 'mirror image', an exact copy of the population being studied. It could be argued that attitudes towards drugs could be linked to age, gender, ethnicity and social class.

In the example two schools could be chosen, one from an inner city and one from a middle-class rural area. Fifty students from each school would be chosen to reflect the balance of gender, ethnicity and age in each school. Each student will then be interviewed.

Quota sampling is slightly different in that one identifies the need to interview 50 males and 50 females across the ages 13–19 and one then goes out to try and find them. The researcher could go to a youth centre and estimate the ages of the young people and when he/she has 20 completed forms from each age their task is complete. The problem with this method is that the researcher is estimating ages rather than identifying individuals and it cannot take into consideration environmental/social class background.

Sampling | Activity 6

1 Describe an appropriate sample that could be used to investigate women's changing role in the workforce.

2 Why is this sample appropriate?

Suitability of methods for collecting the data

In an ideal world a researcher should use a number of different methods when studying a particular topic. This is called triangulation:

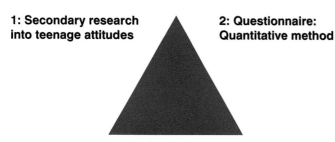

1: Secondary research into teenage attitudes

2: Questionnaire: Quantitative method

3: In-depth interviews with a smaller number of teenagers: Qualitative method

However, because of time and budget constraints, it might not be possible to use triangulation. It is important to choose the most appropriate method for the topic being investigated. For example, a questionnaire would be useful to research into people's attitudes towards marriage and cohabitation, or their use of health and social care services. However, sensitive issues such as domestic violence and the possible effect of divorce upon children would best be approached using a more relaxed and qualitative method such as informal interviews which would focus upon the thoughts and feelings of the respondents.

Problems with methods used for collecting the data

A number of problems need to be considered:

- Is the group studied representative of the larger group or population? (Can one draw conclusions for the whole population?)
- Is the data *reliable*? (Would other researchers using the same method come up with similar results?)
- Is the research free of *bias*? (Has the researcher remained objective and not allowed his/her own views to influence the results?)
- Is the data *valid*? (Does the research method measure what it sets out to measure?) Research into domestic violence carried out by a closed questionnaire would probably be less valid than research using in-depth interviews. The latter is likely to provide a more accurate picture because it is more appropriate for the topic and the respondents will 'open up' more and be willing to talk.
- Is the research *ethically* correct? (Has the researcher followed the Code of Ethics for social research?)
- Is one able to draw conclusions from the research?
- Are the respondents willing to take part and will they ensure a high response rate?

Ways of overcoming data collection problems and ethical issues in research

To some extent following the British Sociological Association's recommendations for informed consent can reduce ethical issues. Everyone involved in research should:

- choose freely to be involved
- suffer no harm as a result of the research
- have their privacy respected
- understand what they are volunteering for
- accept that they can withdraw at any time
- know what the purpose of the research is.

Covert research should not be used, as those taking part cannot give informed consent. Bias is not necessarily a bad thing; what is wrong is to claim to be objective when in reality the results have been influenced by personal values and opinions. In fact it can be argued that it is impossible not to allow one's own values to play a part in the research. 'Sitting on the fence' often means avoiding the issue. If one states one's views at the start of the research then everyone knows where they stand.

Using a qualitative approach to the research can increase validity. A true picture is most likely to be achieved through observing the group as it really is. The researcher is not imposing his/her values in any way as long as the group continues to behave in their normal way.

Reliability is increased with quantitative data. It is easier for another researcher to repeat the research with a structured interview or closed questionnaire than with observation or informal interviews.

If the results are to be made representative of the wider population then large-scale quantitative research should be used, such as a survey with a questionnaire. This is called macro research. Small-scale research such as using observation does not produce results which can be generalised for the whole population. This is known as micro research.

Research method	Validity	Reliability	Representative
Official statistics	Low	High	High
Personal letters, documents and diaries	High	Low	Low
Observation	High	Low	Low
Structured questionnaires	Low	High	High
Structured interviews	Low	High	High
Informal/in-depth interviews	High	Low	Low

The relationship between research and validity, reliability and representativeness

When analysing social trends a number of skills are required:

- interpreting data from tables
- understanding line graphs and pie charts
- understanding projections
- awareness of percentages and scales of convention such as millions and thousands.

Good or bad health — CASE STUDY

A number of studies of health show that there is a direct link between good health and factors such as social class. The middle classes are likely to live longer, have better health and suffer less illness than the working classes. Infant mortality rates are higher amongst working-class children.

1. Explain how one could use secondary and primary research to investigate the possible link between social class and health.

2. Which secondary sources could be used?

3. Which primary research method(s) would be most appropriate?

4. What problems might arise?

When interpreting data from secondary sources it is important to follow some guidelines:

- Read the title of the source carefully: What is the source? – The government, a newspaper, an opinion poll survey?
- What convention are the figures in? – Millions, thousands, percentages, etc.?
- What area is covered by the figures? – The UK, Britain, England and Wales, or Europe?
- If the figures cover a period of time, check carefully which years are included. Are the gaps between the years at regular intervals?
- Look carefully for trends over time. Are the trends steady over time or are there sudden jumps and falls? Are the changes large or small increases/ decreases?
- Does the question ask for identification, description or explanation? For example:

Identification	Description	Explanation
Very brief answer. State what the trend is, for example the birth rate has fallen.	A short and precise answer is required – one or two sentences, with examples.	This requires a number of reasons why the trends and patterns take the form they do.

Take time to read the data carefully so that silly errors are avoided.

Assessment activity 15.2.4 - 1

CASE STUDY

'Teenagers in no rush to have sex, biggest survey shows.

- **Seven out of ten wait until at least 16 to lose virginity**
- **But despite health risk, many fail to use condoms.'**

These findings are revealed by the survey BareAll06, an online poll supported by the Department of Health and conducted by Radio 1, the BBC's black music station 1Xtra, MTV and Durex.

A sample of nearly 2,000 young people, aged 16–24, took part in the survey.

- 10% claimed to have had no sex education at school and
- 79% learned only the basics.

- 36% did not always use a condom with a new partner.
- 24% used no contraception the first time they had sex.

Source: adapted from the Guardian Unlimited website: 15.08.06

1 Identify two characteristics of the data.

2 Outline two reasons why some of the data may not be valid.

3 Describe two ethical issues involved in this type of research.

4 Explain an alternative primary research method that could be used to investigate young people's sexual behaviour in order to increase the level of validity of the findings.

Assessment activity 15.2.4 - 2

CASE STUDY

A local doctors' surgery became concerned over the apparent increase in incidents of domestic violence amongst both male and female patients. One of the nurses was asked to investigate the issue to see if the problem was increasing and why the violence was happening. The surgery was concerned about the possible impact upon children in abusive relationships.

1 Identify an appropriate primary research method one could use.

2 What sources of secondary research could one use?

3 Describe the primary research method in detail. How would one ensure that the aims of the research are met?

4 What potential problems are likely to arise and explain how they might be overcome?

Unit 16 Research Methods in Health and Social Care

Contents

About this unit

Within this unit you will investigate:

- purposes and methods of research
- ethical issues, sources of error and bias in research
- planning, presenting and analysing findings from research
- evaluating findings from research.

Research is a complex task

Introducing this unit

Research is exploring a topic to find out new information. In Health and Social Care, practitioners have a duty to ensure they keep up to date with the latest research, for example doctors have a duty to follow medical research into prescription drugs and their side effects – they can then use this information to make the best decision for the treatment of their patients.

However, it is not just in the Health and Social Care discipline that research is used. Lots of different people in many different types of occupations use research to help them to expand their knowledge or to improve their customer service or their efficiency. Shoppers are often stopped by market researchers and asked for their views on various products. This information will be collated, analysed and presented to the manufacturer who will use the findings of the market research to improve the product.

To investigate effectively, the researcher must be well organised and have a systematic approach to the topic being looked at. Choosing a sustainable, interesting, manageable topic is essential. The length of time available for the research will have a bearing on the final decision. Thorough planning is essential whatever the research topic.

Throughout the investigative process the researcher has to be aware of ethical issues such as confidentiality and respect for interviewees and their beliefs. Care must be taken to avoid personal bias which could lead to a misrepresentation of the picture. The findings from the research must be presented in a well organised, easy to follow format. Anyone following a presentation which is disorganised and difficult to understand will soon lose interest.

Research is important as it is only through accurate research that people can find out if some common social assumptions are true. For example, it is often said that it is common knowledge that teenagers become pregnant so they can go to the top of the housing list. This is an assumption or an opinion and not necessarily based on fact. It is only after careful research into teenage pregnancies that this statement could be confirmed or refuted.

Doctors can use medical research to prescribe new drugs

16.2.1 Purposes and methods of research

Different methods of research

Research is the investigation of a topic for a specific purpose. Research can be drawn from a number of Health and Social Care areas including medical, health, sociological, psychological, and special and early years care and education. The purposes of research could include:

• reviewing and monitoring changes
• exploring specific needs of local populations
• exploring social science hypotheses
• extending and improving practice and collective knowledge.

The National Census which is carried out every ten years is the biggest piece of social research

in this country. This piece of research, which began in 1801, is the source of vital information for both central and local government. It allows the government, the health authorities and other organisations to target their resources more effectively, spending money where it is needed most. Education, housing, health and transport services will be planned using National Census information.

The National Census counts the number of people in every city, town and country area of our country. It gives the balance of young and old, the jobs people do and the type and condition of the housing they live in. The National Census takes the form of a large questionnaire which is normally completed by the **householder**. The questionnaire asked questions on:

National Census questions

This major piece of social research, although scanned electronically, took around ten months to process. However, the finished **compilation** gives a complete picture of the nation. Unlike other research questionnaires, this one is not optional. People have a legal **obligation** to complete it and could be prosecuted if they fail to do so.

From the completed census local and central government have data on the age and socio-economic make-up of the population. They have a clearer picture of the health of individuals. If there is any long-term illness and if so, how many carers there are. This allows the government to plan health and social services and to allocate resources.

Local governments' housing departments, too, are able to measure the number of people who have **inadequate** accommodation. This would indicate if there is a need for new housing. The census also indicates the occupations of people which would help the government and industry to make informed decisions about investments and possible future training programmes. From the census results you can see that the government can:

(i) Review and monitor changes, for example in local government there could be a change in the ratio of younger children who need to be catered for in junior school, as the birth rate could have dropped since the last census. Conversely, the number could have risen due to people moving into the area. Whatever the result, the local government department will be able to review their provision as they have an up-to-date picture of their area.

(ii) Exploring specific needs of local populations, for example if there is a surge of unemployment in a local area due to the failing fortunes of a local employer, then the local government may have to channel more money than usual into retraining people for other jobs.

(iii) Exploring social-science hypotheses, for example local government will have a much clearer picture of the wealth and well being of the people living in their area. Has the standard of life improved for the majority of people? Are people living in the area better off or healthier than people living in neighbouring areas?

(iv) Extending and improving practice and collective knowledge. For example, not only will local government have a clearer picture of progress in their area but they will be able to speak to other local councils who have made better progress whilst dealing with similar issues – they could then share good practice.

Medical research

Medical research aims to improve human health throughout the world. The Medical Research Council supports research 'across the biomedical spectrum, from fundamental lab-based science to clinical trials, and in all major disease areas'. They work with the NHS and UK Health Dept to try to make a difference to clinical practice and therefore to the health of the population. To find out current medical research go to www.mrc.cc.uk

Health research

Health research is needed to examine the increasing effect that ill health and disease have on the population. In the UK research programmes are funded by the Department of Health, which sets the overall policy on all health issues including public health matters and the health consequences of environmental issues. Visit www.dh.gov.uk and for recent health research projects such as 'Bird flu and pandemic influenza' click on news.

Sociological research

Sociological research involves investigation into social institutions such as the family, law and order or education, or any facet of the society in which people live. An example of a sociological research project could be the examination of the diet of different socioeconomic groups or the life expectancy of different groups within a named area.

Psychological research

Psychological research is carried out to identify why people behave the way they do. Psychologists carry out research on ordinary people to find out how they function, which will help them to understand human behaviour. Scientific methods of study, such as observations or experiments, are often used but so, too, are questionnaires and structured interviews. An example of a psychological research project could be why some teenagers develop anorexia and others do not.

Special and early years research

Special and early years research aims to investigate what gives a child the best start in life; whether it is health, family support, early education or childcare. There are lots of suitable topics for research within this area – for example, examining how special educational needs are catered for in different schools, or which toys offer value for money, or nursery provision and its impact on primary education.

Purpose of research	Activity 2

Look at the four purposes of research suggested at the beginning of 16.2.1.

Either

1 Explain in detail how the health services can use the information from the National Census to help them improve services.

Or

2 Explain in detail how the housing services can use the National Census information to help them improve services.

Data collection

There are many different methods that can be used to collect information and data. These include:

- quantitative and qualitative research
- primary research
- secondary research.

Quantitative and qualitative methods

Some research is quantitative, some is qualitative and some uses a mixture of both to collect data. Data is the name given to the information which is collected.

Quantitative

As the name quantitative suggests, this research is related to quantity. Usually quantitative research produces large amounts of facts which can be analysed **statistically** or mathematically. It is a good way to measure something, for example the number of people who would use a proposed gymnasium and how many times they would use it. The answers to these questions could be analysed and used to help the gymnasium owners decide where would be the best place to site the proposed gymnasium.

Quantitative data is often collected by researchers who use questionnaires consisting of questions with a choice of specified answers – opinions are not wanted. Charts, graphs and diagrams are ideal for presenting this quantitative data. This makes the data fairly easy for people to follow and understand.

QUESTIONNAIRE

Can you please fill in the following questions as best you can?
Please circle the most appropriate answer.
Thank you very much for taking time to complete this questionnaire.

1. Are you male or female?
   Male   Female

2. How old are you?
   11–12   15–16
   13–14   17–18

3. Do you eat fruit and vegetables?
   Yes   No

4. How many pieces of fruit and vegetables do you eat on average per day?
   None   3–4
   1–2   5–6

5. What types of fruit and vegetables do you eat?
   ....

6. Do you enjoy eating them? Explain why or why not.
   Yes   No
   ....
   ....

7. How many pieces of fruit or vegetables do you think you are supposed to eat per day?
   0–2   6–8
   3–5

Sample of a questionnaire

Qualitative

As the name suggests, qualitative research is related to quality, in the sense that participants qualify or give a reason for their answer. In this method of research, researchers are interested in people's opinions, thoughts and reasons. Quality answers or answers which are qualified give researchers a better understanding of participants' views and feelings.

If the example of the proposed gymnasium were used in qualitative research then researchers would be interested in the reasons why people did/did not want to use this proposed facility. Qualitative data cannot easily be analysed mathematically as feelings, views and thoughts do not convert readily into mathematical formulae. Many participants' views and the quality of their answers would be lost if their interviews and observations were reduced to numbers.

Both qualitative and quantitative research is useful and one is not better than the other. Often researchers use a mixture of both. For example, a researcher examining under age drinking could use quantitative research to find out the age teenagers started drinking, when they drink, where they drink, how many units, etc. The resultant data could be analysed mathematically. However, qualitative research would be used when asking the teenagers how they felt whilst they were drinking and why they felt they had to start drinking.

Finding out about a person's opinions

Quantitative and qualitative research methods   Activity 3

Adam has to produce a questionnaire using both quantitative and qualitative research methods. He has to find out about teenage eating habits.

1   Write **five** questions that Adam could use in his questionnaire that demonstrate his understanding of *quantitative*.

2   Write **five** questions that would demonstrate Adam's understanding of *qualitative*.

Primary research methods

Primary research is research that a researcher has carried out themselves. It need not be an original idea. For example, many different people have researched into the transition period for Year 7 joining a big new school. If you used this idea (which is not original) and carried out the research within a local school then the information you found out for yourself would be unique. It would be new, first-hand, original research.

Primary research   Activity 4

On 1 September 2006 a new law came into force which means that relatives lose the right to block organ donation. Up until now a family could stop doctors from taking their loved one's organs even if the brain dead person carried an organ donor card.

1   Produce a short questionnaire to find out if people are aware of this new law.

2   Do they agree with this law?

The following are all examples of primary research:

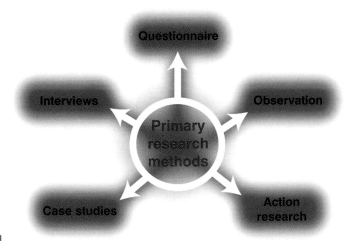

Examples of primary research

Interviews

Interviews can be used for both quantitative and qualitative research. Generally, they provide more detailed information than a questionnaire. However, they are more time consuming as they take longer to carry out since they are on a one-to-one basis. Researchers often gain more information as participants tend to say more than they would write on a questionnaire. There is usually a high response rate as participants are asked the questions directly with the researcher writing down their answers. This allows the researcher to collect more information as participants are usually keener to talk than they are to write. However, researchers can often influence participants by using **affirmative body language**.

Advantages	Disadvantages
1. Higher response rate as participants are asked questions directly. 2. More information gained as participants like to talk rather than write.	1. Time consuming as carried out one-to-one. 2. Researcher can influence or lead participants by smiling or nodding.

Advantages and disadvantages of interviews

Interviews can be:

- structured or formal
- unstructured or informal
- semi-structured.

Structured or formal interviews are useful for collecting quantitative data. Answers are controlled by the use of **closed questions** which do not allow the participants to expand of any of their answers. Everyone interviewed is asked the same set of questions. The researcher is less likely to influence the participant's reply. However, there is a total lack of **flexibility** and any extra valid comments from the participants are lost.

Advantages	Disadvantages
1. Everyone answers the same questions. 2. Researcher less likely to influence participant.	1. No flexibility. 2. Valid comments from participants not used.

Advantages and disadvantages of using structured interviews

Researchers have more control over **unstructured** or informal interviews as there is not a rigid list of pre-set questions. Participants are allowed to develop their answers and researchers can encourage them to do so. Although there is no list of pre-set questions, researchers usually have a list of topics or areas that they need to cover during the interview. Researchers have to be careful to direct the interview otherwise it could become a cosy chat for the participant and would be very time consuming for the interviewer.

Advantages	Disadvantages
1. Flexible as questions are used as a guide for interview. 2. Participants can expand on answers and researchers can probe further.	1. Although questions are similar not all participants are asked the same ones. 2. Researcher has to control interview or it could become a cosy chat. 3. Could be very time consuming.

Advantages and disadvantages of unstructured interviews

Semi-structured interviews are a mixture of **structured** and unstructured interviews. The researcher has a set list of questions but s/he can ask extra questions where appropriate.

It is important that the researcher puts a time limit on interviews otherwise participants may feel they have to give up too much of their time. During unstructured interviews a researcher may be considerably detained by someone who just wants to talk.

Points for the researcher to consider when interviewing are:

1. If s/he is taking notes then s/he must be sure to have a system of recording the answers.
2. Using a tape recorder could free up the researcher from having to write notes during interview therefore s/he is able to concentrate on participant. However, the participant must be asked, in advance, if they agree to this and *must* be given the option to refuse.
3. Confidentiality must be respected at all times.
4. The researcher must be careful to avoid bias, so it is very important that questions are carefully worded and not slanted in any way.

Interview using a tape recorder — Activity 5

1 Ask an older person with children over 21 if you can carry out an unstructured interview with them. Seek their permission to tape record the interview.

2 Your topic for the interview will be 'Being a Parent'. Draw up a list of topics you wish to cover in your interview.

3 Record the interview.

4 Afterwards listen to the interview. Was it useful to record it? Would you have been able to keep up if you had been taking notes?

Interviews should have a time limit!

Questionnaires

Questionnaires are often used to gather primary data. A questionnaire is a series of questions designed by a researcher. The questions often have a '**forced choice**' answer which gives the participant a limited range of answers to choose from. Opinions are not asked for.

Do you work:

☐ Full-time

☐ Part-time

☐ Student

☐ OAP

☐ Unemployed

Example of 'forced choice' question

Some questions are open, others are closed. For example, a closed question could be, 'Do you smoke?' 'Yes' or 'No'. An **open question** could be, 'What do you think about smoking?'. Whether open or closed questions are used will depend on the depth of information needed.

Questionnaires should be:

- as short as possible – if a question is not relevant do not ask it;
- logically arranged and should not jump from topic to topic;

- **unambiguous** and should make sense;
- written in straightforward and simple language;
- careful about asking for personal information.

Questionnaires are a good way for researchers to obtain a large amount of quantitative data.

Discussion point

Kathryn was carrying out research (during a work placement) into 'My treatment for breast cancer on the NHS'. She produced a questionnaire which met the approval of the hospital. She planned to ask women who came to the Oncology Dept to complete the questionnaire. However, this was not successful as women were reluctant to complete it.

At the end of her work placement Kathryn had two completed questionnaires. The receptionist on duty in Oncology suggested that Kathryn should leave the questionnaires in the waiting room with a sealed box for the completed ones. Two weeks later when she returned Kathryn found ten completed questionnaires.

Why do you think the first approach was unsuccessful yet the second one achieved results?

It is a good idea to pilot the questionnaire within a small group of people (five should be sufficient). This is to ensure that any anomalies, e.g. questions that could be misunderstood, are picked up before the questionnaire goes out to too many participants. Any comments from the pilot group should be acted upon.

Advantages	Disadvantages
1. Researcher's time is used effectively.	1. Time consuming to produce good questions.
2. Cheap and easy to produce.	2. Return rates can be low.
3. Offer anonymity to participants.	3. If questions misunderstood, it will affect outcomes.
4. Can produce a large amount of data quickly.	4. Questionnaire must be piloted.
5. Participants can answer questionnaire at their own pace.	5. No opportunity to probe answer given.

Advantages and disadvantages of questionnaires

Questionnaire on organ donation — Activity 6

Topic: People's decisions on organ donation should be respected by their families.

1 Draw up 5 or 6 questions on the above topic.

2 Was it easy or difficult to think of the questions?

3 Pilot your questions.

4 Did people understand your questions and answer them in the way you thought they would?

Observation

As the name implies, this research method involves watching people and/or events. Meaningful observation is not easy and is a skill that researchers develop over many years of practice. Behaviour is studied as it happens. Researchers do not have to ask people what they do – they watch them doing it!

Observations need to be well planned and the researcher must be open minded and not have any pre-conceived ideas about what will happen or how someone will behave.

Researchers often use observation when they are studying young children because questionnaires and interviews are not usually suitable with this age group. It is a good way to observe physical, intellectual, emotional and social development. Observations are also a good way of looking at **social relationships**. For example, how service users in residential care relate to one another.

Observations — Activity 7

Working with a partner, spend twenty minutes observing the same scene. It could be students in the common room, lower school playing in the yard, students in a PE lesson, students queuing for lunch, etc.

Working independently, write down what you see. Do not talk about this:

1 Was it easy to observe?

2 Compare notes – have you both noted the same things?

3 Discuss any differences in what you have reported.

4 Why do you think there were differences when you were observing the same group?

There are two main types of observation:

- **participant**
- **non-participant**

Researchers using participant observation will join in with the individuals they are observing. The picture below gives an example where the researcher is helping the children to complete a jigsaw but is still observing them.

An example of participant observation

A researcher observing social interaction in a residential home may form the staff as part of the caring team and record any observations as part of normal daily life. However, although the observer blends in with the group it may be difficult to record everything as it happens.

Non-participant observation is where the researcher takes no part in any activities within the group. Researchers look on from the sidelines and have no interaction with the people they are observing. An example could be an Ofsted inspector watching a lesson in a school. With this type of observation the researcher may have an effect on the group behaviour. This is because the people in the group know they are being observed and may change their normal behaviour. This would give the researcher a false picture. Observers need to be good watchers and listeners who are not easily distracted from the task in hand.

Advantages	Disadvantages
1. Researcher can collect data 'as it happens'.	1. Participant observers can be distracted and 'too much involved' with the group to remain objective.
2. Researcher can 'narrow down' his/her topic during the observation. For example, a study on play could be narrowed down to gender differences or most used equipment.	2. Very time consuming.
3. Able to observe body language and non-verbal as well as verbal behaviour.	3. Small groups are normally observed; therefore behaviour observed in one nursery, for example, may not be representative of other nurseries.
4. Detailed data can be collected.	4. Observer may affect group's behaviour and give a false picture.

Advantages and disadvantages of observation

An example of non-participant observation

Action research

This is related to observation and is used when a researcher wishes to **evaluate** changes or solve a problem in their own working environment.

This means that the research carried out relates only to the hospital, care home, nursery, school, etc., where it was carried out. An example of action research could be:

Veryan has decided to monitor the new security system in the nursery where she is manager. After a scare, when one of the children was nearly taken from the nursery yard, the owners decided to have a more rigorous security operation. In practice this means that a member of the nursery staff must be on hand every day to monitor the arrival and the departure of the children. A CCTV system has also been fitted. Veryan must now evaluate the new system and decide if it will help to keep the premises safe and protect the children from strangers. Has the system solved the original problem or can Veryan spot other unforeseen problems?

Another example could be the monitoring of more flexible mealtimes in a residential home. Do the residents appreciate the new flexibility and how much extra pressure does it place on the staff? The manager of the residential care home could evaluate the success of the new meal regime and see if it was worth the extra staff time and effort.

Action research — Activity 8

1 Can you think of any action research you could carry out in your setting? Are there any problems you could monitor? Or changes you could evaluate?

Case studies

A case study can be used to illustrate a point. In any research project a case study can add weight and substance to a claim.

Example case study

Amber has been researching into cyber-bullying and how it was easier for the bullies this way but just as distressing for the victim. Amber knew someone at school, Suz, who had been bullied this way. She interviewed Suz and asked her permission to include her story in her research project – obviously her anonymity was assured. The girl's story backed up Amber's findings that the victims were easy targets as they tended to be loners who had few friends at school. Amber added weight to her project by reporting that Suz had been cyber-bullied over a two-year period which had led her to become severely depressed, anorexic and suffering from panic attacks.

Secondary research methods

Secondary research is using existing material which has been produced by someone else. This can make a researcher's job easier as it is useful to look at existing sources as they are a good starting point and can suggest useful ideas.

The following are examples of types of secondary research:

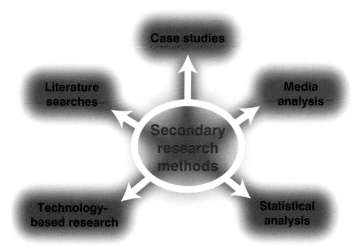

Examples of secondary research methods

Literature searches

This is one of the main sources of secondary research materials. It can include:

- books
- magazines
- newspapers (daily and weekly, local and national)
- specialist journals.

Points to remember when choosing suitable books:

- Make sure the information is current and up-to-date. It is no good using a book from 1952 if the topic is latest medical advances for the millennium! Check the age of the research and statistics in any book.
- Sometimes specialist books are difficult to understand and it is better to refer to a condensed, simplified version that could be found in a textbook. It is essential to understand any information used in a piece of work otherwise the information may be used in the wrong context.
- Do not assume that just because the data has been published, it is correct. It is a good idea to look for similar data which could add validity to the original material.

Points to remember when choosing suitable newspapers, magazines and journals:

- Remember that newspapers can slant information to their readers' views – it is what the readers want: to see that other people have similar views to themselves – this is particularly true of political issues.
- Tabloid newspapers often seek sensationalism and exaggerate facts. They take a small fact and blow it up out of all proportion as this is what sells these newspapers.
- Generally, articles in newspapers and magazines will be factual and easy to understand.
- Professional journals may use technical language so, although they are more reliable than a newspaper, they could be more difficult to understand.

Remember that any information produced by a pressure group will be heavily **biased** towards their particular message. For example, information produced by any green organisation will heavily reflect their green ideals and may **distort** facts to back any claims.

Generally, as an inexperienced researcher, it is a good idea to restrict research to the UK, as education and social services statutory law are usually applicable to a specific country. There is a huge amount of information available for the United States which is not relevant to this country.

It is very important to keep an ongoing updated record of books, newspapers, etc. used, as it is very difficult to remember all the literature used throughout the research. It is a good habit to note any references as soon as you use them. Record the name of the author and textbook title or the date and title of the newspaper used. Even if you have only used the textbook for ideas, still acknowledge it. Remember to give credit to other people's work.

Secondary research   Activity 9

1 Carry out a literature search on Alzheimer's disease.

2 List the secondary sources of information or data available.

3 Is the data current or up to date?

Media analysis

This incorporates certain areas of the media. Sometimes media coverage can be biased so it is important to look at other viewpoints in order to achieve a balanced view.

The diagram gives some examples of media analysis.

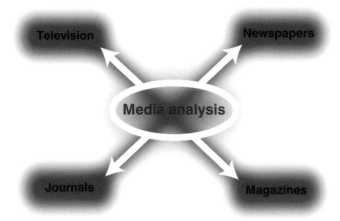

Examples of media analysis

Current affairs programmes and television documentaries can be a useful source of information. It is a good idea to record relevant programmes. If the programme has been recorded it is then easy to re-watch specific areas and to take notes. Recent research shown in the programme could give ideas for further investigation or could establish new facts and figures.

The programme could supply further websites, information addresses or fact sheets available to the general public.

Television   Activity 10

Look through the television listings for the next week.

1   List any Health and Social Care topics which are covered by documentaries and current affairs programmes.

Back issues of newspapers, magazines and journals can be researched in the local library. If the subject is topical there should be a lot of media interest in it.

An example of media interest

Discussion point   IVF treatment

Quote from the Daily Mail 2 September 2006:

'The British Fertility Society has urged the government to ban fat women from free IVF treatment on the NHS on the grounds that being overweight reduces success rates and adds to health risks.'

1   Do you agree with the British Fertility Society?

2   Research this topic in newspapers, magazines and journals. How much useful information is there?

Technology-based research

Technology research can be exciting

The advance in technology has provided many different technological resources for researchers.

Here are some examples of technology-based research.

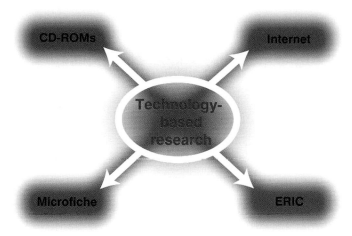

Technology-based research

CD-ROMs

There are many different CD-ROMs covering a multitude of different subjects. Libraries usually carry a wide range of them. CD-ROMs make it easy to explore topics in a short period of time. National newspapers often produce past articles on CD-ROM and sometimes give free copies of educational interactive material.

CD-ROMs	**Activity 11**

1 Carry out research in a local library and find out how many CD-ROMs are available in the Health and Social Care discipline.

2 Borrow one and run it for ten minutes. Was it useful? Did it teach you anything in that short period of time?

3 Contact a national newspaper and enquire if they have produced a CD-ROM on a Health and Social Care topic that you find interesting. What would be the cost of the CD-ROM.? Is it value for money? Why?

4 Does the library stock any national newspaper CD-ROMs?

The Internet

The Internet offers many **search engines** which help researchers find their way through huge amounts of information to the specific areas that are of interest. Examples of search engines include Google, Ask Jeeves and Yahoo.

There are also online encyclopaedias and online libraries. Some of these are downloadable and copyright free. However, always check that copyright laws are not broken.

National newspapers are available online as are some of the BBC's news reports. Hansard (transcripts from Parliamentary debate) is also available.

It is wise to remember to use reputable, recognised sites as anyone can set up a website and the information found on it may be inaccurate.

The Internet	**Activity 12**

1 Get the web address of a broadsheet newspaper (e.g., www.timesonline.co.uk) and go online to the web address. Look at the range of reports available. How useful would this be to someone researching?

2 Visit www.bbc.co.uk. How useful is this site for a researcher? Did you know this BBC website allows you to listen to programmes you have missed over the course of the last week?

ERIC (Educational Resources Information Centre) is usually found in higher education libraries. ERIC searches for the key words it has been asked for and produces a list of further sources such as books or articles from journals. It may suggest books which are difficult to obtain because they have gone out of print or there were not many published in the first place.

Microfiche

Microfiche is one of the most compact storage systems. It is used to provide a comprehensive research library in further/higher education institutions. Copies of books, journals, periodicals and newspapers are usually stored on microfiche. The image is too small to read without a special reader that projects full size images on a ground glass screen.

Case studies

Case studies have already been mentioned in primary research but case studies presented by other researchers can be used as secondary research. They could be used to add weight to primary research. For example, a researcher looking into gender differences (related to play) in a nursery school found a case study in a professional journal which backed up her findings. She used the secondary research case study as she felt it gave weight to her own findings.

Statistical analysis

National and local government produce lots of different statistics which may be useful to researchers. The information collected by the Census is likely to give a researcher an accurate picture of income, housing, etc. in Britain as the survey is carried out extremely carefully. Similarly, health statistics collected by the Census would be useful if researching into coronary heart disease within a county district. Remember to check that the research is the most recent set of data available.

The Office for National Statistics (ONS) is useful for **demographic**, economic and social statistics which are up to date. Their website is www.ons.gov.uk.

Whatever the choice of research topic it is very likely that someone else has conducted research into the chosen area. It is important to consider the relevant theories put forward by the previous research. That is why a search using all the secondary research methods referred to in this assessment objective is necessary. Reading around a research subject is vital otherwise the final publication will lack depth and relevance. One of the best ways to start to research would be to look at what is available in a city or town library. Librarians are a good resource, so do ask for advice as they can save a lot of wasted time and frustration as they will often know where to find the information needed.

A rationale is an introductory statement about the research which goes into detail or expands the hypothesis, issue or research question. It may describe what the research is trying to find out or demonstrate links to previous knowledge or research.

Assessment activity (AO1)

1. Give an in-depth explanation of the purposes of research and three different research methods which are available.

2. Give a sound explanation of the rationale for your chosen research area.

The work will be coherent and demonstrate an understanding of the subject area. There will be no inaccuracies or omissions within the evidence.

16.2.2 Ethical issues, sources of error and bias in research

Ethical issues are very important considerations when carrying out any research. These include:

- considering the participants' rights
- the importance of confidentiality
- issues relating to anonymity
- issues relating to the nature and type of research.

These issues will be dealt with throughout this section but it is important to understand what ethical issues are.

Ethical issues

Ethics are codes of behaviour or sets of moral values. They are what people know or feel is the right type of human behaviour. Ethics can be related to conscience. Before any researcher carries out any investigation they must be sure that any participant would not be damaged by their study. A researcher must **adhere** to a recognised code of conduct.

In research, ethics are rules which dictate what good practice is during the course of research. Bad behaviour is to behave unethically during the research process. The researcher has the responsibility to behave ethically to anyone taking part in the research. Remember, when dealing with sensitive topics, that some participants might find it difficult to discuss their feelings or even answer questions if they have been personally involved.

Participants must decide to join the research **voluntarily**. The aims of the research must be fully explained to them and they must freely agree to take part. This is called **informed consent** as participants have been told what they have to do, and they have then agreed to take part in the research. If they wish to withdraw from the research at any time, then this is well within their rights.

It is **unethical** to involve participants with mental impairments in research, as it would be very difficult to be sure such participants understood the type of research, the requirements of the research or any potential risks of the research. Parent/carer permission must be obtained in the instance of very young children. If research is to be carried out in a school, then the permission of the headteacher must be obtained. The headteacher is *in loco parentis* (in place of the parent) while the child is in school.

Researchers must never harm any participant. Their research must not damage the participant either physically or mentally. This would be unethical behaviour. Researchers must look at what has to be considered in relation to the participants involved in their research project. These include:

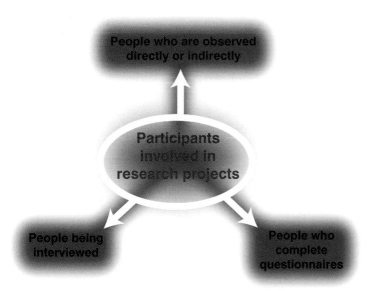

People who are observed directly or indirectly

Participants involved in research projects

People being interviewed

People who complete questionnaires

Participants involved in research projects

People being interviewed

The researcher must be careful to allow the participant to have their own view and must not try to control the situation. Leading questions can be used by the researcher to give a personal bias to the interview. For example, if a participant were to be asked a question beginning with, 'You do think...' then this is a leading opening to a question which leads to the answer, 'Yes, I do'. The approach is then **subjective** rather than **objective**. Sometimes the participant may find subjects sensitive and it is up to the researcher to handle the questioning in a suitable manner. The participant will need to be reassured about how the interview will be used. It would be distressing as well as unethical for the participant to find out that the interview had been discussed with people who were not part of the research project. Confidentiality and anonymity will also have to be agreed. Sensitivity to the participant is important.

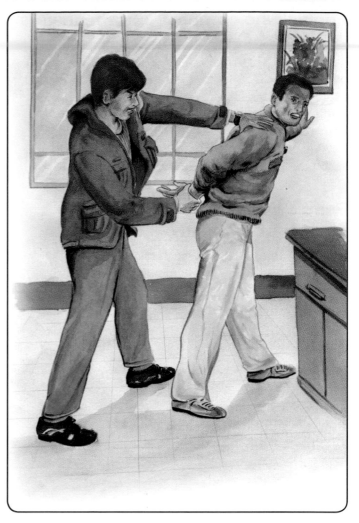

'You do think overweight people shouldn't have IVF funded on the NHS don't you?'

Research benefits should be balanced with the research risks

People who complete questionnaires

The information given in the interview section also applies to participants who complete questionnaires. Beware of leading questions such as, 'You do think the NHS is not giving value for money don't you?'. Again, confidentiality and anonymity is important to the participant and they should be reassured. Handle delicate subjects in a sensitive way.

People who are observed either directly or indirectly

Permission must be sought for both direct and indirect observations. This is especially important if the participant is too young or has mental impairments and is unable to give permission themselves. Anonymity and confidentiality are important here, too.

Sometimes ethical considerations are unnecessary, for example if a researcher were observing in a public place, such as a supermarket or shopping centre. This is because the participants are:

- not asked any questions, therefore don't give personal opinions
- watched very briefly
- not identifiable
- part of a large number of people.

Ignoring the importance of ethics

Ignoring ethics could cause a lot of distress to the participants and cause problems for the researcher. If participants complained or were distressed because the research was not handled sensitively then the whole research project could be called into question. In research, benefits should balance with the risks of the research.

The importance of ethical consideration must be understood when carrying out research, including:

- considering the participants' rights
- the importance of confidentiality
- issues related to anonymity
- issues related to the nature and type of research.

Considering the participants' rights

Before carrying out any research it is very important to consider the participants' rights.

Here are the rights of participants:

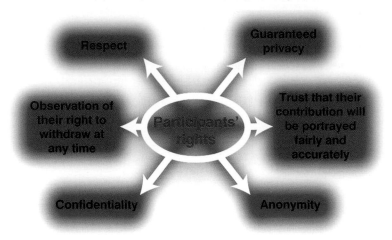

Participants' rights

Before carrying out research the researcher must:

- respect the participants' views and record their answers correctly – there should be no distortion of facts
- ensure any information is kept confidential (this will be dealt with in more detail in the next section)
- be sure the participant remains nameless or anonymous
- respect the participant throughout the research process
- allow the participant to leave the study if they wish to do so – participants should not feel pressured to stay in the research programme
- allow the participant guaranteed privacy – views recorded should remain private and not be broadcast to other people.

Disregard of any of the participants' rights would be morally or ethically wrong.

The importance of confidentiality

It is important to be aware of the right to confidentiality of the participants:

- individuals
- organisations
- people who have assisted in the research through work placement or place of employment (internal research).

Individuals

Any individual who agrees to take part in any research will need to know who will have access to the information. They will also need to know how, when and where the research will be published. They have the right to expect that any information they have given to the researcher will remain private. Any data produced in the research must only be used for the purpose for which it was originally collected. No part of the research data should be passed on to other researchers.

Organisations

Permission must be sought from the organisation as well as the participant. If this is not done at an early stage in the research process, then the organisation might withdraw from the project, which could cause the researcher problems, particularly if the research was well underway. Be careful not to offend anyone by comments which are less than complimentary.

Internal research

If working or on work placement in a care setting, school, etc., the researcher has to be careful not to upset anyone, as it is important to maintain cordial relationships with colleagues. Unfavourable comments could have repercussions on the promotion prospects of the researcher. Unhappiness about the results of the research could stop future research as the manager may feel that the current research findings have had a demoralising effect on staff and service users.

Guaranteed privacy

Any participant has the right to privacy and the researcher must respect this. Any information that is collected by the researcher should be kept secret or private and only used without identifying the participant. The information should not be broadcast as this may cause embarrassment to the participant.

Observation of their right to withdraw

The researcher must respect the participant's right to withdraw at any stage in the research process. The research must not pressurise the participant to remain in the programme by making comments that make the person feel guilty, for example, 'I've spent a lot of time with you, where am I going to find someone else now?'.

Issues related to anonymity

Participants have the right to remain anonymous – their names should not be published nor should they easily be identifiable by information contained in the research report. For example, if a teacher was interviewed in a school and the researcher mentioned that this participant taught Year 3 in a named primary school, then it would be easy to work out who this participant is. People are more likely to give truthful answers if they know they will not be identified.

Respect at all times

The researcher must show respect to the participant at all times even if their views and beliefs are contrary to those of the researcher.

Trust that their contribution will be portrayed fairly and accurately

Any views given by the participant must be recorded exactly as they have been given and must not be interpreted in a slightly different way to give a different meaning to the original statement. Researchers must be careful not to let personal bias creep in to their recording of material.

Ethical issues   Activity 13

As part of their Health and Social Care course, two students decided to carry out a study into anti-social behaviour in a street known to have a problem with underage drinkers. The students designed and piloted a set of standard questions. They then knocked on residents' doors and asked if they would be prepared to be interviewed on the anti-social behaviour. Out of 32 residents 21 agreed to be interviewed. On the bus back home the students discussed the interviews openly. Next day back at their Centre they asked another student on a different course, if he lived in that street. When he said he did, they told him what the other residents had said – giving him house numbers but not names. When the results of the interview were published, they mentioned someone with twins living in that street.

1   Was there any good practice in the above case study?

2   Had ethics been applied when carrying out the study? What evidence do you have for your answer?

Issues relating to the nature and type of research

It is important to understand the issues relating to:

- covert observation
- the building up of trust
- ensuring true representation of participants' views.

Covert observation

Covert observation is where the researcher hides their identity, rather like a police detective working undercover. The participants do not know who the researcher is or what they are doing – both the identity and the purpose of the researcher are kept secret. Sometimes covert observation is the only way of collecting information. This is especially true of unco-operative or hostile groups where a researcher would not be allowed near, if their real purpose were revealed. For example, homeless individuals or gangs of youths would not necessarily welcome researchers into their midst. Covert observation throws up serious ethical issues.

> **Discussion point 'Covert observation'**
>
> Can you think of all the ethical issues involved in covert observation?
>
> Which ethical codes are broken?

Building up trust

Trust must be built up – it does not happen overnight. Would anyone trust someone they had just met? Probably not, as they would not know enough about them, so would feel reluctant to share personal information. If the participant does not trust the researcher then it is possible that real thoughts, feelings and answers will not be shared. The participants might be less than honest if they feel they cannot trust the researcher to keep information confidential and anonymous. Time should be taken to earn the trust of the participant especially if sensitive issues are to be aired.

Ensuring true representation of participants' views

The researcher needs to choose the appropriate research method as this will have an impact on the way their findings regarding their views are presented. For example, a questionnaire to find out the most popular toy in a pre-school nursery might not be the best method as two- to three-year-old children may

misunderstand the questions. It would be far better to carry out an observation over several days.

Issues of objectivity and subjectivity

When carrying out any research it is important that the researcher is **objective**. This means that they are able to examine any material that has been collected without any bias or prejudice. Research results must not be distorted by the researcher's feelings. They must report what they have found and must not add extra points which have not been demonstrated by their research. It is very easy for personal opinions or views to affect research findings, therefore the researcher must try to be sure that any conclusions made are proven through the research. For research to be valuable a researcher must be as objective as possible. Findings should not be interpreted as a result of a researcher's life experiences even if the results were not as expected. The facts as they appear should be analysed and presented. Recognising that personal opinions and views can affect objectivity will help the researcher to be as objective as possible. Subjectivity is when personal opinion and views are allowed to influence the conclusions of the research. This can happen when the researcher does not base their comments on the information they have found out from participants but allows their personal opinions to colour that information. **Subjective** research is therefore not valuable as it does not given an objective view of what is happening.

> **Poppy** — **Activity 14**
>
> Poppy has decided to research into the most popular toy for two-year-old males in her local nursery. She has decided to observe the children playing and count the number of times a toy is played with. She thinks she knows the answer before she starts the research as her two-year-old son Byron loves playing with his toy garage.
>
> **1** Is Poppy being objective about her research?
>
> **2** Explain how her final conclusions could be affected.

Sources of error

Errors can happen at any stage during the research process. The following can affect the research and be sources of error:

- *Low response rate* – perhaps the researcher gave out a sufficient number of questionnaires but there was a very poor return rate. For example, a student left 20 questionnaires in the waiting room of an oncology ward but only two people

Research Methods in Health and Social Care
16.2.2 Ethical issues, sources of error and bias in research /
16.2.3 Planning, presenting and analysing findings from research

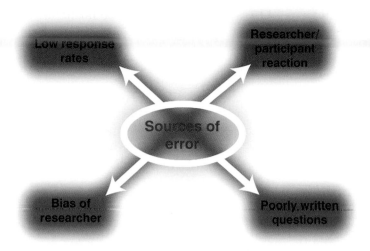

Sources of error

completed them. Could the student then say one hundred per cent of people surveyed thought that their treatment was very good?

- *Researcher/participant reaction* – during an interview perhaps the researcher was tired and did not give full attention to the participant or there could have been a personality clash which led the participant to be less than co-operative.

- *Bias of researcher* – maybe the researcher tried to influence the participant's answer either by offering their opinion or by the way the question was phrased or by their body language, for example nodding their head.

- *Poorly written questions* – the question could be biased (as discussed earlier in the unit) or may have confused the participant. Possibly the question was misunderstood by the participant. This is why it is important to pilot any questions. Biased or leading questions should be avoided, as this will affect the objectivity of the research.

Assessment activity (AO2)

1. Give an in-depth detailed explanation of the range of ethical issues which relate to your chosen research area.

2. Show a comprehensive understanding of the ethical issues, sources of error and bias which would apply to your chosen research area.

Specialised vocabulary will be used with accuracy. And you will write in a manner which conveys appropriate meaning.

There will be no inaccuracies or omissions within the evidence.

16.2.3 Planning, presenting and analysing findings from research

Any researcher needs to plan, present and analyse their findings in a manner that is suitable for a research project. The process needs to include:

- choosing the subject area
- setting out the hypothesis, issue or research question
- writing the aims and objectives for the research
- selecting appropriate research methods
- identifying ethical considerations
- time management
- record keeping.

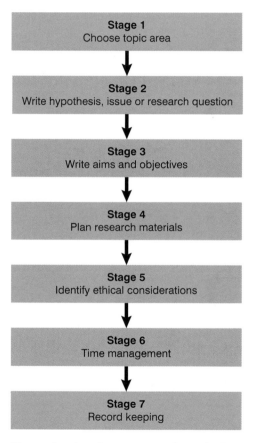

Stages in planning a research project

As set out above, it is a good idea to plan the research project in stages. It is essential for the researcher to complete the following stages.

Choose the subject area

When choosing the subject area for a research project it is good practice to choose a subject which interests the researcher. It is useful to make a list of possible topics. At this stage broad subject areas

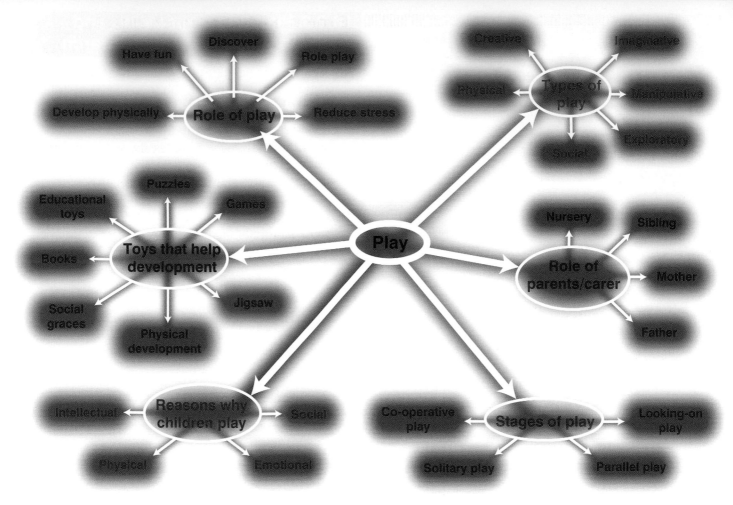

Spider diagram examining aspects of play

are fine; they can be narrowed down at the decision stage. A spider diagram is a useful tool when trying to decide on the focus of the research. For example, Fatima wants to become a nursery nurse and has decided she would like to look at play. However, it is such a wide subject area that she could spend years researching the overall topic. She decided to draw a spider diagram to help her choose her area of play.

From this spider diagram Fatima has decided that her main area of research will be toys that help development. This will be her main subject area. From this she will be able to write a hypothesis, issue or research question.

When choosing a research topic, remember to:

- Choose an area of particular interest, otherwise it may be difficult to sustain the study – boredom may set in.

- Check the amount of time available for the research project to be carried out.
- Narrow down the topic so it is specific and therefore manageable.
- Check on the availability of resources for the chosen topic. Remember that secondary research has to be used in the project so it is useful if there are a variety of materials available for use.
- Be realistic – it is a good idea to keep the research project confined to a local area and not the whole county or country. For example, it would be manageable if a project took in an area around the researcher's Centre rather than the whole of their geographical area. Similarly, deciding on a specific age group would keep the research manageable. If researching toys, for example, it would make sense to keep the study to 0–2 year olds or 3–4 year olds rather the right across the age ranges.

Mohammed — Activity 15

Mohammed decides to look into the uptake of the flu jab in Tyne and Wear across the age range of 0–75. He has 12 weeks to finish and present his research.

1. What do you think about Mohammed's topic?

2. Do you think his topic is manageable? If not, why not?

3. What suggestions would you give Mohammed regarding this project?

Setting out the hypothesis, issue or research question

Once the researcher has decided on the area of research then the **hypothesis** can be formulated. A hypothesis is a statement which is identified at the start of the chosen research. This statement makes a prediction about what the researcher will find. The researcher tests the hypothesis by finding evidence that will either support or contradict it. However, the researcher need not set a hypothesis but might prefer to set an issue or research question for the subject area. When setting the hypothesis, research question or statement, be sure the focus or end result of the project is clear, otherwise the wrong methodology could be selected. This could lead to data which does not relate to the original research idea and is difficult to explain. For example, in Fatima's spider diagram on play, unless she had narrowed her focus to toys that help development, she could have had a project which was so large that data could have been collected on 'bits' of everything, whilst finding out insufficient information about any one topic. So be clear and specific.

Example of hypothesis

New mothers often feel pressured into breastfeeding whilst in hospital but start to bottle feed once they return home.

Example of an issue

In today's society a lot of new mothers are more concerned about keeping their figures rather than giving their babies a good start in life, therefore they reject breastfeeding.

Example of a research question

To what extent have attitudes towards breastfeeding changed in the last twenty years?

Write aims and objectives for the research

An aim will clarify the hypothesis, issue or research question. The aim is the overall purpose of the research. Aims usually begin with verbs which explain what the research hopes to achieve. For example, the researcher could say they were going to find out about teenage drunkenness or to establish if teenagers feel pressured into drinking by their peers.

Objectives explain the ways the researcher is going to achieve the aim. For example, some objectives could be:

- to interview teenagers about their drinking habits
- to research facts and figures on teenage drinking
- to write a questionnaire for parents of teenagers.

Objectives break down the aim into specific tasks or things to do.

Select appropriate research methods

Primary research methods that could be used:

- questionnaires
- interviews
- action research
- observation
- case studies.

Secondary research could be:

- literature searches
- media analysis
- technology-based research
- case studies
- statistical analysis.

Please refer back to 16.2.1 for more detailed information on primary and secondary research methods.

The researcher must choose methods that are suitable for their project. For example, if the researcher was looking at Alzheimer's disease it would not be sensible or ethical to interview a person who was in the advanced stages of the disease, as they would not understand what the research was about and would not be able to answer the questions, nor be able to agree to take part in the project.

Considerations to bear in mind:

- Choose the participants to be interviewed, observed or questioned carefully as this can make a difference to the outcomes and validity of the research.
- Questionnaires need careful consideration as too many questions can put participants off.
- Always pilot questionnaires to 'iron out' ambiguous questions.
- Interviews can take a long time.
- Always seek permission well in advance for any interviews, etc.

If the research is to be carried out in a school or similarly large establishment, the headteacher or person in charge needs to give their written consent.

Identify ethical considerations

Ethical issues were covered in 16.2.2 but remember:

- confidentiality and anonymity
- seek permission from those involved in the research or, if too young, then permission must be sought from their parents/carers

- is the issue sensitive? If so, how? Examples of sensitive issues include any topic where participants are asked about their feelings on personal issues, e.g. divorce
- what about participant rights?

Time management

A very important part of managing a research project – a well planned timetable is essential. It is sensible to set realistic time spans. Both primary and secondary research can take more time that the researcher may estimate; therefore it makes more sense to over-estimate rather than under-estimate the time it may take to find out information. Do not leave research until the last minute so there is little time to research properly. If timings do not go according to plan then rearrange them. Always allow plenty of time if the headteacher or parent needs to be approached to gain permission to observe/interview children. The advice is to seek permission well in advance of any proposed action.

There is no right or wrong way to write a time plan. Setting out a time plan can give the researcher direction and purpose. Achievable time plans are vital if the researcher is to keep motivated. An example of the beginning of a time plan can be seen below:

Information needed	How to get it	Date	Achieved	Further action
Think of topics of research (what is a topic of interest?)	Look in Health and Social Care books, professional journal	16/9	Partially – now have some ideas	Make final decision by 18/9
Write hypothesis, issue or research question	Clarify own ideas	23/9	Yes	X
Write aims and objectives	Help from tutor	25/9	Yes, partially	Some objectives a bit shaky – firm up by 27/9

Example of a time plan

This is the beginning of a time plan; the next stage would be to plan the research methods which were to be used. It is a good idea to explain and justify the choice of research methods. Allow lots of time for primary research to be carried out, as questionnaires, interviews and observations can take more time than expected. This will be one of the most time-consuming areas of the research project, although finding existing research, too, can be very time consuming as facts will need to be checked to ensure reliability and validity. Collating and presenting the data will need an adequate time allocation, as will the analysis and conclusion.

Record keeping

Always note down information sources as they are found – it is almost impossible to remember which book, journal, CD-ROM was useful. It is a good idea to mark down the page number within the book or journal as it saves time in searching for the relevant comment or text.

Always reference authors' ideas within the work. For example, 'Jackson (2003) came to the conclusion that...'. As well as acknowledging the authors' work, referring also allows readers to follow up the original sources. Full details of the book should appear in the bibliography, e.g. Author; Date; Title; Publisher; Place where published.

Presenting research and the findings

When presenting findings the researcher must be sure that other people can access and understand the work. Any research projects must have a title page which gives the title of the research project and the name of the researcher producing the report. A contents page should follow the title page giving the page number of each section of the report.

Example of contents page

A report must include:

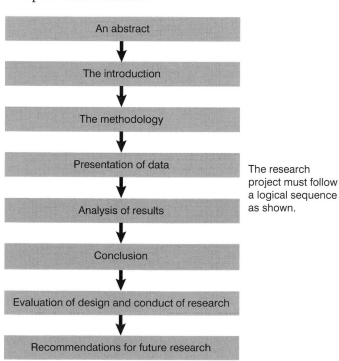

An abstract

↓

The introduction

↓

The methodology

↓

Presentation of data

↓

Analysis of results

↓

Conclusion

↓

Evaluation of design and conduct of research

↓

Recommendations for future research

The research project must follow a logical sequence as shown.

Contents of research report

An abstract

This is a brief summary of the research project. It would contain the aim, research methods used and the conclusions drawn. Be concise.

Example of an abstract   Activity 16

Barbara produced this abstract for her research project:

This research project examines how a child with special educational needs is accommodated within mainstream primary schools. It considers the views of early years workers and, using school provisions, it looks at special needs within that setting. This study focuses on the workplace, X primary school.

The research methods used in this dissertation are personal observations taken throughout the year, interviews, primary research taken from the workplace and secondary research.

This study concludes that there is scope for improvement in the way special needs are accommodated for within mainstream schools.

1. Her research question was: 'How is a child with an identified special need accommodated for within X Primary School?' Do you think this is an achievable research question? Explain why.

2. Using the abstract information above, decide if Barbara's abstract meets the criteria for a research abstract.

The introduction

This is where the subject area of the project is introduced. It would contain the aims and objectives of the hypothesis, issue or research question.

The methodology

Here is the justification of the choice of research methods. Is qualitative or quantitative data used or is there a mixture of the two? The choice of primary and secondary research methods is justified. Ethical issues are considered and addressed. The validity and reliability of the project are included in this section, so, too, is confidentiality.

Example of methodology — Activity 17

Barbara produced this methodology for her research project:

Research is the investigation of a topic for a purpose. I have found that choosing research methods requires some experience and judgements. In this research project I have chosen to use a variety of research methods.

In my project I have used both quantitative and qualitative research methods. An example of my quantitative research is the various figures and statistics on topics related to special needs. An example of my qualitative research methods is my interviews. In these, participants have expressed personal feelings and viewpoints.

Primary research involves me, the researcher, carrying out my own line of enquiry. An example of my primary research is my interviews and observations. Interviews are particularly useful to find out people's individual opinions and experiences. Observations are a useful option as they allow you to see what is really happening. Observation is useful because, whereas when you are carrying out an interview, the participant may tell you that they consider 'x' to be their preferred option, during observation you may see in practice that they really follow 'y' instead. In this respect observation can obtain a truer overall result. I also used a case study (child B).

Secondary research is the use of material which has been researched or written by someone else. As an inexperienced researcher it is likely that I have used a lot more secondary research than primary research. I have used a range of books, CD-ROMs and the Internet.

I was looking forward to completing a questionnaire as one of my forms of research but unfortunately I was unable to do so as the Head Teacher of X Primary School thought it was inappropriate due to confidentiality. She also thought it might worry parents and cause problems. Therefore, I chose the research method of interviewing instead.

1. Evaluate Barbara's methodology.
2. Did it meet all the criteria suggested in the methodology section?

Presentation of data

As the name suggests, this is all the data collected and presented in the form of bar charts, pie charts, graphs, etc. These should be carefully labelled and presented in the same order as the analysis of results. Be very careful when changing raw data into percentages to ensure that figures are accurate.

Analysis of results

This is the main body of the report where the findings from the research are discussed. Results must be summarised and those that are important to the hypothesis or research question or statement should be used to support and emphasise it. Results can support or disprove the original hypothesis. Secondary research could be used by the researcher to support or refute their findings. If the researcher's results do not support the hypothesis then on no account should the findings be 'massaged'.

It is very important that the data collected is analysed carefully and is not falsified to fit the hypothesis. Do not distort the findings.

Conclusions

Here all the findings of the report are pulled together and conclusions are drawn. The researcher should not add any new information in this section. Conclusions should only be drawn from the information which has been presented in the project. The hypothesis should be referred to and the researcher should state if the aims of the research have been met.

Evaluation of design and conduct of research

This section reflects on the research carried out and how successfully it was carried out. Strengths and weaknesses are identified. Reflecting on the work carried out is a key area in this section. The whole research project must be examined here.

- Was the hypothesis suitable or achievable?
- Were the aims and objectives sensible?
- Were the primary and secondary methods chosen the best ones for the project?
- Were ethical considerations taken into account by the researcher or did they have to be pointed out as in Barbara's case (see Activity 17)?
- Was the time well planned?
- Were resources recorded and records kept throughout the project?
- Did the project go according to plan?
- What went well, what did not?
- What should be changed?

Recommendations for future research

The conclusion will help the researcher to make recommendations or suggestions for future research in the subject area. For example, Barbara could have suggested that now this study has been completed within the primary sector it would be a good idea to carry the project through to the secondary sector. This would allow the researcher to build on the previous research.

Remember to include a bibliography which lists all the books, newspapers, websites and other resources used in the research.

Example of recommendations for improvements
Activity 18

Barbara's recommendations:

I feel my research went well. I found out a lot about special educational needs within a primary school. However, I do think I limited the research by choosing to carry out the research in one school. If I were to carry out a similar project I would widen my research to include at least three schools. This would show me if schools had similar policies for special educational needs. As it was, in my study I had nothing to compare to my chosen school.

I would like to have been able to carry out a questionnaire on how parents feel about their children and their education. I feel the project would have benefited from it. The next time I would find parents willing to participate before I started the study.

1 Do you feel Barbara's suggestions for improvement were realistic?

Any results from collected data need to be presented in the appropriate format. This could include:

- tables
- bar charts
- line graphs
- pie charts
- pictographs
- sociograms
- Venn diagrams.

The same information can be presented in different ways – it is often a matter of the personal preference of the researcher.

Tables

Tables are very versatile and are a useful way of presenting information especially if data is compared. The table below shows how many students opted for a vocational course in Year 10.

When using tables always:

- label all rows clearly
- include units of measurement if using numerical data
- have an informative title for the table
- have a source of the information.

Bar charts

A bar chart is a type of graph. They are a popular method of presenting data because they are easy to understand and easy to draw. They are useful for presenting descriptive data such as how many

Students opting for vocational courses

Course	2000		2001		2002		2003	
	Boys	Girls	Boys	Girls	Boys	Girls	Boys	Girls
Business	10	15	6	21	12	21	9	23
Engineering	10	0	15	1	18	2	24	0
Art and Design	0	15	4	8	6	12	4	5
Health and Social Care	2	23	0	29	4	27	2	31
Information Technology	20	5	23	8	24	7	29	8

Source: X Comprehensive School

Example of table showing students opting for vocational course

219

students chose to follow a vocational course as the one below demonstrates.

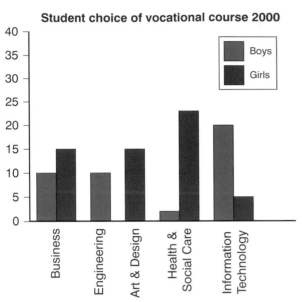

Source: X Comprehensive School

Example of bar chart

When using bar charts remember:

- have all bars the same width
- one axis has scale – the other has descriptive groupings
- bars can be vertical or horizontal
- presentation is enhanced if bars are coloured
- to include a key to colours used
- to have a clear informative title.

Bar chart   Activity 19

1   Draw a bar chart using the 2002 data from your Centre on the number of students choosing vocational courses.

Line graphs

Another type of graph, this is useful for showing changes over a period of time. If a meaningful line graph is to be produced, which does not distort facts, then a large amount of data is needed. Line graphs can be used as comparisons between sets of figures.

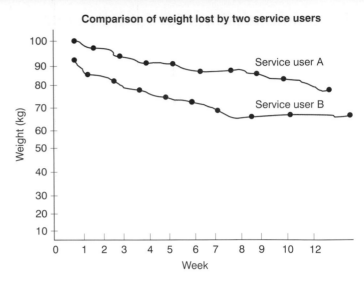

Example of line graph showing comparison

When using line graphs remember:

- axes should be clearly labelled
- units of measurement must be indicated
- good for comparisons
- horizontal axis is variable, such as units of alcohol, weight of service user, number of cigarettes smoked
- graph must have clear informative title.

Pie charts

So called because the chart is circular and when divided it looks like pieces or portions of a pie. The circle or pie represents the whole number or one hundred per cent. Any data collected must be converted into percentages in order to fit it into the chart or pie. For example, if the table below was converted into percentages for boys in 2000 the percentages would be:

Business	- 25 students out of 100	= 25%
Engineering	- 10 students out of 100	= 10%
Art & Design	- 15 students out of 100	= 15%
Health & Soc. Care	- 25 students out of 100	= 25%
Information Technology	- 25 students out of 100	= 25%

When using pie charts remember:

- have an informative title for the pie chart
- pie charts are useful for showing relative proportions

Percentage of students who chose vocational courses in 2000

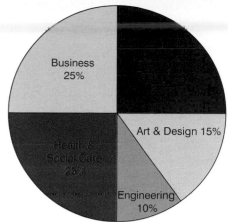

Source: X Comprehensive School

Example of a pie chart

- using different colours for different portions of the chart helps to clearly divide the portions
- each portion must be labelled or have a clear key
- too many different portions makes it difficult to draw.

Pie chart — Activity 20

1. Draw a pie chart showing the number of students who choose vocational courses in your Centre in 2003.

Pictographs (or Pictograms)

As the name suggests, a pictogram is a chart shown in a picture format. It is easy to understand and they are used for their eye-catching qualities.

When using pictographs remember:

- symbols used should relate to subject
- should have an informative title
- should have key to show what symbols represent.

Symbols for pictographs — Activity 21

1. Make a list of symbols you could use for various subjects represented by pictographs.

Number of students owning dogs and cats

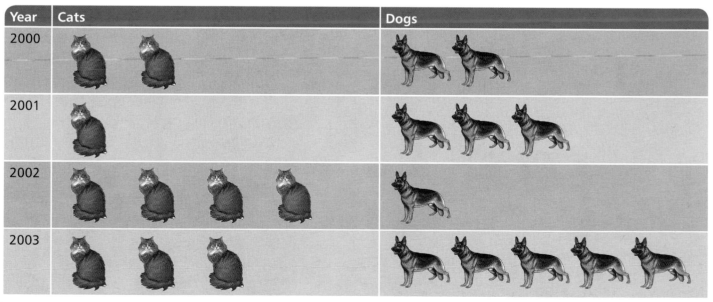

Year	Cats	Dogs
2000		
2001		
2002		
2003		

Key:  = 5 dogs   = 5 cats

Example of a pictogram

221

Sociograms

Sociograms can show the relationship between each group member or just one member of the group. They are a good way of representing a social structure with a group.

Sociogram of Vanda's social relationship with the group

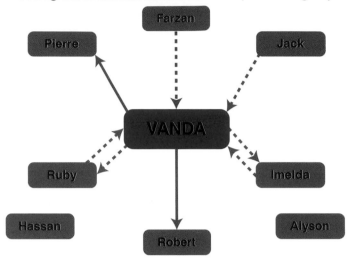

Key

- - - - - - - ▶
Denotes negative relationship

─────────▶
Denotes positive relationship

Example of sociogram (individual)

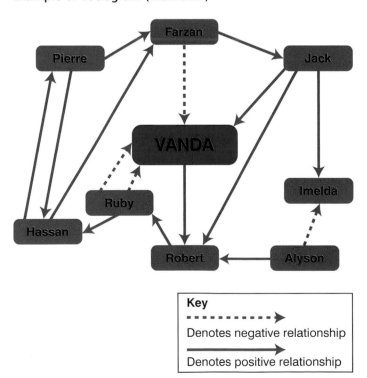

Key

- - - - - - - ▶
Denotes negative relationship

─────────▶
Denotes positive relationship

Example of group sociogram

1   From the individual sociogram is Vanda popular or unpopular?

2   Who are the most and least popular people in the group sociogram?

When using sociograms remember:

- individual members should be clearly identified
- can be useful if used in early years to see who is popular and who is not
- an informative title should be used for the sociogram
- sociograms must have a clear key.

Venn diagram

A Venn diagram consists of circles which interlink. The circles can be free standing or can overlap demonstrating a link or relationship.

Chart to show students on Health & Social Care course

Students on the AS Level Health and Social Care course	Students taking Psychology	Students taking NVQ Level 2	Part-time students
Aisla	Temal	Aisla	Katie
Jermain	Ursula	Laura	Max
Ross	Adrian	Ross	Jermain
Temal	Max	Jermain	Ross
Katie	Ross		
Ursula			
Laura			
Adrian			
Max			

This chart could be shown on a Venn diagram as below:

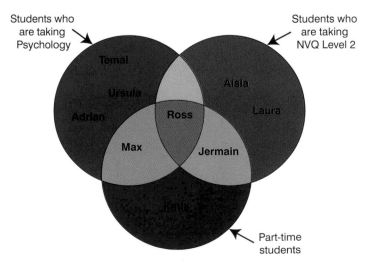

Example of Venn diagram

Research Methods in Health and Social Care
16.2.3 Planning, presenting and analysing findings from research /
16.2.4 Evaluating findings from research

The Venn diagram on page 222 shows that Ross is the only student who is part-time; taking Psychology and NVQ Level 2.

It is important that the research undertaken needs to support the hypothesis, question or research issue which was used as the research project. The range of research methods and data sources must be sufficient to provide depth and breadth to the research project. Presentation of the data needs to be relevant and any diagrams need to be supported by a brief description of what is shown. The data collated must be used to analyse the findings.

If the findings are to be presented orally, then it is a good idea to produce a CD or video recording of the presentation. However, there must be written material to support this oral presentation.

An oral presentation is much enhanced by the use of visual aids such as:

- audio-visual resources (videos, CDs/DVDs, computer-aided slide show)
- tables, charts and graphs
- handouts
- posters
- photographs.

Assessment activity (AO3)

1 Use three different relevant information sources to undertake research in your chosen area of study ensuring there is a balance of primary and secondary sources of data.

2 Evidence will be presented in an appropriate and coherent format, followed by a comprehensive analysis of your findings.

3 Research methods and analytical techniques will be justified.

There will be no omissions or inaccuracies within the evidence.

16.2.4 Evaluating findings from research

Any researcher must evaluate their research project to include their plans, actions and the written (and oral if applicable) presentation of the research work.

Strengths and weaknesses must be identified, as should successes and failures.

Discussion of the following issues must take place:

- reliability
- validity
- representativeness.

Reliability

If the findings of research can be **replicated** or repeated again (carried out by a different researcher) with the same or similar results, then the data is said to be reliable. Reliability relies on the researcher using appropriate research methods. It is therefore important to choose the best method for the study. Could other methods have been used? Would they give similar results?

If the consumption of alcohol among teenagers was the topic then it is likely that interviewing different age groups of people (for example, 14–19 year olds and 45–50 year olds) would give very different results. So, too, would the area you chose to carry out the survey, for example a village, a city, small town and so on. Culture would also affect the result – if alcohol were banned as part of a religious belief, then the results could be very different than if alcohol were tolerated.

Validity

Validity refers to whether the researcher has actually measured what they said they were going to measure. If something is valid it is said to be true. Validity gives a true picture of what was being researched. It has to address what it said it was going to address.

Do the questions that the researcher asked the participants measure what the researcher said they wanted to measure? Do the questions address what they say they address? For example, if the researcher is measuring alcohol consumption amongst teenagers, is this what their questions actually address? To claim validity the researcher has to feel as sure as they can be that the participants have told the truth. It is often difficult to know for certain if participants have told the truth. Could the researcher have influenced their answers? Would the researcher get the same answers if they went back and asked the same questions at a later date? Would a different researcher reach a similar conclusion?

Validity addresses what is true and reliable.

Representativeness

Researchers must target participants who are representative of the group they wish to represent. If not, the results will be unreliable.

Judi	Activity 23

Judi decides to research the type of healthy food that would sell well in the school canteen. She asks a group of 25–30 year olds who work in local offices.

1 Is this representative?

Sometimes researchers generalise their findings. They may interview a very small group or sample of people who are not typical of the average group. On the basis of this study they then apply their conclusions to a whole section of the community. This is not representative of the section of the community. For example, if a student interviewed twenty Year 7 students about their school which has 1255 students, then this small number is not representative of all the pupils in the school nor does it represent all the different age groups. If Year 7 students in the same school were interviewed about the fairness of Sixth Form rules, then this group is not representative as they do not have experience of the Sixth Form rules.

Evaluation of the research

All evaluations contain elements of:

- reflection
- analysis
- making informed judgements
- drawing conclusions
- making recommendations for future planning.

Evaluating a research project is no different as all of the above need to be taken into consideration.

- Reflection means thinking about what has been done in the research project. The researcher should look back on the actions taken during the project and think about them. Were they the right actions to take? What were the alternatives?
- Analysis is examining the whole issue of the research project and then breaking it down into the small parts or components. This would make it easier for the researcher to draw conclusions.
- Making informed judgements is about the researcher measuring what they have found out

in their primary research against any knowledge that they already have. For example, if they were looking at Piaget's theory on conservation, then they may be able to apply knowledge they had from Health and Social Care lessons to practical work in a primary school classroom.

- Making reasoned judgements is where the researcher examines their decisions against facts and knowledge supplied by people who may be experts. For example, if the researcher were looking at a project which involved psychology, then they may use information which is from a psychology textbook.
- Drawing conclusions means that the researcher reflects on everything that has been done during the project. They weigh up facts from primary and secondary research and they then come to conclusions about how satisfactory the whole research project has been. Decisions are made about the hypothesis, aims and objectives, time planning, methodology, presentation and analysis of results. Once conclusions are drawn, it is the natural progression to make recommendations for future planning.
- Future planning would involve the researcher thinking about how the project could be improved if it were to be carried out again. This would be building on good practice. There are bound to be areas which were well carried out and other areas which were not.

Evaluation of the research project should include questions which help the researcher to identify:

- strengths and weaknesses
- successes and failures
- achievements.

Useful questions to start the evaluation process could be:

1. Were the aims and objectives clear?
2. Were they met? If not, why not?
3. Was the hypothesis proved or disproved? A researcher must not worry if the hypothesis set is not supported by the data collected. It is quite common and does not mean that the researcher has been unsuccessful. The researcher must remain objective and try not to change the data to suit the original hypothesis.
4. Was the research question answered?
5. Was the primary research successful? Or were the wrong methods chosen? Could different methods have been more successful?

6. Was the secondary research current and up to date and sufficiently supportive for the chosen research? How many secondary sources were used? Was the material found critically evaluated?
7. Had all the ethical issues been identified?
8. Was data collected analysed correctly? Was data produced easy to interpret and explain?
9. How well was data presented?
10. Was objectivity retained?
11. If there were problems, how were they overcome?
12. Was a conclusion drawn?
13. How well was the time managed?
14. Were all references collected as the project proceeded?
15. What changes would be made if research was carried out again?

Valid recommendations for improving the research project must be made. Suggestions need to be made for the continuation of the research project which addresses the issues raised by the evaluation of the research findings.

Assessment activity (AO4)

This assessment depends on your evaluating the success of your research.

1 Using the pre-determined aims and objectives from your research project, give a comprehensive evaluation of its success. Remember you must apply the issues of validity, reliability and representativeness to your study.

2 Make realistic and detailed recommendations for improvements and continuation of the research.

3 The strengths and weaknesses of the evidence will be explained in detail and the work will demonstrate detail and coherence.

There will be no omissions or inaccuracies within the evidence.

Unit 10: Care Practice and Provision

Every Child Matters – A Practical Guide for Teachers Cheminais R (2006), David Fulton Publishers

GCE AS Level (Double Award) Fisher A et al (2006), Folens

The Insider's Guide to the NHS Lilley R (2003), Radcliffe Medical Press

Sociology as Applied to Medicine: (5th edition) Scambler G (editor) (2005), Saunders

Websites

Every Child Matters: http://www.everychildmatters.gov.uk

Irish Heart Foundation: http://irishheart.ieopen24/catalog24

NHS inspections: http://www.bma.org.uk/ap.nsf/Content/InspectionsNHS

Patients' survey: http://www.nhssurveys.org/

Skills for Care: http://www.skillsforhealth.org.uk

Star Ratings: http://.nhs.uk/England/AboutTheNHS/StarRatings/Default.cmsx

The General Social Care Council (2005) Codes of Practice and FAQS: http://www.gscc.org.uk/

The NHS in England: http://www.nhs.uk

http://www.kc-pct.nhs.uk/news/NewEraOfPatientInvolvementInTheRunningOfHealthServices.htm

http://www.alzheimers.org.uk/After_diagnosis/Getting_support/info_communityassessment.htm

http://www.healthcarecommission.org.uk/serviceproviderinformation/annualhealthcheck.cfm

http://annualhealthcheckratings.healthcarecommission.org.uk/annualhealthcheckratings.cfm

http://www.addenbrookes.org.uk/trust/perform/Health_Check.html

http://www.cgsupport.nhs.uk/About_CG/CG_Glossary.asp

http://www.hedweb.com/bgcharlton/clingov.html

http://www.papworthpeople.com/clinical.asp?section=clinical&nav=governance

http://www.nnuh.nhs.uk/docs%5Cleaflets%5C36.pdf

http://www.southbirminghampct.nhs.uk/_services/elderly/success_charter.html

http://www.csci.org.uk/about_csci.aspx

http://www.ukhca.co.uk/mediastatement_information.aspx?releaseID=8www.ukhca.co.uk/pdfs/whocaresnow.pdf

http://www.healthcarecommission.org.uk/_db/_documents/State_of_Healthcare_2006_-_English.pdf

Unit 11: Understanding Human Behaviour

Applied AS Health and Social Care Fisher A et al (2006), Folens

BTEC National Care Walsh M, Stretch B, Moonie N, Herne D, Millar E and Webb D (2003), Heinemann

Care in Practice for Higher Still Miller J (2000), Hodder & Stoughton

Child Care and Education Bruce T and Meggit C (1999), Hodder & Stoughton

Further Studies for Social Care Holden C et al (2000), Hodder & Stoughton

Human Behaviour in the Caring Context Moonie N et al (1995), Nelson Thornes

Human Growth and Development for Health & Social Care Thompson H and Meggit C (1997), Hodder & Stoughton

Psychology for Childhood Studies Kanen T (2000), Hodder & Stoughton

Teach Yourself Psychology Hayes N (2003), Teach Yourself

The Biological Basis of Personality Eysenck H (1967), Charles C. Thomas

The Scientific Study of Personality Cattell R (1965), Penguin

Understanding Children's Challenging Behaviour Mukherji P (2001), Nelson Thornes

Websites

Cognitive theories of learning, humanistic approaches to learning, also has info on behaviourism:
www.learningandteaching.info/learning/piaget.htm,

Link to websites about Cattell:
www.psy.pdx.edu

Unit 12: Anatomy and Physiology in Practice

Anatomica the Complete Home Medical Reference Cheers G (2000), Global Books Ltd

Anatomy and Physiology (7th edition) Seeley R, Stephens T and Tate P (2006), McGraw-Hill

Principals of Anatomy and Physiology Tortora G and Grabowska S (2000), Wiley & Sons

Royal Society of Medicine Health Encyclopaedia Young R (2000), Bloomsbury Publishing

The Atlas of the Human Body Abrahams P (2002), Silverdale Books

The BMA Complete Family Health Encyclopaedia Smith T (1997), Dorling Kindersley

The Nursing Times (monthly periodical magazine)

Websites

www.archive.official-documents.co.uk/document/doh/ohnation/ohnch4.htm

www.bbc.co.uk/health

www.bupa.org.uk

www.howstuffworks.com

www.innerbody.com/htm/body.html

www.nhsdirect.nhs.uk/

Unit 13: Child Development

Advanced Early Years Care and Education MacLeod-Brudenell I et al (2004), Heinemann

BTEC National Early Years (2nd edition) Tassoni P (editor) (2006), Heinemann

Children's Care Learning and Development Tassoni P et al (2005), Heinemann

Planning Play and the Early Years Tassoni P (2005), Heinemann

Early Years Educator Vol. 7 No. 5 September (2005), MA Education

Websites

BBC – Lifestyle – Parenting:
www.bbc.co.uk

National Children's Bureau – Children's Play Council:
www.ncb.org.uk

Qualification and Curriculum Authority:
www.qca.org.uk

Skills Active – The National Network of Playwork Education and Training:
www.playwork.org.uk

Unit 14: Mental-Health Issues

A Level Psychology Flanagan C (1994), Letts Educational

Abnormal Psychology (2nd edition) Rosenhan D and Seligman M (1989), Norton

Abnormal Psychology (9th edition) Davison G et al (2004), Wiley & Sons, Inc.

Applied AS Health and Social Care Fisher A et al (2006), Folens

Current Concepts of Positive Mental Health Jahoda M (1958), Basic Books

Foundations of Psychology (3rd edition) Hayes N (2000), Thomson

GCE A2 Level Health and Social Care Moonie N (editor) (2006), Heinemann

GCE AS Level Double Award Health and Social Care Moonie N (editor) (2005), Heinemann

Human Nature and the Social Order Cooley C (1902), Scribner

Introduction to Psychology Weber A (1991), HarperCollins

Overview: A current perspective on twin studies of schizophrenia Kendler K (1983), *American Journal of Psychiatry* 140

Psychiatric and Mental Health Nursing Barker P (editor) (2003), Arnold

Psychiatric disorders in the biological and adoptive families of adopted individuals with affective disorders Wender P et al (1974), *Archives of General Psychiatry* 30

Psychology (5th edition) Gross R (2005), Hodder Arnold

Social Welfare Alive (3rd edition) Moore S (2002), Nelson Thornes

Social Work and Mental Health (2nd edition) Golightley M (2006), Leaning Matters

The Psychology of Interpersonal Behaviour (3rd edition) Argyle M (1978), Penguin

Websites

www.bbc.co.uk/health/mental

www.direct.gov.uk

www.mentalhealth.org.uk

www.mind.org.uk

www.psychonet_uk.com

Unit 15: Social Trends

Asylums: Essays on the social situation of mental patients and other inmates Goffman E (1961), Penguin

Complete A–Z Sociology Handbook Lawson T and Garrod J (2003), Hodder & Stoughton

How to Do Social Research: Sociology In Action Dunsmuir A and Williams L (1997), Collins Educational

Social Trends National Statistics (2006 edition) Office for National Statistics (2006), Palgrave Macmillan

Sociology AS for AQA: Kidd W, Abbott D and Czerniawski G (2003), Heinemann

Sociology AS the Complete Companion: McNeill P, Blundell J and Griffiths J (2003), Nelson Thornes

Sociology for AS Level Moore S, Chapman S and Aiken D (2001), Collins

Sociology Review (published quarterly) Philip Allan Publishers

Websites

BBC News is useful for constant updating of social change and statistics:
http://news.bbc.co.uk

Newspaper websites recommended for current data and articles:
http://society.guardian.co.uk

www.independent.co.uk

www.timesonline.co.uk

www.telegraph.co.uk

An example of a pressure group working in the relationships field:
www.relate.org.uk

An example of a voluntary group working on behalf of informal carers:
www.carersuk.org

National Statistics Online:
www.statistics.gov.uk

Unit 16: Research Methods in Health and Social Care

AS Level for OCR Health and Social Care Moonie N (series editor) (2005), Heinemann

BTEC Nationals Health Studies Stretch B (2002), Heinemann

BTEC National Care Walsh M, Stretch B, Moonie N, Herne D, Millar E and Webb D (2003), Heinemann

Research Methods Green S (2000), Stanley Thornes

Research Methods in Health, Care and Early Years Hucker K (2001), Heinemann

Websites

BBC Television:

www.bbc.co.uk

National Census information 2001:
www.statistics.gov.uk/census2001/B 2.asp

Statistics – demographic, economic, social:
www.ons.gov.uk

Times newspaper:
www.timesonline.co.uk

Accommodation	transferring action to a different shaped object and the schema will need to be adapted
Acute	short-term, active condition requiring treatment as opposed to a *chronic*, long-term continuing condition; short, sharp and over in a relatively short time
Adaptation	assimilation and accommodation are the two parts of adaptation
Adaptive	able to change its way or form
Adhere	to stick to or hold fast or to follow closely
Advocate	a person who speaks or acts for another person who is not able to manage by themselves
Affirmative body language	body language which is confirming or agreeing with the other person, for example nodding or smiling encouragingly
Ageing population	a population in which the proportion of people of retirement age is increasing faster than other age groups
Aggression	hostility
Aim	the intention of the activity
Antibodies	substances produced in response to an antigen; molecules of protein
Anti-discrimination	making sure everyone is included; being against discrimination
Antigens	a substance that stimulates the production of antibodies; any organism or foreign material that is not recognised by the body as being part of the body
Anxiety	worry
Assessment	observation and discussion about what a person can or cannot do and making decisions about their needs
Assimilation	transferring action to another similar shaped object, e.g. grasping a rattle then a ball
Atria	smaller upper chambers of the heart
Aversion	strong dislike
Beveridge Report	named after William Beveridge, a report in 1942, which formed the basis of the Welfare State. The report set out proposals to eliminate the five 'evils' of society – poor education, poverty, unemployment, bad housing and illness
Biased	prejudice or preference for the researcher's own argument
B-interferon	a drug used to reduce the severity of multiple sclerosis
Biopsy	a microscopic examination of tissue taken from the body to aid diagnosis
Biphosphonates	drugs used to reduce the effects of osteoporosis
Bolus	a soft mass of chewed food produced in the mouth prior to swallowing
Bone marrow	cell material found in the centre of bones where blood cells are produced
Braille	system to help severely visually impaired people to read
Bronchodilator	a drug that widens the bronchioles, (small airways in the lungs), to increase the flow of air and improve breathing
Buccal	relating to the teeth or mouth
Calcitonin	drugs used to reduce the effects of osteoporosis
Cardiologist	a doctor who specialises in heart dysfunction
Care plans	a detailed plan of the care a service user is entitled to
Centile	linked to 100 points
Centile chart	growth chart indicating normal weight and height
Chronic	disease or dysfunction that lingers on and does not go away
Chronic obstructive pulmonary disease (COPD)	collective term for chest diseases such as bronchitis and emphysema
Chyme	ingested fluid and stomach secretions mixed together
Classical conditioning	association learning
Clinicians	qualified medical practitioners
Closed questions	questions that generally have a yes or no answer
Closed society	not accepting ideas/ways from outside
Cognitive	linked to intellectual, thought processes and skills
Colic	sharp and debilitating abdominal pain

Commissioned	entering into an agreement for services to be provided	**Diffusion**	transfer of molecules across a membrane due to pressure
Commissioning levers	incentives to save money when purchasing	**Dissidents**	those who disagree with the government
Communicate	transference of ideas and knowledge usually verbally or in writing	**Distort**	twist or contort or misrepresent
		DNA	deoxyribonucleic acid, genetic building blocks
Community empowerment	the population of the local area being able to make decisions for themselves	**Dopamine**	a drug found in nerves that maintains their function
Compilation	something that is collected or compiled, such as list, report, etc.	**Effectively**	successfully; well
		Effluent	liquid industrial waste
Compromised	affected	**Ego**	the part of us that helps to resolve conflicts
Conception	the beginning of life		
Concepts	ideas	**Egocentric**	only considering self; self centred
Conditional positive regard	receiving regard depends on behaviour	**Elements**	(small) parts of
		Empathise fully	understanding from another's position
Conformist	following the accepted way; self denying	**Empathy**	understanding and compassion
Congruence	to agree	**Emphysema**	a lung disease in which the alveoli become damaged
Conscience	the inner self that determines right from wrong	**Empowerment**	to enable a service user to be in control of their lives and to make their own decisions
Continuum	the range between the two points		
Co-ordination	synchronised, working together	**Empty nest family**	a family in which the children have grown up and moved out of the parental home, leaving the adult partners as a couple again
Covert observation	studying the behaviour of a group by going undercover. This is highly unethical		
		Empty shell marriage	a couple relationship which stays together for the children but there is little emotional or physical relationship between the partners
Cyanosis	a bluish colouration of skin and mucous membranes due to too much deoxygenated haemoglobin in the blood		
		Encompass	include; surround
Delayed development	development that is behind the norm	**Endometrium**	the lining of the inside of the uterus
Deliberate	on purpose	**Environment/ Environmental**	surroundings; the area around us
Demographic	the science of the population to include the description of factual characteristics such as age, gender or income level		
		Epithelium	type of cell found in the lining of the respiratory system
		Erythrocytes	red blood cells
Determinism	the doctrine that all things, including the will, are determined by causes	**Euphoria**	exaggerated sense of well being
		Evaluate/ Evaluating	considering the advantages and disadvantages and making judgements against theory or the views of others
Detrimental	harmful		
Devolution	not making decisions at the top of the structure; allowing local organisations to make decisions for their area	**Exertion**	to make an effort
		Experiment	a research method occasionally used in social science which is based upon the experimental method used in the natural sciences such as Chemistry. This approach creates a number of ethical issues as one is researching people and consequently other methods are more commonly used
Diagnose	identify; detect		
Dialysate	chemical used in dialysis to extract waste from the blood		
Diarrhoea	faeces or stools in liquid form		

Fear	to be afraid; frightened
Feminist	follower of a movement that developed in the 1960s which promoted women's rights both in the home and at work
Fine	small (muscles)
Flexibility	room for movement from a set format; adaptable or variable
Foetus	developing baby when it is no longer just a collection of fast dividing cells
Forced choice	questions where the participant has to choose from a range of answers – there is no room for individuality in the answers
Gaseous exchange	the transfer of oxygen into and carbon dioxide out of the blood in the alveoli
Genes	DNA molecules that make up who we are
Genetic	relating to origin
Genetically	linked to genes and inherited characteristics
Gestation period	period of development before birth
Glass ceiling	an invisible barrier that prevents some women from fulfilling their potential in the workplace and explains why there are relatively few females in senior positions
Gross	large (muscles)
Haemoglobin	oxygen-carrying protein found in red blood cells
Hazards	anything with the potential to cause harm
HDL-cholesterol	form of blood fat that does not deposit in the walls of arteries
Health professionals	e.g., nurse, doctor, physiotherapist, health visitor
Helicobacter pylori	a bacterium responsible for the onset of some stomach cancers
Histamine H2-receptor blockers	drug used to slow down the production of stomach acid
Holistic	considering the whole person, not just a part, e.g. physical
Householder	person who rents or owns a house
Hypothermia	body temperature at a dangerously low level

Hypothesis	this is a statement about what the researcher thinks they will find
Id	'I want' demands.
Identity	individuality
Impaired	flawed; faulty; not working fully
Inadequate	not sufficient, not enough
Incision	a cut made into a body
Independence	self sufficiency
Individual education plans	a programme of learning to help a specific person
Individualism	a view that as a society people are becoming more concerned about their own lives and are less prepared to sacrifice their own opportunities for other members of their family
Inferior	to have a low opinion of; no self regard
Informed consent	when someone has been given the facts about the research to be carried out and on this basis has agreed to take part
Innate	inborn; natural to the mind
Integral	fundamental
Integrated	interwoven with other aspects
Intellectual	linked to cognitive thought processes and skills
Interaction	to mix and to talk and exchange ideas with others
Inter-dependence	dependent upon each other
Internalised	to think about and understand; to make an idea one's own
Intervention(s)	involvement; interference; interruption to the pattern
Ions	an element in a free form
Irrationality	not rational or logical
Itemise	list
Learning aid	something used to assist learning
Leukocyte	any type of white blood cell
Logical	coherent; reasonable
Lumen	inner lining of a vessel
Lymphocytes	type of white blood cell involved in the protection against infection
Macro research	any research that is large scale, for example a study of family patterns across society using a questionnaire and a large sample
Macromolecules	large molecules with long chains of chemicals

Magnetic resonance imaging	studies the behaviour of protons when they are subjected to a very strong magnetic field
Maladaptive	faulty
Malena	the presence of blood in the stools
Malignant	cancerous; derived from the Latin meaning evil or nasty
Mature	to age; to develop; to grow wiser
Means-tested benefits	benefits which are given to individuals who are in need as shown by drawing a poverty line below which one is unable to achieve a minimum standard of living. Nearly all government support today is based upon this principle
Micro research	small scale research, for example interviewing informally five families in depth in order to see how family life has changed across different generations
Milestones	major points in a child's development
Minimise	lessen
Mitral (or bicuspid) valve	a valve that permits blood flow from the left atrium into the left ventricle of the heart, but prevents blood flowing in the reverse direction
Monitoring	to check to see how something is going, e.g. quality practice
Mucous membrane	linings of cavities and tubes in the body that secrete mucus for lubrication
Multi-cultural society	a society which embraces and accepts a wide range of people with different religious and ethnic backgrounds. The census clearly identifies the many varied backgrounds of the population of the UK
Multi-disciplinary approach	several sectors working together, e.g. social services and childcare
Multi-faceted	having many characteristics or parts
Multi-skilled	having the ability to complete more than one task
Myocardial infarction	the sudden death of part of the heart muscle, commonly known as a heart attack
Nature	already present at birth
Nature vs. nurture	ideas about inherited factors vs. ideas about how the environment around us influences our development
Negative identity	to have a low self opinion
Neurological dysfunction	poor functioning of the nervous system
Neurotransmitter	a chemical that allows nerves to send messages
New Labour	the current Labour Party who have moved away from their traditional left wing policies of socialism to the centre ground with more moderate less controversial policies. They believe in competition between health and social care providers
New man	a term applied to those men who have apparently moved away from the stereotypical traditional male 'macho' figure to one that shares equally all tasks with his partner/wife
New right	a view of the family that is based upon tradition and is reluctant to accept changes that have occurred, such as the increase in lone parent families and the divorce rate. It believes that the two parent family is a more stable unit and should take care of its children without too much government intervention
Non-confrontational	not to be aggressive towards others
Norm	average, e.g. the norm for that stage of development
Norms of development	average levels of development
Nuclear	an atom; small amount
Nurture	affected by the environment
Objective (adj.)	this is research which is not distorted by emotional involvement or personal bias
Objectives (n.)	steps to make it possible to meet the aim; what should be achieved by the end of activity
Obligation	legal requirement or moral duty, that is it has to be done or completed – there is no choice in the matter
Open questions	questions that allow a completely free response by the participant

Open societies — groups of people who are prepared to accept new ideas and views from outside their own culture

Outcome — can be used instead of objective

Palette — upper part of inside of mouth

Paramount — most important issue to be considered. Mainly identified with the Children Act which stated that the interests of children must always be placed at the top of the agenda in any issue involving them

Paraprofessional — working alongside a professional and having some training, e.g. support worker

Participant observation — joining an organisation such as a doctors' surgery to see the reality of people's behaviour in a real-life setting

Pathogens — bacteria, virus, fungi and other substances that harm the body

Perception — a view

Performance indicators — criteria for measuring performance

Perineum — area of skin just in front of the anus

Peritoneum — inner lining in the abdomen

Personalised — particular to the needs of the person being considered

Perspective — viewpoint

Pharmacological — relating to the science of the study of drugs

Placenta — the organ through which the foetus obtains food and oxygen and gets rid of waste matter

Plaques — small pieces of waste material that stick to the walls of arteries

Potential — possibility

Precise — specific; accurate

Pre-coded — a question often found in questionnaires and structured interviews which is designed to gain factual data or an opinion whereby a series of alternative answers are provided for the respondent to choose from

Pre-programmed — already in place

Prevailing — common

Preventative approach — using methods to prevent illness

Primary — first-hand knowledge or experience

Primary colours — colours not created by mixing others, i.e. red, yellow, blue

Professionals — those working in the vocational sector

Prognosis — indication of what is to happen

Progression — development

Progressive — becoming more severe or extensive with time

Prolactin — a hormone that promotes and stimulates growth of the mammary glands

Proteases — an enzyme used in the digestive process

Proton pump inhibitor — drug used to slow down the production of stomach acid

Providers — people or organisations who give a service or make services available

Psychologist — professional whose work covers all aspects of behaviour

Psychosocial — co-operating with others

Pulmonic/ Pulmonary — pertaining to the lungs

Purchaser- provider — an organisation that buys or provides goods or services

Qualitative — research based mainly on interviews

Quantitative — research from which numbers result

Questionnaire — a list of questions used to gather facts and/or attitudes from a large sample of the population

Refined — polished; honed

Reinforcement — support; strengthen

Remission — to get worse

Replicate — to copy or reproduce

Representational meaning — represents something else

Resources — materials

Responsibility — accountability

Restrictive — limited; unable to escape from

Role model — individual who is looked up to and whose behaviour is copied

Saturated fat — fat molecules that have the maximum number of hydrogen atoms attached to each carbon atom

Schema — early concepts

Scope — the breadth and depth

Seamless (of service) — unbroken

Search engines	piece of software that looks at a vast amount information on the World Wide Web to find a specified topic	**Stratification**	several levels
Secondary	obtaining information from books, magazines, etc.	**Stroke**	cerebro-vascular accident/incident (CVA/CVI); a burst blood vessel or clot in the brain that leads to severe dysfunction
Secondary (approaches)	early detection and treatment	**Structured**	ordered; pre-arranged
Secrete	produce and release chemical substances needed for metabolic processes	**Structured interview**	similar to a questionnaire but with a smaller sample and usually in more depth
Self actualisation	fulfilling our topmost needs	**Subclavian vein**	large vein found just beneath the clavicle or collar bone
Self awareness	being aware of who we are/what we can do	**Subjective**	this research is coloured or affected by personal views, emotions or prejudice
Self completed	to complete oneself	**Superego**	demands made by parents or society about the way we behave
Self concept	the view we have of ourselves	**Symbolic representation**	symbol representing something else
Self empowerment	able to take control without help	**Symphysis pubis**	hard ring of bone in the front of the pelvis just above the genitals
Self esteem	self confidence	**Target**	goal
Self regard	having respect for ourselves	**Temper tantrum**	angry outburst in young children
Sensitivity	sympathy and understanding	**Tension**	difficulties; torn between two things
Sequential	in order	**Tertiary (approaches)**	minimising illness
Skeletal muscle	striated muscle that helps to maintain posture	**Thrombocytes**	platelets in blood that aid clotting
Social evolution approach/theory	concentrates on the whole human race not on the individual	**Tomography**	radiography of a layer in the body by moving the x-ray tube and photoplate in such a way that only the chosen plane appears in clear detail
Social relationships	the way people react or relate to one another in their social grouping, e.g. children in a nursery, residents in a care home		
Socially acceptable	accepted by people in society	**Treat**	address the problem; to make better
Society	the community in which we live	**Tricuspid valve**	a valve that permits blood flow from the right atrium into the right ventricle of the heart, but prevents blood flowing in the reverse direction
Spleen	organ that filters blood and is part of the immune system		
Stakeholder	a person who has an interest in buying an item or in a procedure		
Standard	a concept which defines the level of performance	**Typology**	types of
Statistically	data that is capable of exact numerical representation	**Ultimate**	the highest or last goal/achievement
Stigmatised	individuals or groups are stereotyped usually in negative ways and are blamed for some of the problems in society, for example young single mothers or asylum seekers	**Unambiguous**	having only one meaning or interpretation
		Unconditional positive regard	accepting someone for who they are without any restraint
		Unethical	not carried out in accordance with the principles of conduct that are considered correct
Stools	fully formed faeces	**Unified budget**	one budget that covers individuals/ professionals from across different sectors
Strata	a level	**Universal**	unlimited

Universal benefits — benefits which everyone receives irrespective of their need – the only remaining example today is Child Benefit

Unpredictable — not foreseeable or anticipated

Unresponsiveness — not reacting

Unstructured (interviews) — no rigid set of pre-set questions, so the researcher has some flexibility

Uraemia — the presence of excess urea in the blood, indicating kidney failure

Urban — a built-up area; not rural

Vaccine — a substance that stimulates the immune system

Values — standards

Ventricles — two larger chambers in the heart

Vertebrae — bones that make up the spinal column

Visually — linked to sight

Voluntarily — performed or brought about by free choice

Voluntary — to work without pay

Vulnerable — at risk; susceptible

Welfare state — a 'safety net' for individuals and families whereby the government will ensure a basic minimum standard of care and support

Wider society — made up of people/countries outside our own society